The Boater's Handbook

THE INDISPENSABLE LOOK-IT-UP BOOK

The Boater's Handbook

A Chapman Nautical Guide

Third Revised Edition

by Elbert S. Maloney

Hearst Books
A Division of Sterling Publishing, Inc.
New York

Copyright © 2002 by Hearst Communications, Inc.

Project Editor: Joseph Gonzalez
Interior Design: Laura Smyth
Cover Design: Remo Cosentino
Cover Photographs: Upper right, courtesy Talon Marine
　　　　　　　　　　Upper left and bottom, Remo Cosentino

Library of Congress Cataloging-in-Publication Data
Maloney, Elbert S.
Boater's handbook : the indispensable look-it-up book : a Chapman nautical guide.—3rd rev. ed / by Elbert S. Maloney.
　　　p.cm.
Updated ed. of: Boatman's handbook / Tom Bottomley. Rev.ed. c1985.
ISBN 1-58816-050-5
1. Navigation—Handbooks, manuals, etc. 2. Boats and boating—Handbook, manuals, etc. I. Bottomley, Tom. Boatman's handbook. II. Title.

VK155.B66 2002
623.88—dc21　　　　　　　　　　　　　　　　　　　　　　　　2001059368

10　9　8　7　6　5　4　3　2　1

Published by Hearst Books,
A Division of Sterling Publishing Company, Inc.
387 Park Avenue South, New York, N.Y. 10016

Distributed in Canada by Sterling Publishing
C/o Canadian Manda Group, One Atlantic Avenue, Suite 105
Toronto, Ontario, Canada M6K 3E7
Distributed in Australia by Capricorn Link (Australia) Pty. Ltd.
P.O. Box 704, Windsor, NSW 2756 Australia

Printed in the United States of America

ISBN: 1-58816-050-5

Contents

9. ELECTRONIC COMMUNICATIONS AND NAVIGATION
Electrical Units, Radio Terminology, Radiotelephones, Using Your Marine Radio, Cellular Telephones, EPIRBs, Depth Sounders, Radar, Electronic Navigation Systems, Electronic Charts

10. LIFE ON BOARD
Customs and Etiquette, Pets and Boats, Housekeeping Hints

11. GOVERNMENT REQUIREMENTS
Federal Equipment Requirements, Registration, Vessel Safety Check Requirements, VSC Recommendations

12. MAINTENANCE
Tools, Cleaning Materials and Procedures, Paints and Painting Procedures, Sealants and Bedding Compounds, Outboard Motors, Inboard Motors, Controls, Electrical System, Sails and Rigging, Plumbing, Trailers

13. INFORMATION SOURCES
Organizations, Publications, Schools and Courses, Museums and Restorations

14. USEFUL TABLES
Time-Speed-Distance, Conversion Nautical-Statute Miles, Propeller Selection, Propeller Shaft Selection, Weight and Strength of Line, Chain, and Wire Rope, Weight of Water and Fuels, Visibility at Sea, Metric Conversions, Technical Values and Equations, Astronomical Data

FOLLOW THE ARROWS ▶
To find desired information quickly, place your thumb at the arrow for the appropriate section, and flip through the pages to the matching tabbed page edges in the book.

EMERGENCIES ▶

SAFETY ▶

SEAMANSHIP ▶

AIDS TO NAVIGATION ▶

CHARTS ▶

PILOTING ▶

TIDES AND CURRENTS ▶

WEATHER ▶

ELECTRONICS ▶

LIFE ON BOARD ▶

GOVERNMENT REQUIREMENTS ▶

MAINTENANCE ▶

INFORMATION SOURCES ▶

USEFUL TABLES ▶

Introduction

This is a handbook of basic information for all boaters, and for all types and all sizes of small craft. It covers essential boating procedures that will enhance your safety and enjoyment of boating.

An important feature of this 3rd revised edition of *The Boater's Handbook* is the inclusion of many Internet addresses where you can find specific information about regional and other boating rules and regulations, as well as maps and other useful aids. It has been truly said that whatever the information you need, it is on the Worldwide Web—you just have to be able to find it! This book will try to help you do just that.

I have been boating so long that it seems to me that the craft in the slip next to my first boat was Noah's Ark! I grew up as a youngster in a house on a beach of the open Atlantic Ocean— our front yard was sand, not grass. Off and on, I had a small boat that I could call my own and spent many hours on the water. There were gaps in my teenage and college years, but even in World War II, when in rear areas, I often found a craft of some sort to get out on the water. My "real" boating began in 1954 in Norfolk, Virginia, with a 30-foot old Wheeler sedan cruiser— "ancient" might be a better word than "old," but it was our family boat. And it soon led to a larger and better new craft. Since those days, we have rarely been without at least one boat, some larger, some smaller; mostly power, but one sail. These have taken us over tens of thousands of miles of inland and offshore waters—in fair weather and foul. And it was the rare day on the water that I didn't learn something! Much of what is in this book is what I have learned from studying and doing, and some from what others have passed on to me.

To give credit where it is due—this book is a continuation of an idea and a handbook originated by Tom Bottomley in the early 1980s. He saw the need for a volume such as this, and created *The Boatman's Handbook*. It went through several editions, but then fell by the wayside, as the saying goes. Now it has been revived, updated, and expanded, and is ready for a new life. Read it for general background learning, and use it as a reference when you have a problem—it's a handy *Handbook* for all.

This book has been produced in a size that will permit it to be carried and used on a boat of any size. Keep it on board your craft—I know that I will on mine!

—Elbert S. ("Mack") Maloney

CHAPTER ONE

Emergencies

Safe boating practices minimize the danger of accidents afloat; indeed, recreational boating is one of the safest of all participant sports. However, the prudent skipper should know what to do in an emergency, and make plans to cope with all foreseeable situations. The first step to boating safety is the preparation of plans and routines. These should be complete, but not too detailed—emergencies will almost never occur just as you have anticipated. Plans have little value if they are not tested and learned to the point where they become automatic actions—a real emergency is no time to be trying to find this book and read what you should do! Even the best plans are valuable only if tried out and evaluated, and they must be practiced on a regular schedule. Plans should never be considered "final"; almost every time that you conduct a drill, you will find some part of the plan that needs major or minor changes—be flexible.

Emergency plans should include actions only for your regular crew; if guests are on board at the time of an emergency or a drill, they should be assigned only the simplest of tasks, or told to stand clear and do nothing. Actions by well-intended, but unknowledgeable and untrained, individuals usually lead to complications and a worsening of the situation.

It is essential for safety to have on board at least one person *other than the skipper* who is capable of operating the radio and who knows what must be included in an emergency call.

Grounding

It has been said there are only two types of skippers — those who have run aground in the past, and those who will run aground in the future. Groundings range from simply running up on a sandbar or mud bank at slow speed, with only minor inconvenience and embarrassment, to a real crisis, such as running onto rocks or reefs at full speed. Whatever the situation, having a planned course of action will minimize the consequences and maximize the safety of the craft and those on board. Here are some suggestions for *your* Emergency Plan for Groundings:

1. Keep calm — it is probably not as serious as you first think. Avoid the instinctive and common mistake of immediately putting your engines in reverse and revving them up — you can make the situation worse, piling up sand or mud under the boat, or clogging up your engine's cooling water intakes and filters.

2. Check for any inflow of water through the hull; if there is any, stopping it takes precedence over any measures you take to become afloat again.

3. Check for any damage to the propellers, shafts, and rudders; check for any injuries to persons on board.

4. Determine your position and make a note of it. This may give you a clue as to why you are aground and in what direction you should move, if or when you can. This will also be needed if you have to call for assistance.

5. If you are in tidal waters, determine the state of the tide and the direction of movement. It might be that if the tide is rising all you have to do is wait for the water to get deeper.

6. Determine the depth of the water around the boat; use a boathook, a sounding pole, or a hand-held leadline. If you have a dinghy in the water, or can launch one, check depths farther away from your craft. Determine the best direction to reach adequate water depths—it is not always back behind you.

7. The method for getting afloat again will vary with the situation. In some cases, all that is required is patience—just wait for the tide to rise. Even if the tide is now falling, it will rise again and may be

STANDARD PHONETIC SPELLING ALPHABET

A	ALFA	N	NOVEMBER
B	BRAVO	O	OSCAR
C	CHARLIE	P	PAPA
D	DELTA	Q	QUEBEC
E	ECHO	R	ROMEO
F	FOXTROT	S	SIERRA
G	GOLF	T	TANGO
H	HOTEL	U	UNIFORM
I	INDIA	V	VICTOR
J	JULIETT	W	WHISKEY
K	KILO	X	X-RAY
L	LIMA	Y	YANKEE
M	MIKE	Z	ZULU

FIGURE 1-1. Many letters, when spoken individually, sound much the same, especially over the radio. The use of phonetic equivalents will prevent misunderstanding and confusion, but don't overuse them. When needed, use the internationally accepted alphabet shown here, rather than one you make up yourself.

enough to get you afloat, assuming you did not have the misfortune to run aground at high tide. You can lessen a boat's draft by pumping out the water tanks or taking off people and gear. Another tactic is to put out an anchor in the direction of deeper water, and then put a strain on the line by pulling, either by hand or using a winch or windlass. (If the tide is rising, and there is any wind or waves pushing you further into shallow water, putting out an anchor is highly recommended to prevent the boat from being blown into shallower water.) You may then be able to get off using your own engines or sail power. In some situations, having a powerboat pass nearby to make a wake may help. Another boat may be able to pull you off after passing a line; if you have hull damage, be sure that pulling you into deeper water doesn't worsen your situation.

8. If you cannot resolve the situation by yourself or with the help of others standing by, call for assistance. Use your VHF radio with correct procedures—speak slowly and clearly, state your position, and describe the situation in as much detail as possible. Consider the use of visual distress signals. In many areas, you may be able to use a cellular phone; this may facilitate the exchange of information, but it does nothing to alert other boats in the area that might be able to assist you. (In an increasing number of areas, dialing *CG will take you to the appropriate Coast Guard unit; check to see if this possibility exists in your boating area.) If you ask for assistance using a cell phone, also make an announcement of your problem on VHF Channel 16. It is a good idea to alert the Coast Guard to your situation even if you haven't yet determined that assistance will be required. They will probably establish a schedule of contacts every hour or half-hour or so to monitor developments. Though this is not a Mayday call, you can use the urgent signal PAN-PAN (pronounced "pahn pahn").

9. If it appears that the situation is serious, and you might have to abandon ship, have all persons put on life jackets without delay.

Flooding

Finding the water level inside your boat rising can be quite a surprise, and it can be a real emergency. Providing that you have not struck some fixed or floating object, the most likely cause is a defective through-hull fitting or related hose. Planning for such an event can only be general in nature, but there are certain actions that are applicable in all cases.

1. Immediately switch on all bilge pumps. The risk of harm to the pumps by running them dry is far less than that of having water in the bilge get a head start. Turn them off as soon as you are sure they are not needed. Assign members of the crew to operate manual bilge pumps, if necessary.

2. As quickly as possible, start a search for the source of the incoming water; pull up floorboards and check the bilges, if necessary. In most cases, the boat should be slowed or stopped to minimize inflow of water; in some cases, however, a hole may be kept above water by remaining on plane.

3. If regular pumps, manual and electric, cannot cope with the inflow of water, stop your engine, shut the water intake seacock, transfer the water intake to the bilge (or shift a valve if you have an emergency pumping setup), and restart the engine so its water pump is also drawing water from the bilge. *Note:* There must be enough water flowing in the bilge to meet the engine's cooling needs, and caution must be exercised to prevent debris from being sucked into the cooling system.

4. If possible, cover the hole from the outside with canvas, bunk sheets, towels, or any other material available; lash the covering in place. The object is to restrict water flow to an amount that can be handled by your pumps.

5. See Steps 8 and 9 under GROUNDING above.

Explosions and Fires

Fires on a boat are serious, but often they can be brought under control if you act quickly and your boat is properly equipped with the required portable and/or fixed extinguisher systems. These should be checked on a scheduled basis.

The best action, however, is to prevent fires and explosions from ever occurring. Be alert for any leaks in your fuel tanks and lines; use proper fueling techniques. If you use a flammable fuel for cooking, make sure that your system meets all safety standards and check frequently for leaks.

EXPLOSIONS

1. In the case of an explosion, prepare all hands to go over the side if the subsequent fire makes it unsafe to remain on board. Grab a life preserver, if possible.

2. If you do have to abandon ship, swim far enough away to be clear of danger. Then check about and account for all those who were on board. Render such assistance as you can to anyone burned, injured, or without a buoyant device. Keep everyone together to facilitate rescue.

FIRES

1. If possible, apply the extinguishing agent by:
   a. Using a fire extinguisher;
   b. Discharging a fixed smothering system; or
   c. Pouring or spraying water on wood, paper, or similar materials.

2. If practical, jettison burning materials.

3. Reduce air supply to the fire by:
   a. Maneuvering the vessel to reduce the effect of wind. It is generally recommended that the boat be turned into the wind, as the fire is usually aft; this allows persons on board not needed for fighting the fire to assemble on the bow.
   b. Closing hatches, ports, vents, doors, etc., if the fire is in an area where this action will be effective.

4. Make preparations for abandoning your boat:
   a. Put on lifesaving devices;
   b. Signal for assistance by radio or any other means available.

Even if it appears that you have put out the fire, be alert to a possible re-ignition and stand by with one or more full extinguishers.

Man Overboard

If a person—man, woman, or child—falls out of or off your boat, anyone seeing that happen should call out "Man Overboard (Port or Starboard, as appropriate)." The following steps should be taken immediately:

1. *Post a lookout.* It is imperative that the person in the water—or at least the spot where he or she was last seen—be kept in sight at all times. Designate a specific crewman to do nothing but act as this lookout. At night, keep a searchlight or handheld flashlight on the person.

2. *Immediately pull the throttles back* to idle and shift into neutral to avoid any danger to the person in the water from the propellers. If under sail, slack the sheets.

3. *Throw over a life preserver.* Throw overboard a life ring, buoyant cushion, or other buoyant device, even though the person may be a strong swimmer. A water-activated strobe light attached to a life ring is extremely effective at night.

4. *Don't let anyone jump in the water to help.* Even if that individual is a strong swimmer, you will then have two persons to get back on board, not an easy task. The only exception is in the case of a small child, or an elderly or handicapped adult. In such a case, be sure the rescuer takes a life ring or other buoyant device with him or her.

5. *Maneuver to return* to the spot where the person fell overboard. Determine *in advance* whether turning to port or starboard is fastest. Stopping and backing down may be the fastest way for some boats, but this should be done *only* in daylight, and *only* when the person in the water can be seen clearly. *Never* back down over the spot where a person went down! If you are alone, note your compass heading, and turn back 180 degrees on the reciprocal heading. Otherwise, follow the signals of your lookout. Sailboat operators should carry out man overboard drills from a variety of headings in respect to the wind, in order to minimize confusion and loss of time in a real emergency. (Many electronic navigation devices have a "MOB" button which should be pressed immediately upon the cry "Man Overboard"—this will record the boat's position and start calculating a course back to that spot.)

6. *Use additional markers.* In some circumstances, particularly at night, it may be helpful to throw over additional buoyant objects to ensure that the path back to the victim can be traced.

7. *Maneuver for the pick up.* In some cases, you can approach from the windward of the victim, and let the boat drift down toward him, providing a lee. In most cases, however, it is best to approach from leeward in order to avoid having your boat blow right over the victim. Just slight amounts of power will be needed to keep your boat under control. A sailboat should approach nearly on the wind so that it can luff up to stop the headway when the victim is reached. In any case, stop the boat a short distance from the victim, and throw him a line, such as a ski tow rope, that floats. It is less hazardous than trying to maneuver your boat right up to him.

8. *Get the victim on board.* If necessary, have someone who is physically able ready to go into the water to assist the victim. This crewman should take a light safety line with him. Where the victim will be brought on board will depend greatly on the type of craft concerned—try various locations on your boat to determine the best procedure. A transom-boarding platform may be a help in getting the victim on board, or you can rig a boarding ladder. A line with a bowline knot tied to form a large loop may be hung over the side to provide a foothold or handhold. Be sure the propeller is stopped whenever there is a person in the water near the stern of the boat.

9. *Call for help if necessary.* If the victim is not rescued immediately, get on the radio with the urgent communications signal PAN-PAN to summon assistance from the Coast Guard, marine police, and nearby boats. Continue the search until the victim is located or you are released by a competent authority.

PRACTICE, PRACTICE, PRACTICE

No emergency plan should be FIRST tried in an actual emergency—this is not the time to find flaws in the plan and make changes. Plans should be written down in specific detail and practiced regularly. Expect to find omissions and mistakes, and revise the plan accordingly. Hold drills with the skipper not participating, as if he were disabled. Rehearse your emergency plans until they are second nature to you and your crew—minimize the extent to which orders and directions must be given. In your drills, include any guests on board as "temporary crew," but do not base your plans on additional persons being on board.

Distress Signals

Accepted forms of distress signals have been written into the International and Inland Navigation Rules. These are illustrated in Figure 1-2. Note that the flying of a national flag upside down is not an approved distress signal—the flags of many countries (France and Japan are two examples) have a symmetrical design, with no "upside" or "downside."

| Flames in a bucket | Red meteor flares | Parachute red flare | Smoke |

| Fog horn sounded continuously | Person waving arms | Position indicating radio beacon | Gun fired at one-minute intervals |

| Black square and ball on orange background | Code flags November and Charlie | Square flag and ball | Dye Marker (any color) |

| Hand-Held flare | Morse code SOS | Mayday by radio |

FIGURE 1-2. Some distress signals are nighttime only, others are daytime only, and some can be used at any time. In an emergency, use any available means of signaling your distress.

Radiotelephone Distress Procedure

1. Make sure that the radio is on Channel 16. If the set is so equipped, activate the Radiotelephone Alarm Signal. (Activate an EPIRB if one is on board.)

2. Give the distress signal Mayday three times.

3. Give the boat's name and call sign three times.

4. Give particulars of your boat's position (latitude and longitude, if in the open sea, or true bearing and distance in miles from a known geographical position). Use the phonetic alphabet (page 12) as necessary for clarity.

5. Give the nature of the distress, the kind of assistance required, the number of persons on board, and any other information that would facilitate rescue.

Accident Reporting

In case of collision, accident, or other casualty involving a boat subject to United States federal law, it is required that the operator, if and so far as he can do so without serious danger to his own vessel or persons on board, render such assistance as may be necessary and practicable to other persons affected by the incident in order to save them from any danger that results. The operator must also give his name and address and the identification of his vessel to any person injured and to the owner of any damaged property. A written report of the accident must be filed under the following circumstances:

1. If the incident results in death or an injury that requires medical treatment beyond first aid;

2. If the incident results in the disappearance of a person from a vessel under circumstances that indicated death or injury;

3. If there is property damage totaling more than $2000.

If death occurs within twenty-four hours of the accident, or a person has a reportable injury or disappears from a boat, the report must be made within 48 hours; otherwise, it must be made within ten days of the accident.

Most state boating laws require that these reports be made to a designated state office or official. In the absence of such a state provision, the report should go to the Coast Guard Officer in Charge, Marine Inspection, at the Coast Guard office nearest the site of the accident. Use USCG Form 3865 or the applicable state form (usually very similar).

CHAPTER TWO

Safety

 Boating is really not an "unsafe" activity, but there is a lot you can do to prevent emergencies from happening in the first place and to make boating safer for you, your crew, your guests, and your craft.

Ensuring maximum safety on board requires more than just a set of emergency preparedness plans, as described in the previous chapter. You must also have the proper equipment on board in sufficient quantities, and you must follow proper procedures at all times.

Fire Safety

For the type and number of fire extinguishers required for boats of each class, see Chapter 11, "Government Requirements," page 204. Keep in mind that the legal requirement is a minimum; safety will often require a greater number. In choosing extinguishers for your boat, you will find the following information valuable:

CLASSES OF FIRES
There are three categories, or classes, of fires:

Class A—fires in ordinary combustible materials such as wood, paper, cloth, etc., where the "quenching-cooling" effect of quantities of water or solutions containing large percentages of water is most effective in reducing the temperature of the burning material to below the ignition temperature.

Class B—fires in flammable petroleum products or other flammable liquids, greases, etc., where the "blanketing-smothering" effect of oxygen-excluding media is most effective.

Class C—fires involving electrical equipment where the electrical conductivity of the extinguishing media is of first importance.

FIRE EXTINGUISHERS

Fire extinguishers are divided into the same three classes—A, B, C—as fires. By law, shipboard extinguishers must be of the B category, effective against fires in petroleum-based and other flammable liquids and products. But most extinguishers can put out more than one type of fire. A carbon-dioxide or dry-chemical B extinguisher will also be effective against a Class C electrical fire, whereas a foam-type B extinguisher will help put out ordinary Class A fires, but is *not* effective against Class C electrical fires. Boaters should remember that for typical small Class A fires in wood, paper, or bedding, the popular dry-chemical extinguishers are *not* as effective as ordinary buckets of water. Get the burning material, especially bedding, over the side as quickly as possible.

Fire extinguishers should be distributed throughout the boat in relation to potential hazards. One unit should be near the boat's control station where it can be grabbed quickly by the helmsman. Others should be mounted near the engine compartment and near the skipper's bunk so that he can roll out at night with it in his hand. Other locations include the galley and any other compartment at some distance from the location of other extinguishers. In the galley, fires involving alcohol fuel from a stove are best fought with water, but a grease fire calls for a regular Class B extinguisher. Fire extinguishers should be mounted where they are clearly visible to both crew and guests as they move about the boat.

It is important to keep in mind that the small extinguishers usually carried on boats normally discharge the extinguishing agent for only *eight to twelve seconds,* and then they are empty and use-less. **Caution:** Never use a dry-chemical extinguisher partially, with the intention of "saving" a portion of its contents for later use. Some of the extinguishing agent will remain in the valve, preventing it from closing completely and resulting in a slow loss of pressure. Always use an extinguisher fully and recharge it, or replace it, at the earliest possible opportunity.

Bilge Ventilation

All boats—including auxiliary sailboats—that use gasoline as a fuel for propulsion, generating electricity, or mechanical power must have proper ventilation for every engine and fuel component, unless the boat is of "open construction." To qualify as a boat of open construction, a vessel must meet all of the following requirements:

1. As a minimum, engine- and fuel-tank compartments must have fifteen square inches of open area directly exposed to the atmosphere for each cubic foot of *net* compartment volume. (Net volume is found by determining total volume and then subtracting the volume occupied by the engine, tank, and other accessories.)

2. There must be no long or narrow unventilated spaces accessible from the engine- or fuel-tank compartments into which fire could spread.

3. Long, narrow compartments, such as side panels, that join engine- or fuel-tank compartments and do not serve as ducts, must have at least fifteen square inches of open area per cubic foot through frequent openings located along the compartment's full length.

REQUIREMENTS FOR OLDER BOATS

Boats not of open construction built prior to July 31, 1980, must have at least two ventilation ducts fitted with cowls at their openings to the atmosphere for each engine and tank compartment. An exception is made for fuel-tank compartments if each electrical component in the compartment is "ignition protected," in accordance with Coast Guard standards, and fuel tanks are vented to the outside of the boat.

The ventilators, ducts, and cowls must be installed so that they provide efficient removal of explosive or flammable gases from bilges of *each* engine and fuel-tank compartment. Intake ducting must be installed to extend from the cowls to at least midway to the bilge, or at least to the level of the carburetor air intake. Exhaust ducting must be installed to extend from the lower portion of the bilge to the cowls in the open atmosphere. Ducts should not be installed so low that they could become obstructed by a normal accumulation of bilge water (see Figure 2-1).

To create a flow through the ducting system, at least when under way or when there is a wind, cowls (scoops) or other fittings of equal effectiveness are needed on all ducts. A wind-actuated rotary exhauster or mechanical blower is equivalent to a cowl on an exhaust duct.

FIGURE 2-1. Natural ventilation system used on some older boats has two intake and two exhaust ducts with cowls. Exhaust ducts start from a low point in the bilge where fumes sink and accumulate.

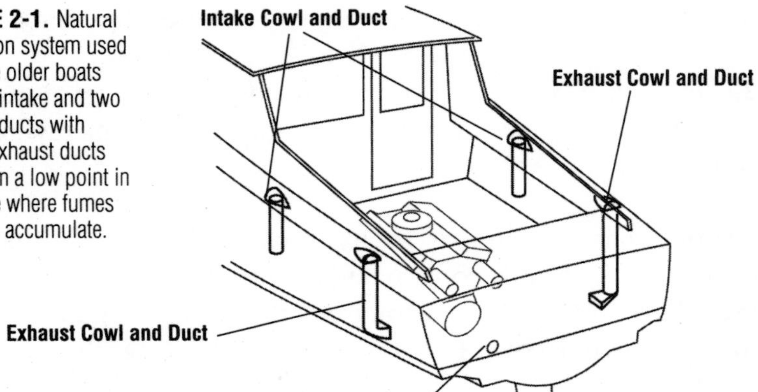

Intake Cowl and Duct

Exhaust Cowl and Duct

Exhaust Cowl and Duct

Power Exhaust Outlet

DUCTS REQUIRED

Ducts are a necessary part of a ventilation system. A mere hole in the hull won't do; that's a vent, not a ventilator. "Vents," the Coast Guard explains, "are openings that permit venting, or escape of gases due to pressure differential. Ventilators are openings that are fitted with *cowls* to direct the flow of air and vapors in or out of *ducts* that channel movement of air for the actual displacement of fumes from the space being ventilated."

SIZE OF DUCTS

Ventilation must be adequate for the size and design of the boat. There should be no construction in the ducting system that is smaller than the minimum cross-sectional area required for reasonable efficiency. Where a stated size of duct is not available, the next *larger* size should be used.

Small Motorboats. To determine the minimum cross-sectional area of the cowls and ducts of motorboats having small-engine and/or fuel-tank compartments, see Table 2-1, which is based on *net* compartment volume (as previously defined).

Cruisers and Larger Boats. For most cruisers and other large motorboats, Table 2-2, which is based on the craft's beam, is a practical guide for determining the minimum size of ducts and cowls.

DUCTING MATERIALS

For safety and long life, ducts should be made of nonferrous, galvanized ferrous, or sturdy high-temperature-resistant nonmetallic materials. Ducts should be routed clear of, and protected from, contact with hot engine surfaces.

TABLE 2-2

Ventilation Requirements for Small Powerboats

		ONE-INTAKE AND ONE EXHAUST SYSTEM	TWO INTAKE AND TWO EXHAUST SYSTEM
NET VOLUME CUBIC FEET	TOTAL COWL AREA SQUARE INCHES	MINIMUM INSIDE DIAMETER FOR EACH DUCT (INCHES)	MINIMUM INSIDE DIAMETER FOR EACH DUCT (INCHES)
Up to 8	3	2	—
10	4	2¼	—
12	5	2½	—
14	6	2¾	—
17	7	3	—
20	8	3¼	2½
23	10	3½	2½
27	11	3¾	3
30	13	4	3
35	14	4¼	3
39	16	4½	3
43	19	4¾	3
48	20	5	3

Note: 1 cu. Ft = 0.028 cu. m; 1 inch = 2.54 cm; 1 cu. in. = 6.45 cu. cm

TABLE 2-3

Ventilation Requirements for Large Powerboats

TWO-INTAKE AND TWO-EXHAUST SYSTEM		
VESSEL BEAM (FEET)	MINIMUM INSIDE DIAMETER FOR EACH DUCT (INCHES)	COWL AREA (SQUARE INCHES)
7	3	7.0
8	3¼	8.0
9	3½	9.6
10	3½	9.6
11	3¾	11.0
12	4	12.5
13	4¼	14.2
14	4¼	14.2
15	4½	15.9
16	4½	15.9
17	4½	17.7
18	5	19.6
19	5	19.6

Note: 1 foot = 0.305 m; 1 inch = 2.54 cm; 1 sq. in. = 6.45 sq. cm.

POSITIONING OF COWLS

Normally, the intake cowl will face forward in an area of free airflow under way, and the exhaust cowl will face aft so that a suction effect can be expected.

The two cowls, or sets of cowls, should be located with respect to each other, horizontally and/or vertically, so as to prevent the return of fumes removed from any space to the same or any other space. Intake cowls should be positioned to avoid picking up vapors from fueling operations.

AIR FOR CARBURETORS

In addition to the ventilation system requirements outlined above, openings into the engine compartments are also necessary in order to allow air to flow to the carburetor.

REQUIREMENTS FOR NEWER BOATS

On boats built after July 31, 1980, each compartment with a permanently installed gasoline engine must be ventilated by a power-exhaust blower system unless it is of open construction as defined above. Each exhaust blower, or combination of blowers, must be rated at an airflow capacity not less than a value computed by formulas based on the net volume of the engine compartment plus other compartments open thereto. The installed blower or blowers must be tested to prove that they actually do move air at a rate determined by other formulas also based on compartment volume. See Figure 2-4.

The engine compartment—and other compartments open to it where the aggregate area of openings exceeds two percent of the area between the compartments—must *also* have a *natural* ventilation system.

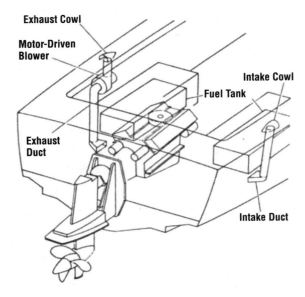

FIGURE 2-4. Blowers are required on newer boats and must be operated before the engine is started. A blower in an exhaust duct should have a minimal effect on the functioning of the duct as a natural ventilator.

There must be a warning label as close as practicable to the ignition switch that advises of the danger of gasoline vapors and the need to run the exhaust blower for at least *four minutes* and then check the engine compartment for fuel vapors *before* starting the engine.

Natural ventilation systems are also required for any compartment containing both a permanently installed fuel tank and any electrical component that is not ignition protected in accordance with existing Coast Guard electrical standards for boats; or a compartment that contains a fuel tank that vents into that compartment (highly unlikely); or one having a nonmetallic fuel tank that exceeds a specified permeability rate. These regulations specify the required cross-sectional area of ducts for natural ventilation based on compartment net volume and on how ducts shall be installed.

RESPONSIBILITIES

The above regulations are the responsibility of the manufacturer of the boat, but there is also a requirement placed on the operator that these ventilation systems be operable anytime the boat is in use. Lack of adequate bilge ventilation can result in an order from a Coast Guard boarding officer for "termination of unsafe use" of the boat.

General Safety Precautions

Ventilation systems are *not* designed to remove vapors in large quantities such as might be caused by breaks in fuel lines, leaking tanks, or dripping carburetors. If gas odors are detected, repairs are generally needed.

Before starting the engine, especially on calm days and on boats without a power ventilation system, the engine compartment should be opened to dissipate any vapors that might be present. The smaller the compartment, the quicker an explosive mixture of gasoline vapors can develop.

Regardless of the ventilation system installed, always open hatches and use your nose to detect any gasoline odors. Even the slightest trace should warn you to search for the cause and to ventilate the compartment thoroughly before pressing the starting switch.

Fueling Precautions

Certain precautions must be carefully and completely observed every time a boat is fueled with gasoline. Step by step, these are:

BEFORE FUELING

1. Fuel before dark whenever possible. Make sure that the boat is securely made fast to the fueling pier.

2. Stop engines, motors, fans, and other devices capable of producing a spark. Open the master switch if the electrical system has one. Put out all cigarettes, galley fires, and open flames.

3. Close all ports, windows, doors, and hatches so that fumes cannot blow on board and below.

4. Make sure all passengers and any crewmembers not needed for the fueling operation disembark before you begin fueling.

5. Prohibit all smoking on board and in the vicinity.

6. Have a fire extinguisher close at hand.

7. Measure the fuel in the tanks and do not order more than the tank will hold. Allow for expansion.

8. When fueling a boat with an outboard motor, remove any portable tanks and fill them on shore.

WHILE FUELING

9. Keep nozzle or can spout in contact with the fill opening to guard against static sparks.

10. Do not spill any gasoline.

11. Do not overfill. The practice of filling until fuel flows from the vents is highly dangerous. Gasoline flowing out of a vent could ignite; gasoline or diesel fuel would pollute the water around the boat.

AFTER FUELING

12. Close fill openings.

13. Wipe up any spilled gasoline; dispose of wipe-up rags safely on shore.

14. Open all ports, windows, doors, and hatches; then turn on bilge power-exhaust blower. Ventilate the boat this way at least *four minutes.*

15. Sniff low down in tank and engine compartments. *If any odor of gasoline is present, do not start engines.*

16. Be prepared to cast off lines as soon as engine starts; get clear of pier quickly. Most explosions from gasoline in the bilge occur not when the engine is started but a few moments later—getting clear of the pier will lessen the danger to the fueling station and other boats.

Lightning Protection

Boats, power or sail, are seldom struck by lightning, yet cases have been reported. A skipper can add to both his physical safety and his peace of mind by obtaining some basic information and taking a few precautionary actions.

PROTECTIVE PRINCIPLES

A grounded conductor or a lightning protective mast will generally attract direct lightning strokes that might otherwise fall within a cone-shaped space, the apex of which is the top of the conductor or mast and the base is a circle at the water's surface having a radius approximately equal to the conductor's height. Probability of protection is considered to be 99 percent within the 45-degree angle as shown in Figure 2-5.

To provide an adequately grounded conductor or protective mast, the entire circuit from the masthead to the ground (water) connection should have a conductivity equivalent to a Number 8 gauge wire. The path to ground followed by the conductor should be essentially straight, with no sharp bends.

If there are metal objects of considerable size within a few feet of the grounding conductor, there will be a strong tendency for sparks or side flashes to jump from the grounding conductor to the metal object at the nearest point. To prevent such possibly damaging flashes, an interconnecting conductor should be provided at all likely places.

Large metallic objects within the hull or superstructure of a boat should be interconnected with the lightning protective system to prevent a dangerous rise of voltage due to a lightning flash.

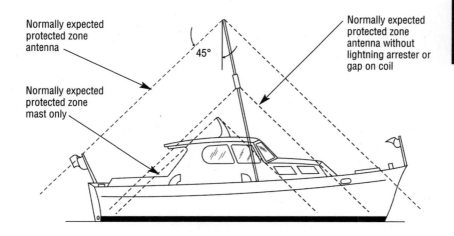

Normally expected protected zone antenna

Normally expected protected zone antenna without lightning arrester or gap on coil

45°

Normally expected protected zone mast only

FIGURE 2-5. Under certain conditions, a grounded metallic—not fiberglass—radio antenna can provide a cone of protection from lightning strikes for a boat and its occupants. A sailboat's grounded metallic mast can serve the same function.

PROTECTIVE MEASURES

For powerboats, a radio antenna may serve as a lightning or protective mast *only* if it is equipped with a transmitting-type lightning arrester or other means for grounding during electrical storms and if the antenna height is sufficient to provide an adequate cone of protection for the length of the craft. Antennas with loading coils are considered to end at a point immediately *below the coil* unless the coil has a suitable gap for bypassing lightning current. The size of the grounding conductor, interconnection, and grounding of metallic masses should be in accordance with principles noted earlier. Ordinary VHF whip antennas provide no lightning protection.

Sailboats with metallic standing rigging will be adequately protected provided that all rigging is grounded and a proper cone of protection exists. Interconnection and grounding of metallic masses should be done as on powerboats.

Metal objects situated wholly on a boat's exterior should be connected to the grounding conductor at their upper or nearest end. Metal objects within the boat may be connected to the lightning protective system directly or through the bonding system that grounds underwater metal parts.

Metal objects that project through cabin tops, decks, etc., should be bonded to the nearest lightning conductor at the point where the object emerges from the boat and again at its lowest extreme end within the boat. Spotlights and other objects projecting through cabin tops should be solidly grounded regardless of the cone of protection.

A ground connection for lightning protection may consist of any metal surface, normally submerged, which has an area of at least one square foot. Propellers and metallic surfaces may be used for this purpose; a radio ground plate is more than adequate. A steel hull itself constitutes a good ground connection.

PROTECTION FOR PERSONNEL

As the basic purpose of lightning protection is the safety of personnel, the following precautions should be taken by the crew and guests:

1. Remain inside a closed boat as much as practicable during an electrical storm.

2. Avoid making contact with any items connected to a lightning protective conductor, especially items that can function as a bridge between two parts of the grounding system.

3. Stay out of the water during a lightning storm.

First-Aid Kit

The container for your first-aid kit should be plastic; avoid a metal that could rust, or cardboard that could soak up moisture. Seal it with tape to keep it moisture-tight, but do not lock it. Commercially prepared kits are available in sizes to match your vessel and its probable cruising area (consider the distance from on-shore medical help). If you should decide to assemble your own kit, consult with your doctor or local paramedics. Prescriptions may be required for some medications; be aware of expiration dates and replace as required. At the least, your kit should contain the following simple instruments and supplies:

INSTRUMENTS

Scissors, small and sharp. If there is room for two pairs, one should be of the blunt-end surgical type.

Tweezers, small and pointed. Tips must meet exactly to pick up small objects.

Safety pins, assorted sizes.

Thermometer, inexpensive oral-rectal type, enclosed in a case.

Tourniquet. Use only on major bleeding that cannot be controlled by pressure; follow instructions exactly.

Eye-washing cup, small, metal.

Cross Venti-breather device to aid in mouth-mouth resuscitation.

Hot water bottle.

Ice bag.

SUPPLIES
Within reasonable limits, substitutions can be made to reflect local availability or personal preferences.

Bandages, 1-, 2-, and 4-inch sterile gauze squares, individually wrapped. Bandage rolls, 1 inch and 2 inch. Band-Aids® or equivalent, assorted size, plus butterfly closures.

Triangular bandage, 40 inches, for use as sling or major compress.

Elastic bandage, 3-inch width, for sprains or splints.

Adhesive tape, waterproof, 1-inch and 2-inch width by 5 or 10 yards.

Absorbent cotton, standard size rolls.

Applicators, cotton-tipped individual swabs, such as Q-tips®.

Antiseptic liquid, such as tincture of iodine or Merthiolate.

Petroleum jelly, small jar.

Antiseptic ointment, 1-ounce tube of Bacitracin® or Polysporin®, or as recommended by your doctor.

Antiseptic-anesthetic first-aid spray, such as Medi-quik® or Bactine®.

Alcohol for sterilizing instruments.

Nupercainal® ointment, 1-ounce tube, for pain.

Painkiller, aspirin or related compounds.

Sleeping pills, Seconal® or equivalent as prescribed by your doctor (not to be used while underway).

Antibiotics, for use only if there will be a delay in reaching a doctor and infection appears serious. Use ampicillin, cephalosporin, or similar drug as prescribed by your doctor.

Ophthalmic (eye) *ointment,* small tube.

Antihistamine, Pyrabenzamine® tablets, or as prescribed by your doctor.

Ammonia inhalants.

Seasickness remedy, Dramamine®, Marezine®, Bonamine®, or Bonine® tablets.

Anti-acid preparation, liquid or tablet.

Laxative.

Antidiarrhea drug, 8-ounce bottle of Kaopectate®.

First-aid manual.

Tools and Parts

The tools and spare parts you'll need to carry on board depend on the type and size of your vessel. Requirements vary so widely for boats of different types and sizes that it is not practical or advisable to make specific and detailed recommendations. The following list is intended as a guide only. If you are not experienced, consult with a seasoned skipper or a boating professional.

TOOLS FOR ON-BOARD REPAIRS

Screwdrivers, various sizes, both flat blade and Phillips.

Wrenches, open-end and box, or combination; sizes to meet all needs; be aware that you may need wrenches in fractional-inch sizes and in metric sizes. Open-end adjustable wrench, several sizes.

Pliers, slip-joint (ordinary), vice-grip (locking), and needle-nose; several sizes.

Wire-cutting and wire-stripping tools.

Hammer.

Knives, various designs and sizes.

Electrical drill and bits, may be corded or cordless.

Soldering iron and solder (if you know how to solder).

Electrical multimeter, simple model for measuring voltage and continuity.

SPARE PARTS AND SUPPLIES

Set of spark plugs, distributor cap, rotor arm, condenser, breaker-point set (for gasoline engines).

Vee belt for each size used on engine(s); matched-belt pairs, if such are used.

Water-pump impeller (for inboard engines).

Fuel pump and strainer.

Small manual bilge pump.

At least two spares for each type of bulb and fuse used.

Fuel and oil filters, at least one of each type.

Hoses, reasonable length of each size used.

Wire, spool or coil of various sizes.

Plugs, softwood, to match each size of through-hull fitting.

Water-Skiing Safety

One of the most popular boating-related sports, water-skiing does present safety problems. The following guidelines should help reduce hazards:

1. Allow no one who is not qualified as a basic swimmer to engage in water skiing. Make sure the skier wears the proper lifesaving device. A ski belt or vest will keep a stunned or unconscious skier afloat.

2. Ski only in safe areas, out of channels, and away from other boats. Some bodies of water will have areas designated for this sport, with skiing prohibited elsewhere.

3. Install a wide-angle rearview mirror, or take along a second person to act as lookout. This will permit watching the skier and the waters ahead. Some state laws require this mirror, or a second person in the boat, or both.

4. If the skier falls, approach him from the lee side; stop your motor before taking him on board.

5. When taking the skier on board, be careful not to swamp the boat. On smaller boats, it is usually safer to take a person on board at the stern.

SKIING SIGNALS

The following set of signals is recommended by the American Water Ski Association (see Figure 2-6). Make sure that the skier, boat operator, and safety observer all know and understand these signals:

Faster—Palm of one hand pointing upward.

Slower—Palm pointed downward.

Speed Okay—Arm upraised with thumb and finger joined to form a circle.

Faster **Slower** **Speed Okay** **Right Turn** **Left Turn** **Back to Drop-Off Area** **Cut Motor** **Stop** **Skier Okay After Fall** **Pick Me Up or Fallen Skier—Watch Out**

FIGURE 2-6. This simple set of hand signals will allow a water skier to communicate effectively with the operator of the towing boat or another onboard observer. All persons involved must be thoroughly familiar with the full set of signals if maximum safety is to be achieved.

Right Turn—Arm outstretched pointing to the right.

Left Turn—Arm outstretched pointing to the left.

Return to Drop-off Area—Arm at 45 degrees from body pointing down to water and swinging.

Cut Motor—Finger drawn across the throat.

Stop—Hand up, palm forward, policeman style.

Skier Okay after Fall—Hands clenched together overhead.

Pick Me Up, or Fallen Skier, Watch Out—One ski extended vertically out of water.

CHAPTER THREE

Seamanship

 Seamanship is one of the most important areas of boating knowledge. The term encompasses knowledge of the Navigation Rules, docking and anchoring techniques, and "marlinspike seamanship"—the use of knots and splices. Acquiring the knowledge and skills of seamanship is a never-ending task.

Obviously, it takes more than a study of these pages to become a seasoned skipper. In this chapter are the basics you *must* know, the minimum arts of good seamanship. To supplement this information, every boater—whether new to the sport or with years of experience—can benefit from classes in safe boating given free by the U.S. Power Squadrons, the U.S. Coast Guard Auxiliary, and the American Red Cross. (See Chapter 13, "Information Sources," for addresses and web sites.)

Navigation Rules

The Navigation Rules (often unofficially referred to as the Rules of the Road) are statutory requirements to promote the safety of navigation. They include requirements for navigation lights and day shapes, steering and sailing rules, and sound signals. There are two sets of Rules of the Road of concern to boaters in the United States: the International Rules for use offshore, and the Inland Rules that must be followed on all waters within the demarcation lines that separate U.S. from International Rules waters (see "Demarcation Lines," below). The U.S. Inland Rules were derived from the

International Rules and are generally similar. The Rules apply to all vessels, from dinghies to supertankers, but there are different requirements for small craft and large ships. The Rules are numbered, and those that are identical, or nearly so, in the two sets carry the same number. Each set of Rules also has Annexes with additional technical details.

Since the requirements of both sets of Rules are almost identical for recreational craft, it is not difficult to learn the actions to be taken, signals to be sounded, and lights to be carried when operating offshore or on inland waters.

The prudent skipper will have a thorough knowledge of the Rules that apply to all types of boats and ships that operate on waters that he or she uses. The official text of the Rules are in the Coast Guard publication *Navigation Rules, International–Inland,* which is available at most chart outlets. The major requirements that apply to recreational boats are listed briefly here.

DEMARCATION LINES

Demarcation lines indicate the boundaries between the 1972 International Rules for the Prevention of Collisions at Sea (termed "72 COLREGS" by the Coast Guard) and the U.S. Inland Rules. They are defined in the publication *Navigation Rules, International–Inland,* generally using identifiable physical objects such as fixed aids to navigation or prominent points on land. They are also shown on charts by a dashed magenta line labeled "COLREGS DEMARCATION LINE" with a reference to the paragraph in the book where they are described in detail.

Navigation Lights and Day Shapes

Navigation lights convey basic information about a vessel by means of specified colors (white, red, green, yellow, or blue), their arc and range of visibility, and their specific location on the vessel (i.e., height, and vertical and horizontal spacing). The basic purpose of navigation lights is to prevent collisions by alerting vessels to each other's presence. Lights also indicate a vessel's status; for example, whether it is anchored, aground, or not under command, or its heading, if underway. Lights can also provide clues as to a vessel's size, special characteristics, and/or current operations. Most important, lights indicate a vessel's orientation with respect to your boat—a fact you must know to determine who has the right-of-way.

A boat manufacturer has the responsibility to install navigation lights of the proper size, type, and placement. The skipper has the responsibility to make sure the lights will work when needed and are turned on when required by the Rules.

RUNNING LIGHTS

The basic lights shown when a vessel is underway—i.e., not anchored, made fast to the shore, or aground—are a white "masthead" light facing forward (high, but not necessarily at the actual masthead), red (port) and green (starboard) sidelights, and a white sternlight. Variations exist for smaller boats and large ships.

The masthead light is white, showing through an arc of 225°, from dead ahead to 22.5° abaft the beam on both sides. The sternlight is white showing through an arc of 135° centered on dead astern. (Note that the sum of these two arcs is 360°, which means that a white light will be visible all around the horizon.) The range of visibility varies between two miles and six miles, depending upon the size of the vessel. Vessels under 12 meters, and any vessel on the Great Lakes, may show a single 360° white light visible all around the horizon in lieu of a masthead light and a sternlight. Large ships show two masthead lights, the after one being higher.

Sidelights are usually shown separately, but on a vessel less than 20 meters in length they may be combined into a single fixture. They are placed lower than the forward white light. Ranges of required visibility vary from one to three miles.

Lights must be shown from sunset to sunrise, and at other times if visibility is reduced. Vessels being propelled by machinery display the full set of lights described above. Sailing vessels, when not being propelled by machinery, display only sidelights and a stern light. When under power, sailboats must show the full set of lights, even if sails are hoisted. A sailboat under 7 meters in length or a rowboat should show proper lights but, if that is not practicable, may have only a white light (usually an electric lantern or flashlight) to be shown when needed.

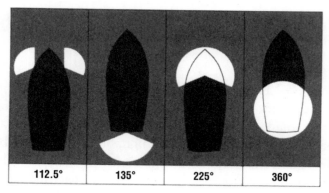

FIGURE 3-1. Each type of navigation light must cover a specified arc of visibility. Some show only from dead ahead and along part of a vessel's side; others can be seen only from the stern area; and some show all around.

RIDING LIGHTS

A vessel at anchor basically shows an all-round white light from a location where it can best be seen. Large ships are required to show two such lights, the aft one lower than the other. A vessel aground must show the proper anchor light(s) plus two all-round red lights arranged vertically; boats less than 12 meters in length do not have to meet this requirement.

SPECIAL LIGHTS

In addition to the basic running lights, there are many special lights to indicate a specific type of vessel or a specific operation in which it is engaged. These may be white, red, green, or yellow; blue lights are used only for law-enforcement vessels. They may be fixed or flashing.

Towing vessels, including those pushing a barge ahead, show additional lights indicating their work. Fishing vessels display additional lights indicating the type of fishing being done. Pilot vessels have special lights to be shown when on duty. Vessels defined in the Rules as having limited maneuverability must show lights to indicate that status; these include diving vessels, vessels with steering or propulsion difficulties, vessels restricted by their draft, etc.

DAY SHAPES

There are a number of shapes, or combination of shapes, to be shown during the day when lights are not effective. There are ball, cone, and cylinder shapes, with a diamond shape being created by placing two cones base to base. They are all black and of a size appropriate to the vessel on which they are to be used.

A vessel at anchor in daytime must show a single ball shape where it can best be seen. A vessel being propelled by sails and machinery must show a cone shape, point down, indicating that she does not have the right-of-way preference of a sailing vessel. Vessels aground should show three balls in a vertical line. (Vessels less than 12 meters in length need not comply with the above three requirements.) There are also various shape requirements for fishing vessels; pilot vessels; vessels restricted in ability to maneuver, such as dredges; and others.

INTERPRETING WHAT YOU SEE

Knowing the rules and requirements described above is fine, but it is only the beginning! You must be able to interpret the navigation lights of a vessel when that is all you can see of her. Study carefully since there will be no time to "look it up in the book" when you encounter another vessel at night.

If you see the red sidelight of another vessel, you immediately know that she has the right-of-way and you must yield—that's why it is red. There are other situations in which you need to figure out light combinations quickly in order to avoid danger; for example, when you encounter a tug and tow, a dredge, fishing vessels, or some other type of unusual vessel.

MISUSE OF NAVIGATION LIGHTS

Boats are often seen underway at night mistakenly showing running lights plus an anchor light. The two white lights, when seen from astern, could easily be misinterpreted for the two masthead lights of a larger vessel. Make sure that your anchor light is turned off if you are underway.

An all-round white running light can also be used as an anchor light if there are separate switches for it and the sidelights. Don't show your running lights when at anchor.

MAINTENANCE OF NAVIGATION LIGHTS

Many boats are used only in the daytime, but the wise skipper checks the navigation lights regularly—once a month is not too often—lest he or she be caught out after dark. Remember, running lights are to be used in any conditions in which visibility is reduced; this includes fog and rain. It is also important to have on board spare bulbs and fuses, one or more of each type and size.

Right-of-Way and Whistle Signals

Although the term "right-of-way" does not appear in the text of the Navigation Rules, it is a commonly understood and often used phrase. The official terms are "stand-on vessel" for the one that has the right to proceed unimpeded, and "give-way vessel" for the one that must turn, slow, or stop to keep out of the other's way. (These were formerly called the "privileged" and "burdened" vessels respectively—these terms are still often used because they are simpler.) The Rules set forth the required actions of both vessels in various types of encounters.

WHISTLE SIGNALS

The U.S. Inland Rules call for whistle signals to be given in certain situations, as discussed below. (Small craft sound "whistle" signals on the boat's horn.) The skipper who signals first signifies his intent to take a specific action; the other skipper responds with the *same signal* to indicate that this intent is understood and that the action will cause no problem. If the action to be taken may lead to a problem, the other skipper responds with the *danger signal* of five or more short and rapid blasts, and the first skipper must not continue with the intended action.

Under International Rules, a whistle signal indicates that a specific action will be taken. Such signals are often called "rudder signals" for this reason, and they are not answered, although in some situations, such as the meeting described below, the second vessel may sound the same signal and take the same action as the first. The danger signal is the same in both the International and Inland Rules and is used in the same manner.

Meeting Head-on

When meeting another power-driven vessel head-on, keep to the right. Show that you intend to do so by swinging the bow of your boat in that direction, even more than necessary so that your action will be obvious to the other skipper. The proper signal is one short blast from either boat, to be answered by one short blast from the other. A short blast lasts one second. Neither vessel is considered privileged or burdened regardless of which first sounds the signal.

If a boat is coming toward you head-on, but is so far to your right that the boats will pass at a safe distance, both can maintain course. One boat may signal his intention to do so with two short blasts of his horn; the other boat should answer with the same signal.

Crossing Situation

Your boat's *danger zone* is the arc from dead ahead to 22.5° abaft the starboard beam. A vessel in your danger zone has the right-of-way if coming toward you — it is the stand-on vessel. Your boat is the give-way vessel and must alter course, slow down, or stop (if necessary) to avoid collision. The stand-on vessel must maintain course and speed, and may sound one

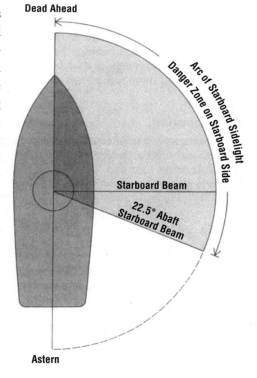

FIGURE 3-2. A boat's danger zone is the arc from dead ahead to a point 22.5 degrees abaft the starboard beam. Any vessel approaching you in that area is a stand-on vessel and has the right of way.

short blast of its horn; if it does so, you must answer with one short blast.

Overtaking

The boat being overtaken has the right-of-way; it is the stand-on vessel and should hold course and speed. The overtaking boat is the give-way vessel and must keep clear until it is well forward of the privileged vessel and no danger of collision exists. A boat is overtaking another when it is approaching a point more than 22.5 degrees abaft the beam of the stand-on vessel on either side. The Rules state that a stand-on vessel, in this case one being passed, must maintain course and speed, but as a practical matter in confined waters it is often wise for that craft to slow down and possibly move toward the side of the channel after sounding the appropriate signals.

If the overtaking boat plans to pass to the left of the privileged vessel (leaving it to starboard), a signal of two short blasts is given, and is answered by the same signal if the stand-on vessel considers such passing to be safe and consents to the proposed action. If the overtaking vessel plans to leave the privileged vessel to port, a signal of one short blast is given, and is answered by the same signal.

No matter which side the overtaking boat plans to pass on, if the overtaken vessel considers passing to be dangerous, it sounds the danger signal of five or more short and rapid blasts, and the other vessel should stay behind.

Initiating Signals

In head-on meeting situations, either vessel can signal first; in overtaking situations, the burdened vessel signals first, to indicate on which side she desires to pass. In crossing situations, the privileged vessel signals first. In any case, on inland water, the second vessel answers with the *same* signal to show that the intent of the first boat is understood. If the skipper of the second vessel believes the action signaled by the first boat will lead to a collision, or is in any other way dangerous, he should sound the *danger* signal. *Never* answer a two-blast signal with one blast, or a one-blast signal with two blasts—this is a "crossed signal" and is strictly prohibited.

Use of Radio
In waters subject to the U.S. Inland Rules, it is permissible to use VHF radio communications in lieu of whistle signals between vessels encountering each other. This is desirable as more information can be passed via radio and thus actions can be taken with greater safety.

POWERBOAT-SAILBOAT ENCOUNTERS
The above situations involve encounters between two power-driven vessels. If a powerboat encounters a sailboat (with no machinery being used for propulsion), the latter has the right-of-way regardless of the configuration of the meeting, except that a sailing vessel overtaking a power vessel (possible, but not likely) is the give-way vessel. Whistle signals are not used.

ADDITIONAL WHISTLE SIGNALS
In addition to the whistle signals described above, there are others you need to know. Three short blasts signify that the vessel is operating astern propulsion even though she may still be making headway. One prolonged blast (four to six seconds duration) is sounded when a vessel is coming out of a slip, entering a channel, or approaching a blind bend.

Fog signals are sounded when underway or at anchor in conditions of reduced visibility. Different signals are prescribed for various types of vessels and situations.

SAILING VESSELS

Different right-of-way rules apply when two sailboats meet. When each has the wind on a different side, the one with the wind on her port side must keep out of the way of the other. When both have the wind on the same side, the windward vessel must keep out of the way of the other. Sailing vessels do not exchange whistle signals.

OTHER MAJOR RULES

Rule 5 requires that *every vessel* must keep a proper lookout by all available means, including sight and sound (and radar, if the vessel is so equipped).

Rule 6 requires that *every vessel* proceed at a safe speed so that she can take proper and effective action to avoid collision and be stopped in a distance appropriate to the prevailing circumstances and conditions. In determining a safe speed, the Rule lists factors to be considered, including, but not limited to, the state of visibility, the amount of other vessel traffic, and the maneuverability of the vessel concerned.

Rule 17 states that if the stand-on vessel's maintaining course and speed might result in a collision, she must alter course, slow down, or stop, or take such other action as might be necessary to avoid a collision.

Rule 2 states that "nothing in the Navigation Rules shall exonerate any vessel or its crew from the consequences of any neglect to comply with the Rules, or of the neglect of any precaution which may be required by the ordinary practice of seamen, or by the special circumstances of the case." It also recognizes that special circumstances may make a departure from the Rules necessary to avoid immediate danger.

Docking Techniques

To handle a boat or a ship, you must first *know* it. Know *what it will do, how fast it will do it,* and *in what space.* No article or text can give you this knowledge—it can come only from actual experience and practice. But knowing certain basic facts will enable you to get much more from your hands-on experience. Some of the most important of these are:

1. *The propeller controls the direction of a boat when docking, almost as much as the rudder.* Most vessels are right-handed, meaning that their propellers turn in a clockwise direction when viewed from astern with the engine turning ahead. A right-handed vessel's bow will usually swing to port slowly when going ahead, even with the rudder amidships, *but* the stern will swing rather sharply to port when the vessel is going astern, often regardless of where the rudder is. For left-handed vessels the effects are reversed.

2. *The "turning effect" of the propeller is much more pronounced when going astern.* Since much of the rudder's effect comes from the wash of the propeller rushing past it, if the engine is reversed, this wash will be directed in a direction away from the rudder and much of the effect of the helm is lost. The propeller takes over in a pronounced fashion.

3. *Brief spurts of engine power may be used to turn the bow or stern of the vessel as desired, without getting the boat underway.* With the rudder to starboard, a brief spurt of engine power (throttle is moved forward momentarily) will swing the bow to starboard *but,* if the power is cut back before the vessel gathers way, most of the power of the engine will have gone into turning the vessel rather than getting it moving through the water. The heavier the boat, the more this is so. Don't be afraid to gun your engine briefly to gain maneuverability. A large boat is quite heavy and won't shoot ahead the moment power is applied.

4. *The wind and current can often be as much help in docking as the engines and helm.* Nature will often dock your boat for you, if given half a chance. Why waste fuel and temper fighting her? A good policy many times is: Ride with the current.

Now to the actual process of docking, which is presented here in a series of diagrams to make it easier to grasp details without wading through a lot of text. The word "wind" will be used to cover whichever factor has the most effect on the vessel at the moment, be it wind or current. In calm or still water almost any of the methods outlined will work equally well. Boats are shown port side to the piers; for the reverse condition, simply reverse the rudder orders but maintain the same engine speeds and directions.

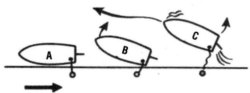

WIND

FIGURE 3-3. Leaving a pier (or wharf), boat alongside, wind ahead: A. Single up to one stern line, no power, no rudder. B. Let wind swing bow out, or push bow out with a boathook. C. With bow out 15 to 20 degrees, swing stern clear by using hard left rudder (right rudder if pier is to starboard) and brief spurts of power. Let stern line go when boat is a few feet from the pier and go ahead slowly. Steer away from the pier with slight rudder.

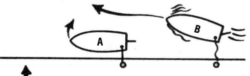

WIND

FIGURE 3-4. Leaving a pier (or wharf), boat alongside, wind off the pier: A. Single up to one stern line and let the wind swing the bow out. B. Ease off on the stern line until clear of the pier. Let go the line and go ahead slowly. Steer away from the pier with slight rudder.

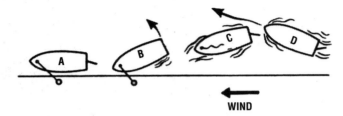

WIND

FIGURE 3-5. Leaving a pier (or wharf), boat alongside, wind astern: A. Single up to an after bow spring line. B. Let the wind swing the stern out, or use the engine in brief spurts with hard left rudder (right rudder if moored starboard side to the pier). C. Reverse engine and back off slowly; cast off line. D. When well clear of the pier, go ahead slowly and use slight rudder to steer away from the pier.

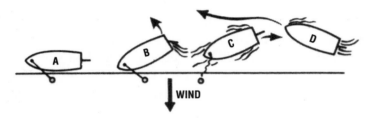

WIND

FIGURE 3-6. Leaving a pier (or wharf), boat alongside, wind onto the pier: A. Single up to an after bow spring line led well aft. B. Use spurts of power ahead to swing stern out, using hard left rudder (right rudder if pier is to starboard). C. Use engine in reverse to back away from the pier; cast off the spring line. D. When well clear, go ahead with engine and steer clear of the pier.

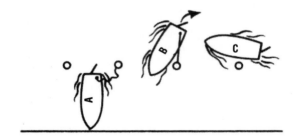

FIGURE 3-7. Leaving a slip: A. Single up to a single stern line, long enough to reach from the stern cleat to a point forward about two-thirds of the length of the boat. Make outboard end of the line fast to the outer end of the slip. B. Go astern slowly until the line is taut, then turn the rudder hard left. Boat's stern will swing to port under full control. C. Cast off when clear. Go ahead, give a slight bit of left rudder to swing the stern out, then use right rudder to steer clear.

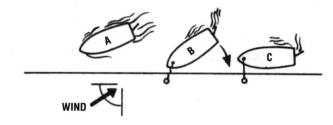

FIGURE 3-8. Docking, wind off the pier (or wharf) or ahead: A. Approach slowly at an angle of 30 to 40 degrees to the pier. B. Put engine in reverse to stop the boat with the bow about one foot from the pier; get the bow line ashore. C. With hard right rudder, use spurts of ahead power to bring the stern in to the pier. Make fast with additional lines.

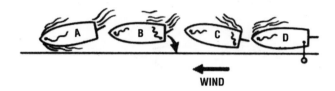

FIGURE 3-9. Docking, wind astern: A. Approach closely to the pier at an angle of 10 to 15 degrees. B. When one to two feet from the pier, use right rudder and brief spurts of power to start the stern swinging in toward the pier. C. As soon as the stern starts to swing in (boat parallel to the pier), reverse engine to stop the boat. D. Get the stern line ashore and let the wind bring the bow in to the pier. Make fast with additional lines.

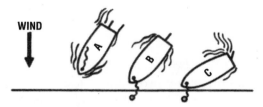

FIGURE 3-10. Docking, wind on to the pier (or wharf): A. Approach at a steep angle of about 60 to 80 degrees. B. Reverse the engine to stop the boat about a foot from the pier; ease boat off with a boathook if possible; get bow line ashore. C. Let the wind bring the stern in, using the engine in reverse and hard right rudder for braking action. Make fast with additional lines.

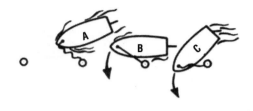

FIGURE 3-11. Entering a slip, wind anywhere but astern: A. Approach slowly, roughly parallel to the end of the slip. Pass a line to the pile or cleat nearest your approach. B. Reverse the engine to slow the approach, and stop the boat just short of the far pile, with the line taut. C. Put rudder hard left and use a spurt of power to bring the boat into the slip, using the pile as a pivot. Ease into the slip, and make fast with additional lines.

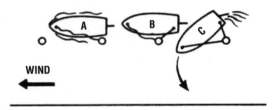

FIGURE 3-12. Entering a slip, wind astern: A. Approach as in Figure 3-11, but use enough power to stop the boat completely after passing the bowline. B. Pass a stern line to the same pile or cleat. C. Pull both lines tight and use the engine, wind, and rudder to ease the boat around and into the slip. Make fast with additional lines.

OTHER TYPES OF VESSELS

The docking and undocking procedures described above involve a single-screw boat, the more difficult type to maneuver. Many craft are twin-screw, with two engines and two propellers. The off-centerline location of these propellers provide an additional turning effect. Such boats can be maneuvered more sharply and even turned around completely without change in position, by going ahead on one engine and astern with the other.

Another type of propulsion can be described as *directed thrust,* typical of outboard motors and inboard-outboard drives in either single- or twin-screw installations. Vessels of this type do not have rudders; instead, steering is accomplished by turning the lower unit and propeller on a vertical axis so that the forward or reverse thrust will move the stern of the craft in the desired direction.

Anchoring

Whether just out for the day or cruising, "anchoring out" can be most enjoyable. But to do it safely, you must have the proper equipment—called "ground tackle"—and the knowledge of how to use it properly.

ANCHOR TYPES
There are many types and sizes of anchors—knowing what anchor to use in different types of vessels, weather conditions, bottom characteristics, and the many possible combinations thereof, is an important part of the "art of seamanship."

Lightweight
Lightweight anchors have long, sharp, flukes designed so that heavy strains bury the anchor completely. Originally called a "Danforth™," there are now many variations on the market, including the Fortress™ anchor made of high-strength aluminum. Lightweight anchors tend to work down through soft bottoms to firmer holding ground below, burying part of the anchor line (rode) as well as the anchor itself. They have a round rod at the crown end to prevent the anchor from rolling or rotating.

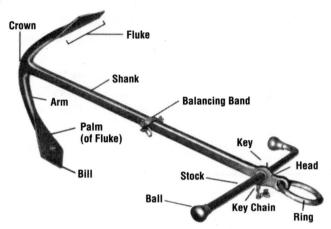

FIGURE 3-13. The parts of an anchor are identified here on a traditional kedge anchor. Some of the same terms are used for corresponding parts of modern anchors.

Plow (CQR)

Resembling a farmer's plowshare, this type of anchor also tends to bury itself completely. When lowered, it first lies on its side on the bottom. When a pull is put on the rode, it rights itself, driving the point of the plow into the bottom; additional strain on the rode buries the anchor completely. Because the shank pivots, this anchor tends to remain buried even when the angle of pull is changed by wind or current, but it breaks out easily with a vertical pull. There are related models in which the shank does not pivot.

Kedge

A kedge is the traditional anchor, with arms, flukes, and stocks as distinguished from modern stockless types. Holding power depends more on anchor weight than design. Dull bills make it difficult to bite in hard bottoms.

The yachtsman and Herreshoff anchors evolved from the kedges and feature changes in the size and shape of fluke relative to the arm. Flukes are diamond-shaped to reduce risk of fouling, and sharpened bills permit better penetration of the bottom. These are not burying-type anchors and serve best on rocky bottoms; they are also useful where heavy grass must be penetrated to get to the bottom soil. Retrieval, using a trip line (see Figure 3-14), is not too difficult if the anchor becomes snagged in coral or a rocky bottom.

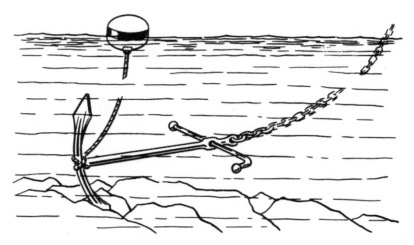

FIGURE 3-14. A buoyed trip line from the crown will permit an anchor that is snagged in a rocky bottom or caught in debris on the bottom to be hauled up flukes first.

Grapnel

This is a stockless anchor with four or five curved, sharp-billed, claw-like prongs at the crown end of the shank. Grapnels are not intended to be used to anchor a boat in position, except on very grassy bottoms. By dragging one back and forth over the bottom, the boater can grapple for a piece of equipment lost overboard.

Other Types

There are many other types of anchors available. These have patented designs and are useful in both general and special situations. Look around your boating area, and ask experienced skippers what they use.

BASIC ANCHORING TECHNIQUES

1. Enough rode (anchor line or chain) for the selected anchorage should be stowed below or coiled on the forward deck so as to run freely and without kinking or fouling. Make sure it is properly secured to the anchor, and that the bitter end is secured on board.

2. Having selected a suitable spot, either from a chart or by eye, run in slowly. Note your position by sighting on ranges ashore, buoys, or landmarks; later these will aid in determining if you are holding or dragging, especially if the marks are visible at night.

3. Give rocks, shoals, reefs, or other boats as wide a berth as possible. Your boat may swing in a full circle while at anchor.

4. As you approach the spot where the anchor is to be lowered, head up against wind or current, as appropriate, on the heading it will assume when anchored. Check other boats of your type that are at anchor in the area to see how they are lying.

5. In a motorboat or sail with auxiliary power, bring the bow up slowly to the point where the anchor is to be lowered. Check the headway by putting the boat into reverse, if necessary. Just as the boat gathers sternway, lower—do not throw—the anchor until it hits bottom, crown first. (If thrown, it is likely that the anchor will come to rest on the bottom pointing in some direction other than the direction of pull; this will delay the anchor in setting. It is also possible that the line will become fouled in the anchor.)

6. With the anchor on the bottom and the boat reversing slowly, pay out the rode, preferably with a turn around a bitt, as the boat takes it. When a scope (see Figure 3-15) of about 5:1 is reached, snub the line by holding it on the bitt; the anchor should take a quick, sure bite into the bottom. Snubbing too soon may cause the anchor to drag. Once the anchor is set, the line can be shortened somewhat if the anchorage is crowded and such a scope would be excessive. A scope of 5:1 is usually enough for normal conditions; more scope should be used if weather conditions threaten.

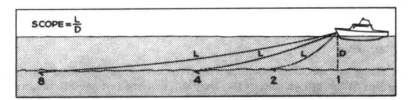

FIGURE 3-15. Scope is the ratio of the length of the anchor line (L) to the height of the bow of the boat above the bottom—i.e., the depth of the water (D), including allowance for tide, plus the height of the bow above the surface. At (1) the length equals the height of the bow above the bottom. At (2) the anchor line length is twice as great. At (4) it is four times as great; in other words, the scope is four. Note how the angle between the anchor line and the bottom decreases. At (8) the ratio is 8:1 and the short length of chain at the anchor lies flat on the bottom.

7. When the proper scope has been attained and the rode secured, apply a backdown load in excess of any that may be anticipated from wind or current. Check your ranges to see if the anchor is dragging. Then, and only then, shut off your boat's engine(s).

8. If conditions permit, put on a mask and snorkel and "swim the anchor," looking to see that it has properly set.

Anchoring Without Power
1. When under sail, approach your anchorage with the wind abeam so you can spill the wind from your sail to slow the boat down, or trim in to gain more headway. Make the approach under mainsail only.

2. When you reach the point where the anchor is to be lowered, you should have steerageway, but no more. Shoot the bow directly into the wind, let the sheet run, and drop the sail. As the boat loses headway, her bow will fall off and the boat will begin to drift to leeward. Now lower your anchor.

3. As the boat drifts back, pay out scope. Occasionally give a few jerks on the line; this helps to set the anchor. Hand test the line by pulling it. Your anchor will be holding when the boat is drawn toward it as you pull on the line. Pay out the usual scope of approximately 5:1.

Rocky Bottoms

If the bottom is foul or rocky in the area where you must anchor, it is advisable to rig a buoyed trip line, as shown in Figure 3-14. Make a light line fast to the crown; the line should be long enough to reach the surface, where it is buoyed with any convenient float. Be sure to allow for a rise in tide. If the anchor does not come free with a normal pull on the rode or by maneuvering the boat while pulling on the rode, haul in on the trip line, and the anchor will be freed, crown first.

Anchor Dragging

1. If it appears that your anchor is dragging, pay out more scope. If you are dragging badly, take a turn around a bitt and snub the line occasionally. If the anchor is not holding by the time you have paid out a scope of 10:1, haul it back on board and try again— preferably with a larger anchor, or one of a different type.

2. If you do not have a larger (storm) anchor, you can add a sentinel (also called a kellet) to the anchor line (see Figure 3-16). This is simply a weight sent more than halfway down the rode. It provides two benefits: lowering the angle of pull on the anchor and putting a sag in the line that must be straightened out before a load is thrown on the anchor.

3. An alternative to the sentinel is a buoy on the anchor line. This carries the vertical hold in the anchoring system and limits the basic load on the boat to that required to hold the boat in position. The buoy permits the boat's bow to rise up easily over wave crests, rather than being pulled down into them, which would increase the loads on both anchor and rode.

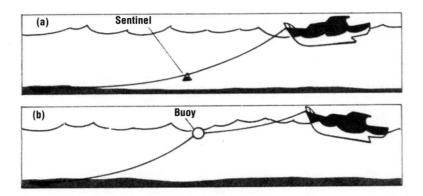

FIGURE 3-16. Two methods of increasing anchor effectiveness (holding power) in rough weather. See text for advantages and disadvantages of each technique.

Getting Underway

When you are ready to *weigh anchor* and get underway, run up to the anchor slowly under power, so that the line can be taken in easily without hauling the boat up to it. Ordinarily the anchor will break out readily when the rode stands vertically.

As the line or chain comes in, it can be whipped up and down to free it of any grass or weed it may have picked up. This clears the rode before it comes back on deck. If the anchor is not too heavy, plunging it up and down near the surface will wash off mud.

SUGGESTED SIZES FOR WORKING ANCHORS

BOAT LENGTH FT (M)	RODE LENGTH FT (M)	RODE SIZE IN (MM)	CHAIN SIZE* IN (MM)	DANFORTH STANDARD MODEL	FORTRESS MODEL NO.	PLOW LBS (KG)	BRUCE LBS (KG)	DELTA LBS (KG)
Up to 15 (4.6)	100 (31)	¼ (6)	3⁄16(5)	4~S	FX~7	20 (9.1)	11 (5)	14 (6.4)
15 to 25 (4.6 to 7.6)	150 (46)	3⁄8 (10)	3⁄16 (5)	8~S	FX~7	20 (9.1)	11 (5)	14 (6.4)
26 to 30 (7.9 to 9.1)	180 (55)	3⁄8 (10)	¼ (6)	13~S	FX~11	20 (9.1)	16.5(7.5)	22 (10)
31 to 35 (9.4 to 10.7)	200 (61)	3⁄8 (10)	¼ (6)	22~S	FX~11	25 (11.4)	22 (10)	22 (10)
36 to 40 (11.0 to 12.2)	250 (76)	7⁄16 (11)	5⁄16 (8)	22~S	FX-16	35 (15.9)	33 (15)	35 (15)
41 to 50 (12.5 to 15.2)	300 (91)	½ (12)	3⁄8 (10)	40~S	FX-23	45 (20.4)	44 (20)	35 (15)
51 to 60 (15.5 to 18.3)	300 (91)	½ (12)	3⁄8 (10)	65~S	FX-37	60 (27.2)	66 (30)	55 (25)

*Recommended chain length: ½ foot of chain for each foot of boat length. Larger vessels should use an all chain rode.

TABLE 3-17. The sizes suggested above are for use in moderate conditions of wind and waves, with good holding ground, and with a scope of 5. For less favorable conditions, increase anchor size by one bracket, and increase scope. For a "lunch hook" under good conditions in the daytime with a person remaining on board, one bracket smaller can be used.

Knots and Splices

Illustrated here are eight knots that every boater should know. They represent just a few of the many that were developed for shipboard use during the age of square-riggers, but they are all that are needed on the average recreational boat.

Also illustrated are the eye splice and short splice. Because the eye splice is used for so many applications, it is shown made with double-braided nylon line as well as standard three-strand line. The method illustrated is that developed by Samson Cordage Works.

FIGURE 3-18. An overhand knot is used to keep the end of a line from unlaying. The knot jams and may become almost impossible to untie.

FIGURE 3-21. The clove hitch is used for making a line fast temporarily to a pile. It is not secure, however, and can slip unless two half-hitches are taken with the free end around the standing end.

FIGURE 3-19. The figure-eight knot can be used as a "stopper" to prevent a line from running through a sheave. It does not jam and can be untied easily.

FIGURE 3-20. The square, or reef, knot is used for tying two light lines together, for tying awning stops, reef points, and similar uses. It can jam if stressed heavily and become difficult to untie.

FIGURE 3-22. Two half-hitches can be used to make a line fast to a ring, pile, or similar structure. Note that the knot consists of a turn around the fixed object and a clove hitch around the standing part of the line.

FIGURE 3-23. The bowline will not slip, does not pinch or kink the line as much as some other knots, and it does not jam or become difficult to untie. By tying a bowline with a small loop, and passing the line through this loop, a running bowline is formed; this is an excellent form of running noose. A bowline is used wherever a secure loop or running noose is needed in the end of a line, such as one to be secured to a pile. It may also be used to secure a line to an anchor.

FIGURE 3-25. A Fisherman's bend, or anchor bend, is handy for making fast to a buoy or spar, or to the ring of an anchor.

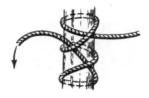

FIGURE 3-26. Shown above is the correct method of making a line fast to a cleat. The half-hitch that completes the fastening is taken with the free part of the line. The line can then be freed without taking up slack with the standing part.

FIGURE 3-24. Use a rolling hitch to make a line fast to a spar or another line. Close the turns up tight and take the strain on the end shown above with an arrow-tip.

EYE SPLICE

1. Start by unlaying the strands about six inches to one foot or more, or six to ten turns of lay, depending on the size of the line. Secure the ends of each strand with masking or plastic tape. With synthetic line, it's helpful to use tape around the unlaid strands every four inches to six inches, to help hold the "turn" in the strand.

2. Form a loop in the line of the desired size by laying the end back along the standing part. Hold the standing part away from you in the left hand, loop toward you. The stranded end can be worked with the right hand.

3. The size of the loop is determined by Point X, Figure 3-27, where the opened strands are first tucked under the standing part of the line. If the splice is to go around a thimble, the line is laid snugly in the thimble groove and Point X will be at the tapered end of the thimble. The thimble may be taped or tied in place until the splice is finished.

4. Lay the three unopened strands across the standing part as shown in Figure 3-27 so the center strand B lies over and directly along the standing part. Left-hand strand A leads off to the left; right-hand strand C leads off to the right of the standing part.

5. Tuck ends of strand A, B, and C under the strands of the standing part; see Figure 3-28. Start with the center strand B. Select the topmost strand 2 of the standing part near Point X, and tuck B under it. Pull it up snug, but not so tight as to distort the natural lay of all strands. Tuck is made from right to left, against the lay of the standing part.

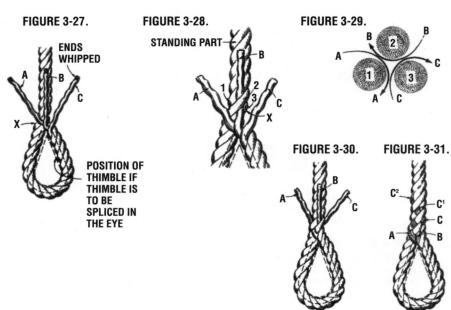

FIGURE 3-27.

ENDS WHIPPED

A   B

C

X

POSITION OF THIMBLE IF THIMBLE IS TO BE SPLICED IN THE EYE

FIGURE 3-28.

STANDING PART

B

A   1   2
3
C

X

FIGURE 3-29.

B   B
A   2   C

1   3
A   C

FIGURE 3-30.

B
A
C

FIGURE 3-31.

C²   C¹
C
A   B

6. Tuck strand A under strand 1, which lies to the left of strand 2. Tuck strand C under strand 3, which lies to the right of strand 2. Tuck from right to left in every case. The greatest risk of a wrong start is in the first tuck of strand C. It must go under 3 from right to left; refer to Figure 3-29. If the first three tucks are correct, splice will look as shown in Figure 3-30.

7. Complete splice by making at least three additional tucks with each strand, in rotation. As each tuck is made, be sure it passes from right to left under one strand of the standing part, then over the next one above it. This is shown in Figure 3-31. Note that C, C^1, and C^2 are the same strand as it appears after successive tucks.

The eye splice with double-braided synthetic line is illustrated and described in Figures 3-32 to 3-39 and their captions.

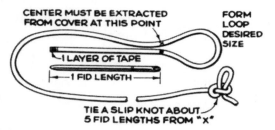

FIGURE 3-32. Tightly tape end of line with one layer of tape. Mark a big dot one fid length from end. From this dot, form a loop the size of the eye you want, and mark with an "X" as shown above. Tie a slip knot about five fid lengths from the "X" as shown.

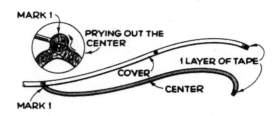

FIGURE 3-33. Bend line sharply at "X" and spread strands apart firmly to make an opening so that the center can be pried out. Mark one big line on the center where it comes out (this is Mark #1), and use your fingers to pull all the center out of the cover from "X" to the end. Pull on the paper tape inside the center until it breaks back at the slip knot; you need to get rid of it so that you can splice. Put a layer of tape on the end of the center.

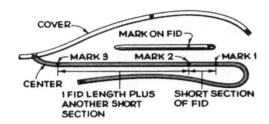

FIGURE 3-34. Pull out more of the center. From Mark #1, measure a distance equal to the short section of the fid, and mark two heavy lines (this is Mark #2). Mark #3 is three heavy lines at a distance of one fid length plus one short section of the fid from Mark #2.

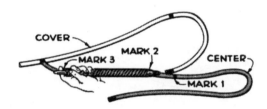

FIGURE 3-35. Insert fid into the center at Mark #2, and slide it lengthwise through the "tunnel" until the point sticks out at Mark #3.

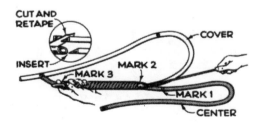

FIGURE 3-36. Cut across the taped end of the cover to form a point and retape tightly with one layer of tape. Jam this point into the open end of the fid. Jam the pusher into the fid behind the tape. Hold the center gently at Mark #3, and push both fid and cover through the center until the dot almost disappears at Mark #2.

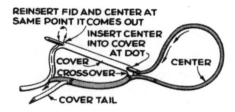

FIGURE 3-37. Note how the center tail must travel through the cover. It must go in close to the dot and come out through the opening at "X." On large eyes, several passes may be necessary for the fid to reach "X." When this occurs, simply reinsert the fid at the exact place it comes out, and continue on to "X." To start, insert the fid into the cover and slide it through the tunnel to "X." Form a tapered point on the center tail, jam it into the open end of the fid, and push fid and center through the cover. After the fid comes out at "X," pull the center tail through the cover until tight, then pull the cover tail tight.

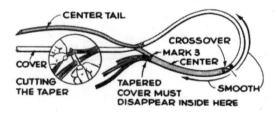

FIGURE 3-38. Unravel the braid of the cover tail all the way to Mark #3, and cut off groups of strands at staggered intervals to form a tapered end. Hold the loop at the crossover in one hand and firmly smooth both sides of the loop away from the crossover. Do this until the tapered tail section completely disappears inside Mark #3.

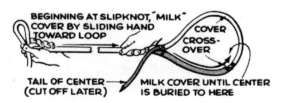

FIGURE 3-39. Hold the line at the slip knot and gently begin to "milk" or slide the cover back toward the loop. You'll see the center begin to disappear into the cover. Go back to the knot and continue sliding the cover more and more firmly until the entire center and crossover are buried inside the cover.

SHORT SPLICE

A short splice is used where two lines are to be permanently joined, provided they do not have to pass through the sheave hole or throat of a block. When a rope must pass through a block, a long splice must be made.

1. Unlay the strands of both ends for a short distance, as described for the eye splice. Secure the strand ends with masking or plastic tape, or fuse them with heat; wrap tape around each line to prevent the strands from unlaying too far.

2. Bring the ends of the lines together so that the strands of one lie alternately between the strands of the other, as shown in Figure 3-40. Tie all the strands of one line in place temporarily, as in Figure 3-41 (some boaters eliminate this step, as it is not essential).

FIGURE 3-40   **FIGURE 3-41**

3. Remove the tape that is keeping the other line from unlaying further and tuck the strands into the line, just as if it were an eye splice, working from right to left with each strand passing over and under the strands of the other line.

4. If the strands from the other lines have been tied back as in step 2 above, release them and repeat the above process. The splice should now appear as shown in Figure 3-42.

5. Short splices and eye splices can be tapered by cutting out yarns from the strands after the necessary full tucks have been made. Never cut end strands off too close to the standing part of the line; a heavy strain may allow them to work out.

FIGURE 3-42

FIGURE 3-43

6. A second method of making the splice is to start as in Figure 3-40, and then tie pairs of strands from opposite ends in an overhand knot (see Figure 3-43). This, in effect, makes the first tuck.

CHAPTER FOUR

Aids to Navigation

Unlike streets and highways on land, water areas have many dangers hidden under their surface, and there are no road signs to direct you toward your destination and alert you to hazards. To guide your way, however, there are charts and *aids to navigation*. To ensure the safety and efficiency of navigation, the Coast Guard establishes and maintains thousands of aids to navigation, such as lighted and unlighted buoys, daybeacons, lights of all sizes and types, ranges, and fog signals (as well as electronic systems, discussed in Chapter 9, "Electronic Communications and Navigation"). There are also aids provided by other governmental agencies and by non-governmental organizations. These *private aids to navigation* must be approved by the Coast Guard before they can be established. The Coast Guard uses the acronym "ATON" for both of these categories. (The term "navigational aid," as opposed to "aids to navigation," is used for such items as books, charts, and instruments.)

All aids to navigation are protected by federal law. A boater must not destroy or damage them, or hinder their operation. Do not tie your boat to an aid to navigation for fishing or any other purpose, except a major emergency. Do not anchor so close as to obscure it from the sight of passing vessels. If you should accidentally damage an aid, report this to the nearest Coast Guard unit without delay. Report any missing or malfunctioning aid by mail or radio.

Minor aids, such as buoys and daybeacons, are normally identified by numbers, or occasionally by letters. More important aids have names, but these are not displayed on the aid. You must learn to recognize each type of aid to navigation and how to use them to make your boating safer and more enjoyable.

Buoys

Floating aids to navigation are termed "buoys"; they are anchored to the bottom with heavy weights and chains in carefully surveyed positions. Buoys may be lighted or unlighted. They are used in various shapes to convey navigational information, and in different sizes to fit the size of the waterway and the vessels using it. Colors, lights, and sound characteristics also provide navigational information.

BUOY SHAPES

Nearly all unlighted buoys are either a *can buoy,* which looks like a cylinder above water, or a *nun buoy,* which looks like a cone-topped cylinder above water. Some buoys are *spherical* in shape. In foreign waters, you may find a *spar buoy,* which looks a lot like a pile of wood floating upright. Lighted, sound, and combination (both light and sound) buoys exist in a variety of shapes; in such buoys, shape has no navigational significance.

   All buoys, lighted or unlighted, will have patches of reflective material and/or reflective numbers and letters that can be readily seen at night when they are illuminated by a vessel's searchlight. Most buoys have a radar reflector that enhances their detection by day and night.

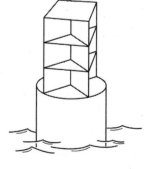 

FIGURE 4-1. Most unlighted buoys are either "cans" with a flat top or "nuns" with a pointed top.

NAVIGATION

SOUND BUOYS

Sound buoys emit an audible signal—bell, gong, or whistle—that facilitates their location in fog or other reduced visibility situations. Different sound signals are assigned to buoys within audible range of each other. *Bell buoys* sound a single note triggered on an irregular basis by the motion of the buoy in swells and waves. *Gong buoys* sound four different notes, also in an irregular pattern. *Whistle buoys* sound signals that are activated by the motion of the water. In a few areas where there is not enough sea motion, buoys will be equipped with an electrically operated horn. There will be only one type of sound signal on any individual buoy.

LIGHTED BUOYS

To facilitate their detection and use at night, buoys that are of greater importance to navigation safety are equipped with lights, whose batteries are kept charged by solar panels. These *lighted buoys* show various colors and flashing characteristics to convey navigational information. The distance at which a light must be seen by the type of vessels using the waterway determines the intensity of the light that is installed on a buoy.

COMBINATION BUOYS

Buoys that have both sound and light signals are called *combination buoys*. The various types are described as "lighted bell buoy," "lighted whistle buoy," etc.

LIGHT RHYTHMS

Lighted buoys will generally flash in one of several specific rhythms. This reduces the electrical power required, makes the buoy more readily detected against a background of other lights, and assists in distinguishing one buoy from another; light patterns

Symbols and Meaning

Illustration	LIGHTS WHICH DO NOT CHANGE COLOR	LIGHT WHICH SHOW COLOR VARIATIONS	PHASE DESCRIPTION
	F. = Fixed	Alt. = Alternating	A continuous light (Steady)
	F. Fl. = Fixed and flashing	Alt. F. Fl. = Alternating fixed and flashing	A fixed light varied at regular intervals by a flash of greater brilliance.
	F. Gp. Fl. = Fixed and group flashing	Alt. F. Gp. Fl. = Alternating fixed and group flashing	A fixed light varied at regular intervals by groups of two or more flashes of greater brilliance.
	Fl. = Flashing	Alt. Fl. = Alternating flashing	Showing a single flash at regular intervals, the duration of light always being less than the duration of darkness.
	Gp. Fl. = Group flashing	Alt. Gp. Fl. = Alternating group flashing	Showing at regular intervals groups of two or more flashes.
	Gp. Fl. (2 + 1) = Composite group flashing	....	Light flashes are combined in alternate groups of different numbers.

FIGURE 4-2. Light Characteristics.

NAVIGATION

	Mo (A) = Morse code		Light in which flashes of different duration are grouped in such a manner as to produce a Morse character or characters.
	Qk. Fl. = Quick flashing		Shows not fewer than sixty flashes per minute.
	I. Qk. Fl. = interrupted quick flashing		Shows quick flashes for about four seconds, followed by a dark period of about four seconds.
	Iso = Isophase		
	Occ. = Occulting	Alt. Occ. = Alternating occulting	A light totally eclipsed at regular intervals, the duration of light always greater than the duration of darkness.
	Gp. Occ. = Group occulting		A light with a group of two or more eclipses at regular intervals.
	Gp. Occ. (2 + 3) = Composite group occulting		A light in which the occultations are combined in alternate groups of different numbers.

can also convey navigational information such as the need for greater caution where a channel turns or narrows.

Flashing lights are the most common on buoys. They are on less than they are off, flashing in a regular pattern. The most common rhythm is a flash every 4 seconds; other rhythms with flashes every 2½ or 6 seconds are often used where multiple buoys are within visible range of each other.

Quick flashing lights, emitting no fewer than 60 flashes per minute, are used where lights must be more quickly detected or where there is a greater navigational hazard.

Other rhythms include *group flashing* (2+1)—two brief flashes, a brief interval, then another brief flash followed by darkness for the remainder of the period—and *Morse Code* (A) lights—a brief flash, a brief interval, a longer flash, then darkness for the remainder of the period.

The term "characteristic" applied to a light refers to its color and rhythm, and sometimes to its nominal range of visibility as well.

CAUTIONS IN USING BUOYS

Buoys are not on an exact position. The chain connecting the buoy to its anchor is always longer than the depth of the water, often several times longer. Thus the buoy moves about horizontally under the influence of wind, waves, and current. Never approach a buoy closely; it might make a sudden shift in position. In recording fixes and plotting courses, make allowance for a reasonable difference between the charted location and the actual position. Remember also that buoys may sink or be dragged off location by vessel collision, storms, ice, or other actions. Lighted buoys may become extinguished or show improper characteristics. Never depend on a single floating aid to navigation for the safety of your craft!

Beacons

Buoys require regular maintenance for the removal of fouling growth, verification of position, service of lights, etc. For this reason, whenever the depth of water allows, *beacons* may be used instead of buoys. Beacons are simple structures fixed to the bottom. They may be a single pile (wood, concrete, or steel I-beam), or occasionally a *dolphin,* a group of piles driven close to each other and fastened together with steel cabling; some beacons consist of a small platform. Beacons have sets of simple signs called *dayboards.* There are usually two dayboards, one facing in each direction along a channel; at junctions, there may be a third dayboard so that the signs can be seen from three directions. Dayboards are typically square or triangular, corresponding to can or nun buoys. They are identified by numbers or letters in the same manner as buoys. Other shapes, such as diamond or octagonal, do exist but are rare. Dayboards have reflective material on background areas, borders, and identification numbers and letters.

Daybeacons are unlighted and may be used instead of unlighted buoys. (Buoys may continue to be used in shallow waters where channels and shoals are subject to shifting.) In a similar manner, lighted buoys are sometimes replaced with *minor lights.* These are no more than daybeacons to which a light has been added. Light characteristics are similar.

Buoyage Systems

The vast majority of aids to navigation in U.S. waters are used in a *lateral* system in which the aids mark the sides of a dredged or natural channel. In wider bodies of water, they mark shoals or projecting points of land. In the Western Hemisphere, plus Japan and the Philippines, aids marking the starboard side of safe water for a vessel coming in from the open sea are *red,* leading to the memory-aid, *Red-Right-Returning.* Aids on the other side are colored *green.* These colors are used on buoys and dayboards, and for the color of lights. Red aids have even numbers, and green aids have odd numbers. Numbers increase from seaward; if numbers get too large, a sequence may be ended and a new set of numbers begun. Numbers may be omitted as necessary to keep opposite or nearly opposite buoys close in step; buoys added after a sequence has been established will have applicable numbers with a letter suffix beginning with "A."

Offshore buoys and minor lights are generally numbered clockwise around the U.S coasts—from north to south along the Atlantic coast; northward then westward along the Gulf of Mexico coast; and from south to north along the Pacific coast. They are numbered on the Great Lakes from the outlet of the lake to its upper end. On the Atlantic and Gulf Intracoastal Waterways, numbering is in the same direction as coastal aids, with many sequences.

Special markers are used where channels divide or come together (if lighted, Group Flashing 2+1); for ranges; to indicate an area of safe water all around (flashing Morse A); to delineate the boundaries of special areas, such as anchorages (flashing yellow lights); and to mark isolated dangers (Group Flashing 2).

The aids to navigation on the Mississippi River and its tributaries are slightly different from those used in coastal waters.

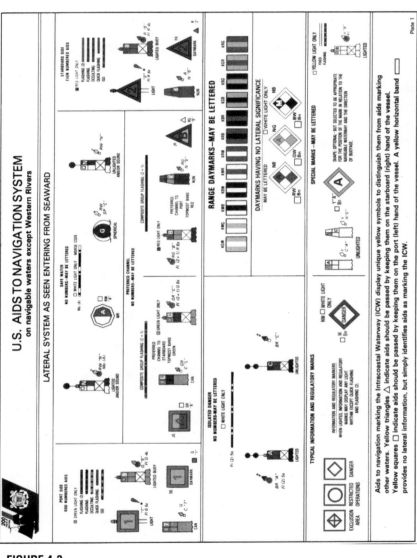

FIGURE 4-3.

NAVIGATION

FOREIGN WATERS

In foreign waters, other than where listed above, a lateral system is used, but one quite different from the one just described. Also commonly used in these waters is a *cardinal system* of buoyage in which the aids indicate the direction of safe water from the aid's position. (Such buoys are used very rarely in U.S. waters.)

Ranges and Directional Lights

A *range* consists of two fixed aids to navigation so located with respect to each other that when they appear to be in line a vessel is in safe water, usually the middle of a channel. Ranges have dayboards of spe-

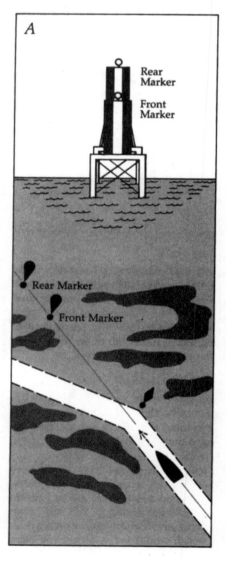

FIGURE 4-4. A boat can be kept within a narrow channel by following a range. At A, the front and rear range markers are in line, with the higher rear mark above the lower front mark. If you get "off the range," the markers will not be aligned, as in B and C. You will be off to the same side of the range line that the rear marker is seen with respect to the front marker. Ranges will often not extend all the way up to the front marker, and you will have to know when to leave the range and take up a new heading; this point is normally marked with another aid to navigation.

NAVIGATION

cial design and are usually equipped with lights of special characteristics, but some lesser ones may be unlighted. These lights usually have a narrow beam only a few degrees wide showing directly down the range. For all ranges, the rear dayboard (and its

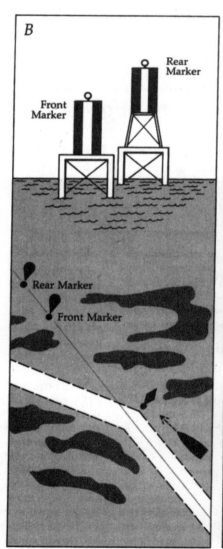

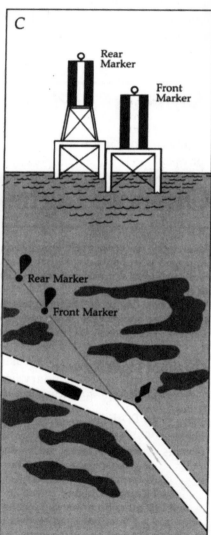

light, if so equipped) is higher than the front aid so when they are seen in line, one dayboard and/or light appears above the other.

A *directional light* is one with a narrow beam of three colors, a very narrow central sector showing white, with narrow red or green sectors on each side. They are not often used, and in rare circumstances, a range rear light will have directional characteristics.

Seacoast and Secondary Lights

Seacoast and *Secondary Lights* differ from minor lights in their physical size, range, complexity of characteristics, and importance to navigational safety. Only broad statements can be made about them as a group.

Seacoast lights (often referred to as "lighthouses") warn the high-seas navigator of the proximity of land. They are usually the first aids to navigation seen on making a landfall; they also enable a coastwise skipper to remain farther offshore at night than if he had to depend on coastal aids. Seacoast lights are normally accompanied by a major fog signal.

Secondary lights are smaller and simpler than seacoast lights, but are distinctly larger than minor lights. They are often found in large harbors and bays, and usually have fog signals.

Seacoast and secondary lights have names rather than numbers and rarely have dayboards, depending instead on their unique appearance for identification. These lights are basically white for greater range, but may have red sectors to mark dangerous areas.

CHAPTER FIVE

Charts

Water areas are much more featureless than land; many hazards are out of sight beneath the surface. Your chart is an essential tool to get you where you want to go without mishap. Have up-to-date charts of your boating area, and know how to use them. There are also many publications with information that can make your boating safer and more pleasant—get them and study them.

Maps and charts are representations in miniature, on a plane surface, of a portion of the earth's surface. A *chart* emphasizes water areas and features that are of particular interest to a skipper. A *map* focuses primarily on land areas, with different types of maps emphasizing physical features, roads, structures, or political boundaries.

Charts are printed very accurately on high-grade paper that will resist moisture. Most are flat sheets, but some are accordion-folded "small-craft charts" intended for use on smaller vessels where space is limited. With the increasing use of technology on vessels, many are now available in digital form for use on computers and "chart plotters."

PROJECTIONS AND DISTORTION

Because the earth is essentially spherical, it is not possible to exactly portray the size and relationship of its various features on a flat surface. To get as good a match as possible, chart makers use various *projections*—graphical and mathematical methods of representing a spherical surface on a flat one—each of which has advantages and disadvantages. Boaters on the high seas and coastal waters will use charts using the *Mercator projection*.

Boaters on the Great Lakes and other inland waters will normally use charts made with the *polyconic projection*. Both projections introduce some distortions, but over the areas covered by charts that boaters use, they are too slight to be noticeable.

GEOGRAPHIC COORDINATES

Locations on the earth and on charts are described in terms of *latitude* and *longitude*. These are shown as a grid of intersecting lines on a chart. *Meridians* run north-and-south and are used to measure longitude in degrees east or west from the *prime meridian,* 0°, which runs through Greenwich, England, to a maximum of 180° in either direction. A statement of longitude must always include the label "E" or "W." *Parallels of latitude* run east-and-west, and measure the distance north or south from the equator, which is 0°. Latitude extends 90° to the North and South Poles, and must always have a label of "N" or "S." Longitude is abbreviated as "Lo" or "Long"; latitude is abbreviated as "L" or "Lat."

Whole degrees are divided into *minutes:* 1° = 60'. Each minute can be subdivided into decimal fractions or into *seconds:* 1' = 60". Check the margins of each chart that you use to determine which method of subdivision is used.

CHART NUMBERING SYSTEM

Charts of U.S coastal waters and some inland waters are produced by the National Ocean Service (NOS), a part of the National Oceanic and Atmospheric Administration (NOAA); such charts are referred to as either NOS or NOAA charts. Charts of more distant waters are produced by the National Imagery and Mapping Agency (NIMA), which now includes the former Defense Mapping and Hydrographic/Topographic Center (DMAHTC).

All NOS and NIMA charts are numbered according to a common system. Boaters will generally be concerned only with charts

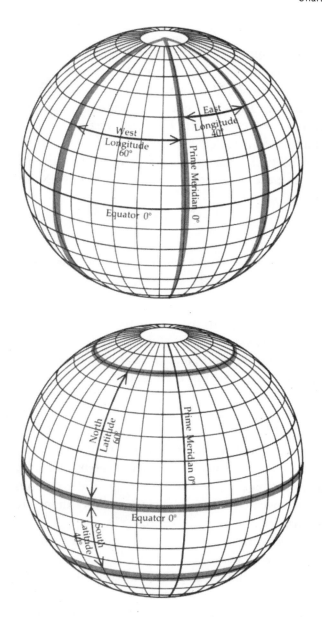

FIGURE 5-1. Longitude, top, is measured from the Prime Meridian (0°) which passes through Greenwich, England, east or west to a maximum of 180°. Latitude, bottom, is measured north or south from the equator (0°) to the poles (90°).

having a *five-digit* number. The first digit refers to a *region* of the world; the second digit, together with the first, refers to a *subregion*. The final three digits are assigned systematically within a subregion to denote a specific chart. Many numbers are left unused so that future charts can be fitted into the system.

Charts, often called "navigational maps," of many major inland rivers and other bodies are prepared by the Army Corps of Engineers; these are not a part of the NOS/NIMA numbering system.

Charting Basics

In order to get the greatest benefits from charts, and the greatest degree of safety, you must be able to read and understand your charts. Direction, distance, and scale are the most important properties of charts you need to understand.

DIRECTION

Direction is defined as the angle made between a line connecting two points and a reference line such as a geographic meridian; these are *true directions*. Boaters also use *magnetic directions*, but these are derived by calculation since magnetic meridians are not printed on charts (see Chapter 6, "Piloting"). The principal difference between Mercator and polyconic charts is the technique used for measuring directions.

To facilitate the measurement of direction, most charts have one or more *compass roses* printed on them. These consist of two or three concentric circles, several inches in diameter, subdivided by degrees with labels around the circumference. The outer circle has its zero at true north and is indicated by a star symbol. The next inner circle is oriented on magnetic north, and is indicated by an arrow over its zero point. There may be a third, inner circle subdivided according to an older system of "points" — 32 points make a full circle. The difference between the orientation of the true and magnetic circles is termed *magnetic variation,* abbreviated "Var." Each compass rose contains a statement of the variation for that general area of a chart, with a date and rate of any annual change.

DISTANCE
Major distances on charts are measured in miles. On oceans and coastal waters, these are *nautical miles,* each equal to 6076.1 feet (1852 meters). For all practical purposes, a nautical mile is the equivalent of one minute of latitude (not longitude!). On the Great Lakes, inland rivers, and the Intracoastal Waterways, the *statute mile* of 5280 feet is used; this is the conventional mile used on land.

Shorter distances are measured in yards, occasionally in feet. Some charts are metric and use meters (but kilometers are not used for longer distances).

SCALE
Because a chart is a miniature representation of a portion of the earth, actual distances must be scaled down. The *scale* of a chart is the ratio of one unit of distance on the chart to the number of such units on the earth; this is true of any unit, yard, mile, meter, etc. Scale is normally represented as a ratio, such as 1:40,000, but it can also be shown as a fraction. (*Equivalent scales,* such as "one inch = 2 miles," are not normally used on charts.)

Large Scale and Small Scale Charts
There is often confusion about the meaning of the terms "large scale" and "small scale" as used with respect to charts. Part of the problem is that the terms do not have exact definitions and are

FIGURE 5-2. NOS charts at scales of 1:80,000 and larger will have a scale of nautical miles and of yards; those for the Great Lakes, inland rivers, and the Intracoastal Waterways will also carry a scale of statute miles. This small-craft chart at a scale of 1:40,000 also has latitude and longitude scales showing subdivisions of one minute.

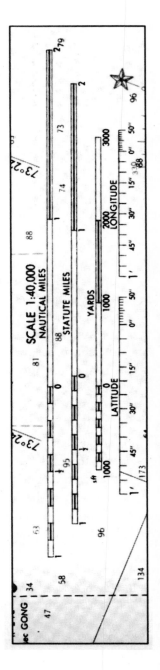

applied to charts relative to each other. Think of the second figure in a chart-scale ratio (e.g., 1:10,000) as the denominator of a fraction. The larger this value, the smaller the fraction. Thus, a 1:80,000 chart is small scale in comparison to a 1:10,000 chart. The small-scale chart, however, covers a larger geographic area than a large-scale chart of the same paper size. Remember: Small scale, large area; large scale, small area.

Chart Features

A vast amount of information is available to you on every chart. To use a chart to best advantage, you must have a good understanding of the various types of information shown and how each is presented.

GENERAL INFORMATION

In addition to being numbered, charts have names, a short statement of the area covered. The *general information block* also lists the type of projection and datum, or reference level, for soundings with the units used—feet, fathoms (1 fathom = 6 feet), or meters. The chart number is shown at several places around the borders. The chart edition and date appear in the lower-left corner of conventional charts, and on the front of folded charts. New editions are printed when features change; the time between editions can range from several months to many years. Between editions, chart corrections are published in *Notices to Mariners*. Issued weekly in Washington, DC, the *Notices* contain world-wide information usually of interest to larger vessels. To be placed on the distribution list, send a request, along with a justification of need, to the Maritime Safety Information Center, National Imagery and Mapping Agency, Bethesda, Maryland 20816-5003. The latest eight *Notices* are available online at http://pollux.nss.nima.mil. Of greater interest to boaters are *Local Notices to Mariners* issued by local Coast Guard Districts with information relating to inshore waters; requests to be placed on the mailing list should be sent to the appropriate District Headquarters. Local Notices of all Districts are available online at www.navcen.uscg.mil. *Only the latest edition of a chart* should be used, as corrections will no longer be published for superseded editions.

USE OF COLOR AND LETTERING STYLES
Most charts use color to emphasize various features. NOS charts use five multipurpose colors in either solid color or tints—black, magenta, gold, blue, and green.

Land areas are shown in gold, with a darker shade being used for built-up areas. Bodies of water are white, except for shallower areas that are shown in one or two shades of blue. The depth division between white and blue areas varies with the type of chart; check each chart before you use it. Areas that are submerged at some tidal stages, but uncovered at others, are shown in green. Magenta, a shade of purple, is used for many purposes as it has good visibility under red light (used to avoid disturbing night vision). Black is used for many symbols and printed information.

NIMA charts of international and foreign waters use colors differently. The major difference is the use of gray for land areas.

Two styles of lettering are used on charts to differentiate between different types of information. *Vertical lettering* is used for features that are dry at high water and are not affected by the movement of water. *Leaning lettering* (slanting, much like italics) is used for water, underwater features, and floating objects, such as buoys. Periods after abbreviations are omitted in water and land areas, but are used in chart Notes.

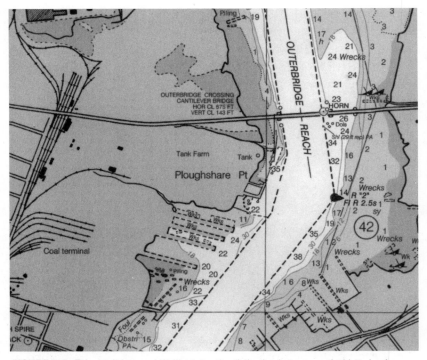

FIGURE 5-3. This detail from a chart illustrates the distinction between vertical lettering for features that are above the water, such as "TANK," and leaning lettering for underwater features such as "Wrecks." Side limits of dredged channels are marked with dashed lines.

WATER FEATURES

Water depths are measured from a *datum,* or reference level. In tidal areas, the datum used is *mean lower low water,* which means the *average* of the lowest level of all days in a 19-year cycle. It is important to note that on some days the lower low tide will be *below* the datum and that actual depths will be *less* than charted depths. In the Great Lakes and other inland areas depths are measured from an arbitrarily established datum as noted on each chart.

Water depths are shown on a chart by many small printed figures, usually in feet or fathoms. Most foreign, and some U.S., charts show depths in meters and decimeters (tenths of a meter); 1 meter = 3.28 feet. The printed depth figures are only a very small fraction of all the depth measurements taken during a survey. Only the more significant and representative depths are shown on a chart. Wide spacing of depth figures means a fairly uniform bottom; wherever the depths vary irregularly or abruptly, the figures will be more frequent and more closely spaced. Depth curves appear on many charts—lines connecting points of equal depth. The depths for each line are indicated on the chart and may vary with the scale of the chart.

Dredged channels are shown by two dashed lines marking the sides of the improvement. Information on depths in the channel and the date of measurement are often shown between the lines or alongside them. Use this information with caution as shoaling may have occurred.

The nature of the bottom—information useful in determining where to anchor—is described in many areas by means of standard abbreviations; these are usually explained somewhere on the chart.

LAND FEATURES

Characteristics of land areas are shown on nautical charts only in such detail as will be useful to a navigator. The general topography of land areas is usually indicated by contour lines (lines connecting points of equal elevation), form lines (broken lines approx-imating contours), or hachures (short lines or group of such lines that indicate the approximate location of steep slopes). Specific heights may be shown for the tops of major land features. Heights are measured from *mean high water* or an established datum for inland charts. The term "sea level" is not used in charting.

MAN-MADE FEATURES

Man-made features on land are shown in detail only when such information will be of interest to vessels; examples are bridges, over-head power lines, and piers. Other man-made features, such as roads and streets, may be shown in detail or generalized, as deter-mined by their usefulness to navigation and by the scale of the chart.

Specific names have been given to certain types of landmarks to standardize terminology; typical of these are *house, stack, spire, tower, tank,* and *flagpole;* abbreviations are also standardized. When two similar objects are so closely located that separate symbols cannot be used, the word *"twin"* is used with a single sym-bol. For groups, phrases such as *"tallest of three"* are used.

Symbols and Abbreviations

The vast amount of information that must be shown on a chart, and the closeness of many items, makes necessary the extensive use of symbols and abbreviations. No skipper could be expected to know all of them, but you must be able to read and interpret those on the charts you use—the safety of your boat may depend on this ability.

Symbols are conventional shapes and designs indicating the presence of a certain object or feature at the location shown on the chart. No attempt is made at an accurate or detailed representation of the object.

Symbols and abbreviations used on U.S. charts are taken from an international set. They are shown on *Chart No. 1*, which is published as a booklet available at many chart stores and also on the Internet at www.chartmaker.ncd.noaa.gov.

Electronic Charts

For a discussion of electronic digital charts, see Chapter 9, "Electronic Communications and Navigation."

Publications

Closely related to charts are *navigational publications*, some issued by governmental agencies and others by commercial sources. All skippers should be aware of their existence; you may even want to keep certain of these publications on board your craft. Most of them can be obtained from local authorized sales agents for charts. Many are also available on the Internet; start your search at http://pollux.nss.nima.mil and www.navcwen.uscg.mil.

Light Lists are published by the Coast Guard in seven volumes covering the coasts, the Great Lakes, and the Mississippi River system. New editions of each volume are issued each year, except for Volume V (Mississippi River system), which is updated every two years. These books provide more complete information on aids to navigation than can be shown on charts.

Navigation Rules, International–Inland is an excellent, well-illustrated small book from the Coast Guard containing the actual wording of the two sets of Rules, with corresponding international and inland Rules conveniently located on facing pages. The annexes of the Rules are included, as are other related regulations, such as the demarcation lines that separate waters governed by each set of Rules. New editions are published when warranted by changes.

Federal Requirements and Safety Tips for Recreational Craft is a Coast Guard pamphlet useful to any skipper.

Coast Pilots are published in nine volumes by the National Ocean Service to supplement charts by providing additional information necessary for safe and efficient navigation, such as descriptions of coastal waters and shores, channels, and dangers to navigation. They provide useful data on ports and harbors, and on the facilities available. Information on canals, bridge and cable clearances, and inland waterways is included where applicable. Four new editions of various *Coast Pilots* are published each year.

Notice to Mariners is issued weekly by the National Imagery and Mapping Agency (NIMA). Prepared jointly with the National Ocean Service and the Coast Guard, this publication is of primary interest to larger commercial vessels, but does include corrections to *Light Lists, Coast Pilots,* and charts that are of interest to small-craft skippers. Recent *Notices* are available on the Internet— http://pollux.nss.nima.mil.

Local Notices to Mariners are published weekly year-round by each Coast Guard District (except the 9th District, Great Lakes, which issues them seasonally). They are generally similar to the "Washington *Notices*" but are focused on coastal and inshore waters of the respective District. They also include information on changes and proposed changes to aids to navigation, bridge restrictions and construction projects, and other local information. Boaters can subscribe to them, or view them online on the Internet at www.navcen.uscg.mil.

Annual tide and tidal current tables are no longer published by the government. Instead, such information is available in commercial publications based on data supplied by the National Ocean Service. Tide information is, however, still included on NOS small-craft folded charts; it can also be obtained for all areas from NOS on the Internet. Tidal and current information is often included in electronic charting programs for personal computers.

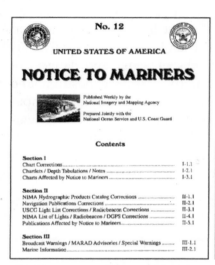

FIGURE 5-4. *Notice to Mariners* is available in two versions: 1) A weekly edition published by the NIMA covers the entire world, except for inland waters not used by ocean shipping; 2) A regional edition is published monthly, with weekly updates, by each Coast Guard District.

CHAPTER SIX

Piloting

Piloting is the form of navigation in which you use landmarks and aids to navigation, charts, and simple instruments on your boat. It takes some serious studying, and practice, but good piloting knowledge can make your boating fun and worry-free. Piloting is usually used in channels, harbors, and along coasts where depths of water and dangers to navigation require close attention to a vessel's position and course. You will enjoy piloting most when you can do it without anxiety. Study thoroughly and practice often—try "over-navigating" when conditions are good, so that you will acquire the skills needed to direct your boat safely through fog, rain, or night without fear or strain.

The Dimensions of Piloting

The basic dimensions of piloting are direction, distance, and time. Other factors that are measured or calculated include speed, position, depths, and heights. Each of these is measured in specified units to varying levels of precision.

DIRECTION
Direction is the position of a point with respect to another point regardless of the distance between them. Types of direction include: True (abbreviated T), which is measured from a reference point of geographic, or "true" north; Magnetic (M), which is meas-

ured from magnetic north; and Compass (C), which is based on the readings of a compass. A direction is stated as a three-digit number up to a maximum of 360°, using leading zeros as necessary for values less than 100. The number should be followed by T, M, or C, as appropriate.

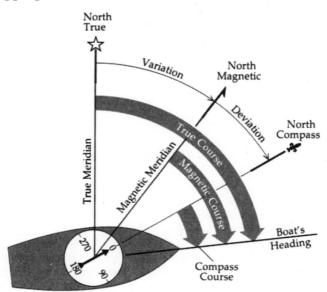

FIGURE 6-1. A course, heading, or bearing can be measured and named using any one of three systems based on the reference direction used. It is, of course, the same line no matter how it's labeled.

Direction is measured in *degrees,* with 360° equaling a full circle. One degree can be subdivided fractionally or decimally, or into 60 *minutes,* each of which can be further divided into 60 *seconds,* but in small-craft navigation, directions are stated to the nearest whole degree.

For every direction, there is a *reciprocal direction,* derived by adding or subtracting 180° to the direction so as to keep the result between 0 and 360. An *angle* is the difference in direction between two lines, expressed as a one-, two-, or three-digit value in degrees.

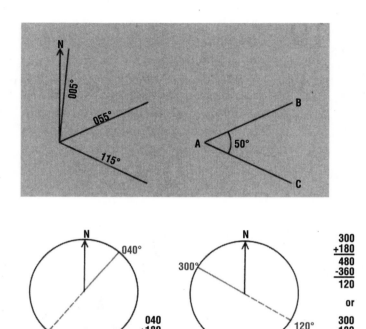

FIGURE 6-2. Directions, *top left,* are always designated by a three-digit number, with zeros added before a single- or double-digit number. An angle between two directions, *top right,* is not expressed as a three-digit number. The reciprocal of a direction, *above,* is found by adding 180° to the given direction. If the total exceeds 360°, subtract 360°—or simply subtract 180° from the given direction.

DISTANCE

Distance is the spatial separation between two points without regard to the direction of one in relation to the other. The basic unit of distance is the *mile,* but as noted in Chapter 5, "Charts," there are two kinds of miles. The *statute mile* of 5280 feet is used on the Great Lakes, inland rivers and lakes, and the Intracoastal Waterways. The *nautical mile,* 6076.1 feet, is used on ocean waters, bays and sounds, and coastal tributaries; conversions between these units are shown in Table 14-1. Shorter distances are typically measured in *yards;* feet are seldom used. In some instances, *metric* units are used. Conversions between conventional and metric units are shown in Table 14-19. Longer distances are usually stated in whole miles or miles and tenths. Calculated values are *rounded* up or down to the nearest tenth or whole number. You may cruise from waters using one type of mile into waters using the other—be alert to the change.

TIME

Highly precise and accurate *time* information, used in celestial navigation, is not needed in piloting. Time is normally stated to the nearest hour and minute, with the possible exception of races and some navigation contests.

In piloting, the *24-hour clock* is used to express time of day; this simplifies recording and calculating by eliminating "a.m." and "p.m." suffixes. The day starts at midnight, 0000; noon is 1200; and afternoon times continue the sequence, with 3:30 p.m. being written as 1530. Hours and minutes are not separated by a colon. In the morning, 1000 is spoken as "ten hundred," not as "one thousand"; likewise, 2000 is "twenty hundred," not "two thousand." In nautical usage, the word "hours" does *not* follow the numbers.

When doing additions and subtractions, and "carrying" or "borrowing," be careful to remember that an hour has 60 minutes, not 100! When cruising, be alert for possible time zone changes.

Correct time information is available on any short-wave receiver at 5, 10, 15, and 20 MHz, broadcast from station WWV, Fort Collins, Colorado. The frequency to be used will vary with your location and the time of day. Highly accurate time is also available on the Internet at www.nist.gov and other locations; computer clocks may be set using public domain or proprietary software programs.

SPEED

Speed is a fundamental dimension of piloting—it can be either measured or calculated. Speed is defined as the number of units of distance traveled in a specified unit of time. Where statute miles are used, the unit is *miles per hour (mph)*. Where nautical miles are used, the unit is the *knot (kn or kt)*—one nautical mile per hour (note that "per hour" is included in "knot" and is not stated with it). Speeds are normally stated in whole numbers and tenths; calculated results with additional decimal places are rounded up or down.

POSITION

A *position* can be described in *geographic* terms, using coordinates of latitude (L or Lat) and longitude (Lo or Long); see Chapter 5, "Charts." It can also be stated in *relative* terms, i.e., distance and direction from a stated object such as a landmark or another vessel. An example of relative position would be: "two and a half miles 030 degrees from Hillsboro Inlet Light." In many instances, the distance can be zero, such as "at Buoy 3."

Positions can be stated in degrees, minutes, and seconds, or in degrees, minutes, and tenths of minutes, as determined by the subdivision of the scales of latitude and longitude around the edges of the chart being used. Statements of latitude *must* end with "N" or "S" as appropriate; longitude values, with "E" or "W."

DEPTHS

Information on the *depth* of the water—the distance from the surface of the water to the bottom—is of value in piloting as well important to a vessel's safety. In coastal and inland waters, depths are measured in *feet;* off shore the unit normally used is the *fathom,* equal to six feet. On metric charts, depths will be in meters, with shallower values in meters and decimeters (tenths of a meter). Check each chart when you buy it to learn the depth unit used; it will be stated near the name of the chart. Depths are measured from a *datum,* or defined level (see Chapter 5, "Charts"). Statements and calculations of depth are usually expressed in feet and tenths, particularly in tidal waters.

HEIGHTS

The *height,* or elevation, of objects above the water may also be of concern in piloting. The height of lights and landmarks will determine the distance from which they can be seen. Vertical clearance under a bridge or powerline may be of critical importance to a boat. Heights are usually measured from a different datum than depths (see Chapter 5, "Charts"). Heights will be stated in feet or meters; check your chart to ascertain which unit of measurement is being used.

Magnetic Compasses

The *magnetic compass* is the oldest and most basic navigation tool used on boats. Its history goes back centuries and improvements over the ages have been in mechanical construction details rather than in basic principles.

Your boat's safety may well depend upon her compass, and on your ability to use it. Electronic systems do much for a skipper today, but there is always the possibility of equipment failure or loss of electrical power. Know the limitations of your compass, but within these, trust it to guide you safely.

HOW IT WORKS

The earth has a *magnetic field,* much as if it had a giant bar magnet inside it. A compass consists of several small bar magnets beneath a *card* that has a scale around its perimeter, graduated in degrees. These magnets align themselves with the horizontal component of the earth's field, and the direction is read from the scale on the card that is opposite an index mark, the *lubber's line,* fixed on the case of the compass. To make compasses more sensitive, the card is supported on a needle-sharp bearing and floated in or on a non-freezing liquid. A top, usually spherical in shape, covers the compass to contain the liquid. The entire assembly is often mounted in *gimbals,* pivots and brackets that allow the compass to remain as nearly level as possible as the vessel pitches and rolls.

SELECTION AND INSTALLATION

Compasses come in a wide range of sizes to match the vessels on which they are used; they are often lighted for use at night. Compasses also come in a wide range of prices. Because your compass is so essential to safety, the basic rule is to purchase the best one that you can afford in the proper size for your boat!

A compass must be properly installed in a place where the helmsman can view it easily, preferably directly forward of the steering wheel. An imaginary line from the center of the compass through the lubber's line must be exactly parallel with the craft's centerline. Consideration must be given to the presence of other instruments or objects that could influence compass readings. If you are not completely sure of how to install a compass, seek the advice and assistance of an experienced skipper or a professional compass adjuster.

USING A COMPASS

Unfortunately, a compass does not give *true* directions. The earth's magnetic poles are not located at the geographic poles, so the invisible grid of magnetic lines of force does not line up with geographic meridians. Worse yet, because of the varying composition of the earth, magnetic lines are not straight and uniform.

Variation

The basic "error" of a compass is called *variation,* defined as the difference at any location between *true directions* and *magnetic directions* as measured by a compass unaffected by local influences. (Although the term is common, it is not truly an "error," but an unavoidable condition.) Variation is different for different locations on the earth; at each location it is nearly constant, but does change very slightly over the years. Variation will be either east or west, and must be labeled "E" or "W" as appropriate; it can be as much as 60° in extreme locations. The amount of variation in any area is indicated on charts by *compass roses* (see Chapter 5, "Charts"). Variation is the same for all vessels in a given area.

Deviation

The other component of compass error is *deviation.* A boat's compass rarely exists in an environment that is free of nearby magnetic material and influences. Objects made of iron and iron-alloys can influence a compass, while electrical currents (DC) produce magnetic fields that can also affect compass readings. The difference between the direction that would be indicated by a compass free of any local effects and the actual reading of an installed compass is termed *deviation.* It can be either east or west, and each value in whole degrees (fractions are not used on small craft) must be so labeled. For all practical purposes, deviation is not affected by the vessel's geographic location. However, *it is dependent upon the vessel's heading*—the deviation of your compass on a heading of 90° may be very different than the deviation at 120°. Deviation will be different for different vessels.

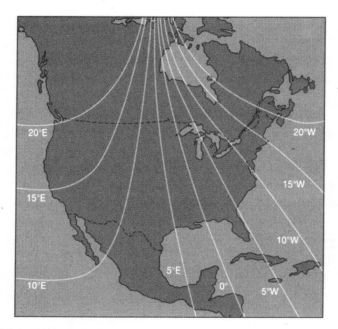

FIGURE 6-3. Variation is the angle between the magnetic meridian and the true geographic meridian; it can be either easterly or westerly. Variation depends on geographic position, and for any given geographic location it is the same for all vessels.

Correcting for Compass Errors

On board a boat, variation cannot be changed. It must be determined from the chart and applied mathematically to courses and bearings. Use the appropriate guide listed below to calculate a Compass or Magnetic direction from a True direction, or a True direction from a Compass or Magnetic direction.

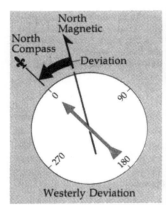

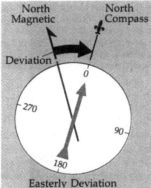

FIGURE 6-4. Deviation is the difference between magnetic north and north as indicated by your compass. It can be either easterly or westerly, and depends on the magnetic conditions on your vessel. It changes with the boat's heading, but is not noticeably affected by changes in position within a geographic region.

From TRUE to COMPASS or MAGNETIC

True

Variation (add W; subtract E)

Magnetic

Deviation (add W; subtract E)

Compass

From COMPASS or MAGNETIC to TRUE

Compass

Deviation (subtract W; add E)

Magnetic

Variation (subtract W; add E)

True

Deviation values can be minimized by proper compass location and installation. Keep it as far as possible from magnetic objects. Keep electrical wiring as distant as possible, and twist together each *pair* of wires so that the magnetic field of one wire will neutralize that of the other.

COMPASS COMPENSATION

Because of the limited options available for compass placement, it is highly likely that some deviation will still exist despite your best efforts. The next step is compass *compensation*. Most compasses will have in their base a pair of very small magnets that can be rotated to vary their effect and so compensate for external influences. One adjustment will compensate for north-south effects, and the other for east-west influences. (If your compass does not have internal compensators, you can mount a pair of external magnets near the instrument.) Even after careful compensation, there may still be some deviation, east or west, on various headings of your boat. You must determine what these are, and record them on a "deviation card," which should be kept close by your compass and charts. Deviation for the heading that your boat is on must be applied in accordance with the above guides to determine either true or compass courses and bearings.

Typical Compass-heading Deviation Table

COMPASS HEADING (DEGREES)	DEVIATION (DEGREES)
000	.0
015	.0
030	.1 W
045	.2 W
060	.3 W
075	.3 W
090	.4 W
105	.3 W
120	.2 W
135	.1 W
150	.1 W
165	.0
180	.0
195	.0
210	.1 E
225	.2 E
240	.2 E
255	.3 E
270	.4 E
285	.3 E
300	.2 E
315	.1 E
330	.1 E
345	.0

TABLE 6-5. This is a typical deviation table with values for each 15° of compass heading.(It is not a table for your boat, you must prepare one specifically for your craft.) Values of deviation for headings between tabulated listings can be interpolated; round off to the nearest whole degree. A similar table can be prepared for values of magnetic heading—it is useful to have both tables.

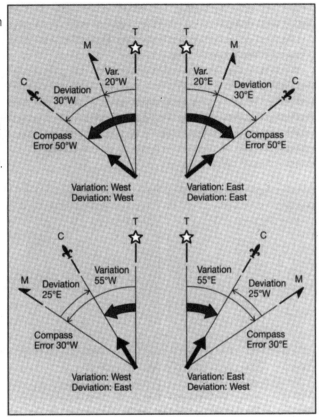

FIGURE 6-6. Variation and deviation are sometimes combined algebraically into a single value, termed compass error (CE). These intentionally exaggerated drawings show the four possible combinations of easterly and westerly variation and deviation.

The term "compass error" is sometimes used for the combined effect of variation and deviation. It is the algebraic sum of the two values, and must be labeled "E" or "W" and applied in the same manner as described above. There are also other "memory aids" for the application of compass corrections; use any one that is easy for you to remember.

OTHER COMPASSES

A small compass (sometimes with a handle) designed to be easily held in front of your face is called a *hand bearing compass*. As its name implies, it is ordinarily used for determining the direction of distant objects. In an emergency, it can be used in steering your boat.

An *electronic compass* uses circuitry to sense the earth's magnetic field and then displays the heading of the craft as a digital value. There are some stand-alone units, but usually they are a part of an autopilot system (see Chapter 9, "Electronic Communications and Navigation").

Large vessels, such as ships, will have a *gyrocompass*. This large, complex, and expensive device is designed to hold a fixed direction in space; explaining its operation and error calculations is beyond the scope of this book.

Other Piloting Instruments

In addition to a good-quality compass properly installed, you will need a few other simple instruments.

For drawing lines and measuring directions, a *course plotter* is a useful tool, but there are others that do the same job and the choice is a matter of personal preference. Whichever one you choose to use will come with directions for its use.

Dividers are used to measure distances on a chart. They are available is several types, but the simplest will be adequate for small-craft piloting.

Every boat should have at least one, and preferably several, timepieces. These may be clocks or wristwatches, and should be able to keep reasonably accurate time. *Elapsed time,* used in determining speed and estimated time of arrival, is of greater importance than absolute time; a stopwatch, or wristwatch with this capability, is handier than having to make calculations. A *countdown timer* with an audible alarm saves you the trouble of having to keep an eye on the clock or your watch, and prevents mistakes from being made, such as a missed turn.

For instant information on speed without having to make calculations, consider installing a *speedometer or log.*

You can measure relatively shallow depths with a *lead line,* a piece of line marked at intervals from a weight at one end. An *electronic depth sounder,* however, is more convenient and can measure greater depths (see Chapter 9, "Electronic Communications and Navigation").

For plotting on charts, well-sharpened, medium (No. 2) pencils are essential. Make sure to have a good eraser on hand, in addition to those at the ends of your pencils.

For finding and viewing distant objects, keep a good binocular on board. They are available in various types; a "7 X 50" model, for example, is excellent for use on the water. The two eyepieces should be individually focusable if the binocular is to be used by more than one person.

Every boat should have several *flashlights* or *electric lanterns* (or both) for regular use and emergencies. To avoid losing your night vision when reading charts and publications, one of these should have a *red* lens.

Dead Reckoning

An essential part of navigation is *dead reckoning* (DR). This is the advancement of a boat's position on the chart from its last accurately determined location, using the courses steered and the boat's speed through the water. No allowance is made for the effects of wind, waves, current, or steering errors.

When operating your boat in large bodies of water, you should always have at least a rough knowledge of your position on the chart. Much piloting is now done with electronics, but equipment can fail—often at the worst possible time. It is dead reckoning that will get you assistance if you need it, or on to your destination if you don't.

DEAD RECKONING TERMS

The *DR track* is the path that a boat is believed to be following as represented on the chart by a line drawn from the last known position using courses and distances through the water. The path actually traveled may be different due to one or more offsetting influences, which will be considered later in this chapter. Dead reckoning plots can also be drawn on a chart in advance, as plans of where you intend to go.

Course (C) is the direction that a boat is being steered, or is to be steered—the direction of travel through the water. Courses are normally plotted as true directions using three-digit figures (add leading zeros as necessary). Some experienced skippers may plot magnetic courses.

Heading is the direction in which a boat is pointed at any given moment, often stated as magnetic or compass. Headings are not plotted.

Speed (S) is the rate of travel through the water. It is used with elapsed time to determine *DR positions* along the track line.

Distance (D), speed multiplied by elapsed time, may be used with a plot of a future intended track; speed is not shown on a plot except for a vessel underway.

DISTANCE-TIME-SPEED

The basic equations for calculating either distance, time, or speed when the other two factors are known are given below:

When time is in hours: $D = S \times T \qquad T = \dfrac{D}{S} \qquad S = \dfrac{D}{T}$

When time is in minutes: $D = S \times T60 \qquad T = \dfrac{60D}{S} \qquad S = \dfrac{60D}{T}$

BASIC PRINCIPLES OF DEAD RECKONING

1. A DR track is always started from a known position.

2. Only courses steered are used for determining a DR track.

3. Only the speed through the water is used for determining the distance traveled to a DR position.

If offsetting influences are known and applied, the plot becomes one of *estimated positions (EP)*.

PLOTTING AND LABELING

The essence of dead reckoning is the chart plot—it must be done accurately, clearly, and completely. Standard symbols and abbreviations must be used so that the plot will be readable by another person.

The label of any line should be along that line.

The label for any point should not lie along any line; it should make an angle with any line so that its nature as the label of a point is clear.

The direction label is placed above the track line as a three-digit number preceded by "C." It may be followed by a "T" for *true directions;* it must be followed by a "M" or "C" for magnetic or compass if such directions are being used. (Quotation marks and degree symbols are not used.)

The speed along the track is labeled by a number under the track line, preceded by "S"; it is usually placed immediately beneath the direction label. (Units, such as mph or knots, are not used.)

A known position is termed a *fix.* It is shown as a small circle across a line; a small dot may be added at the center (but is often not needed) for example, at the intersection of two lines of

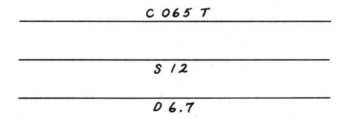

FIGURE 6-7. Course is labeled above the line with direction as a three-digit number, which may be followed by T for "true direction" and must be followed by M if direction is magnetic. Speed is labeled below the line, with the letter S before the numbers. Alternatively, distance can be shown below the line, with the designator D. Note the space between the letters and the numbers.

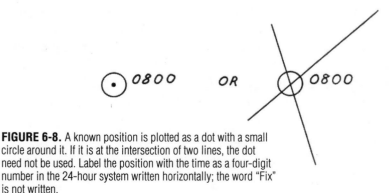

FIGURE 6-8. A known position is plotted as a dot with a small circle around it. If it is at the intersection of two lines, the dot need not be used. Label the position with the time as a four-digit number in the 24-hour system written horizontally; the word "Fix" is not written.

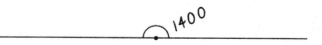

FIGURE 6-9. A dead reckoning position along a track line is plotted as a small half-circle around a dot. Add the time in the same manner as for a fix, but not horizontally nor along the line.

position. A fix is always labeled with a four-digit time reading placed horizontally. The word "Fix" is not shown.

A *DR position,* calculated as a distance along the track, is shown as a half-circle with a dot at the center. Time is labeled at an angle to the track, but not horizontally. "DR" is not shown.

When you plot a passage beforehand but are not sure of the speed that will be run, *distance* can be substituted for speed. It is written below the track line and labeled "D". Units are not shown.

To prevent clutter, all lines on a chart should be erased when no longer needed.

DEAD RECKONING PLOTS

There are several specific rules for maintaining a DR plot:

1. A DR plot should show true directions (or magnetic directions if properly labeled); never plot compass directions.

2. A DR plot should be started when leaving a known position.

3. A DR position should be shown whenever there is a change in course or speed.

4. A DR position should be shown at regular intervals, typically hourly, more often in reduced visibility.

5. A new DR track is started each time the boat's position is fixed. The old DR position for the same time as the fix should be plotted at the end of the old track, which is no longer carried forward.

Positioning

At the heart of piloting is the determination of the vessel's position. Underway on a body of water of any size, it's not "where you ought to be" or "where you think you are," but "where you are for sure" that counts. Dead reckoning is a must, but you must also take advantage of every opportunity to determine where you truly are.

DEFINITIONS

A *line of position (LOP)* is a line, in actuality or on a chart, at some point along which the observer is located. This may be found by observation or measurement, either visually or by radar. An LOP may be straight, as from a bearing; or it may be circular, as from a distance measurement, in which case it may be called a *circle of position.*

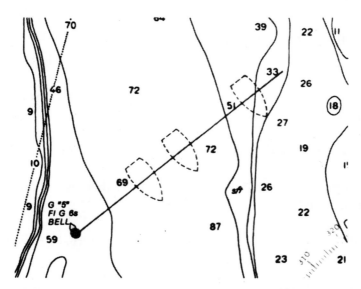

FIGURE 6-10. A line of position, in actuality or on a chart, is a line somewhere along which the observer is located. A single line will not determine a position, but it does tell the observer where he is *not* located, and such information can be useful in itself in many situations.

A *bearing* is the direction of an object from the observer. A bearing may be True or Magnetic depending upon which "north" is used (uncorrected or corrected for variation). A *compass bearing* is one taken from the north direction indicated by the compass. A *relative bearing* is one referenced to the boat's heading, measured clockwise from 000° dead ahead.

A *range* consists of two identifiable objects that are seen in line with each other.

A *fix* is an accurately located position determined without reference to any prior position. A *running fix* is a position that has been determined from LOPs, at least one of which was taken at a different time and advanced to the time of the latest observation based on the movement of the vessel during the interval. *An estimated position (EP)* is the best position that can be determined short of a fix or running fix; it will normally involve the effects of wind and current.

LINES OF POSITION

By definition, an observer is somewhere on a line of position. If he is on both of two lines of position, he must be at their intersection, and a fix is established.

Visual bearings are the most likely source of LOPs for small craft. A range, either from aids to navigation or landmarks, provides an excellent LOP.

Radar bearings are also a source of LOPs, but are less precise than visual observations. Radar has an advantage in that a single bearing plus a distance measurement, plotted as a circular LOP, can provide a fix.

A bearing is labeled with the time of the observation *above* the line and the direction—three digits followed by T (or M)—*below* the line. A circular LOP is normally plotted as an arc (portion of a circle) with time above and distance below. A range is labeled only with time above the line. An LOP that has been advanced will be labeled with both times. *Always label all LOPs immediately;* unmarked lines can be a source of confusion.

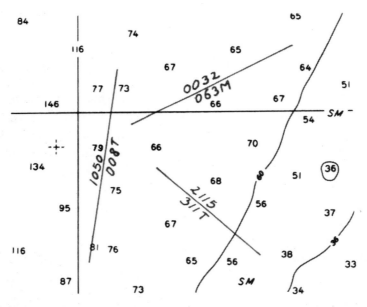

FIGURE 6-11. Correct labeling of lines of position is important; unlabeled or mislabeled lines cause confusion. Time is shown above the line in the 24-hour clock system, and direction below the line as a three-digit number, labeled T for true direction (or M for magnetic).

FIXES
The simplest fix, and the one most often used by boats, is obtained by passing close by an object that can be identified on the chart, usually an aid to navigation. No additional symbol is plotted, merely label the position with the time, written horizontally. Because of the scale of the chart, draw a track line directly from the chart symbol without any offset to indicate the slight distance the boat is from the buoy or other object.

Fixes can also be obtained from two lines of position. These should intersect as near to 90° as possible, never less than 60° nor more than 120°. At lesser or greater angles, the exact point of intersection becomes more uncertain. If you must use such bearings, do so with caution. Even with a good angle of intersection, the certainty of the fix can be compromised by inaccuracy in either LOP.

If three LOPs can be obtained, the credibility of the resulting fix will improve considerably; the ideal crossing angles in this case would be 60°. Do not, however, expect to have a single point of intersection; this is unlikely due to unavoidable small inaccuracies in observations. Expect to get a small triangle, and then use its center, gauged visually, as the fix. If the triangle is large, discard the observations and try again. Normally, more than three LOPs are not taken.

A fix is labeled as described above. A running fix is labeled with the time of the last observation and "R FIX."

Value of a Single LOP
While a fix based on two or three lines of position is the most desirable kind, the value of a single LOP should not be overlooked. This cannot tell you where you are, but it can, within its limits of accuracy, tell you where you are *not*. If you are somewhere along the line, you are not somewhere appreciably distant from the line — this can often be a desirable reassurance.

A single line of position can often be combined with other information to provide better location information than a DR position. If the depths are varying relatively uniformly, a depth value can be combined with an LOP for an estimated position.

VISUAL OBSERVATIONS
On a typical motorboat or sailboat, visual observations will be the primary, almost sole, source of lines of position. Correct identification of the object sighted upon, in actuality and on the chart, is essential.

Bearings Dead Ahead

The simplest, and probably most accurate, bearings are those taken dead ahead with the steering compass. No auxiliary equipment or other person is required. If you are sure that you are in safe waters, you can momentarily swing a powerboat off course for a few seconds to take such a bearing. This procedure will not normally work on a sailboat where the mast blocks direct forward vision.

Beam Bearings

If the object you wish to sight on is too far off your course, you may be able to use the beam bearing technique. Determine some structural part of your boat that is at a right angle to its centerline. Use that for sighting, and add or subtract 90° to or from your boat's *heading* at the time of observation.

Other Bearings

Within a limited arc of forward visibility, bearings can be taken by sighting across the steering compass. The extent to which this can be done is determined by the layout of the helm position and the compass installation. A hand-bearing compass will normally allow observations to be taken essentially all around the horizon.

Correction of Compass Bearings

Compass bearings must be corrected before they can be plotted. The first correction is for deviation. *This is deviation for the heading of the boat at the time of observation, NOT for the value of the bearing—a common misapprehension!* (That is, if your boat is on a heading of 120° and the object's bearing is 0°, you must correct for your compass's deviation at 120°—not 0°. Deviation for a hand bearing compass will not be the same as for the steering compass. The former must be determined for each location from which the instrument will be used. After correction, you will have a magnetic bearing that can be plotted as such, or more often, one that is further corrected for variation and plotted as a true bearing.

You should be consistent as to which procedure you use. Whichever bearing is plotted, either magnetic or true, it should be labeled immediately as described above.

Ranges
Ranges provide highly accurate lines of position and should be used instead of bearings whenever possible. No matter how small your boat, or how bad the conditions are, if you can see the two objects come into line, you have an excellent LOP. The objects may be two aids to navigation, whether formally designated as a range or not; two landmarks or other man-made structures; or one of each. Do not use floating objects, such as buoys, as their positions are not sufficiently exact. Note the time of observation and label as described above.

OTHER POSITIONING METHODS
More complex visual observations include vertical and horizontal angles, danger angles, and combinations of relative bearings. Information on these and other piloting procedures will be found in *Chapman: Piloting, Seamanship and Boat Handling*.

Positioning by electronic navigation systems — LORAN and GPS — is covered in Chapter 9, "Electronic Communications and Navigation." But always remember, electronic equipment can fail — make sure that you learn the basic procedures covered in this chapter, and practice with them often enough to maintain and improve your capabilities.

PILOTING

CHAPTER SEVEN

Tides and Currents

Millions of boaters do their thing on waters subject to tides, while other millions enjoy non-tidal waters. But with more and more skippers trailering their craft far from home, both groups should have general knowledge of tidal effects.

Tide is the rise and fall of ocean level as a result of the gravitational attraction among the earth, moon, and sun. It is a *vertical* motion only; tides do not "ebb and flow" except in poetry and non-technical writings. *Current is the horizontal* flow of water from one location to another. *Tidal current* is the flow from tidal changes; river flows and ocean currents such as the Gulf Stream are other types of currents.

Tides and currents will affect your boating—you may run aground because you didn't allow for the tide, or you may run out of gas because you forgot to allow for an adverse current. Learn the ways of tides and currents and put them to work to aid your boating, not to cause trouble for you.

Tides

Tides originate in the open oceans, but are only significant near shore. They are noticeable along coastal beaches, in bays and sounds, and up rivers as far as the first rapids or dam. Oddly, the rise and fall of tide may be greater a hundred miles or more up a river than it is at its mouth.

DEFINITIONS

The *height of tide* at any specified location and time is the vertical distance between the surface of the water and a designated *tidal datum,* usually mean lower low water (the average over a 19-year cycle of all of the lower levels of the two low waters of a tidal day, which usually are not the same). Do not confuse this measurement with the depth of the water!

High water (sometimes called "high tide") is the highest level reached by a rising tide. *Low water* (or "low tide") is the lowest level of a falling tide. *Tidal range* is the difference between high and low waters.

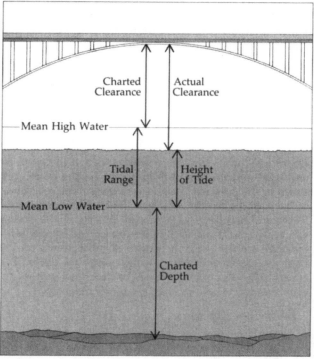

FIGURE 7-1. This diagram illustrates some of the terms used to describe tidal conditions. Mean lower low water is the reference datum for all NOS tide levels. Bridge clearances are measured from mean high water. Tidal range is the difference between these two levels.

The change in levels does not occur uniformly. From a low water, the level starts to rise slowly, the rate increases to a maximum near the middle of the rise, then slows as high water is approached; the opposite occurs with a falling tide.

TIDAL THEORY

A skipper need have only a general knowledge of tidal theory, but it is an interesting subject. The major cause of tides is the relationship of the earth and moon; the relationship of the earth and sun has a lesser effect. Because the paths of the moon around the earth and of the earth around the sun are not circular, the distances, and consequential tidal effect, vary. In fact, the *tidal cycle,* the time between dates that will have the same tides at the same times, is approximately 19 years!

When the sun and the moon are in line with the earth—at full and new moons—tidal ranges are at their maximum, with higher highs and lower lows. These tides are called *spring tides* (the name has nothing to do with the season of the year). At quarter and three-quarter moons, the gravitational effect of the sun partially offsets that of the moon, resulting in tidal ranges that are less than normal. Such tides are called *neap tides.* Due to the complexities of lunar and solar motion, spring and neap tidal ranges will vary from month to month.

Types of Tides

As tides move inland from offshore, their heights and frequency are greatly influenced by the nature and shape of the coastal waters and tributary bodies. Tidal ranges can be as little as a foot or less, or more than 50 feet. Common along the Atlantic Coast are *semidiurnal tides* with two highs and two lows on most days; the heights of the two highs and the two lows of any day will not necessarily be the same, but will not be greatly different. The daily tidal cycle varies, but averages about 24 hours and 50 minutes, so there will be some days with only three tides. When this occurs there will be a high water or a low water early on the next day.

A *mixed tide* is one in which there are marked differences in the height of the two highs or of the two lows, or both; these are often found along the Pacific Coast.

Another type of tide is *diurnal,* with only one high and one low on most days. Such tides are found along the Gulf of Mexico coast.

THE IMPORTANCE OF TIDES

A good knowledge of tides is essential for safe navigation. The skipper of a boat of any size will often need to know the time and height of high or low water, or the height at some intermediate time. A shoal may be passable at some tide stages, and a hazard at other times. The depth of the water and the tidal range may affect where you choose to anchor and how much line to put out. Making fast at a pier in a harbor requires knowledge of the tidal state when arriving and the range that may be expected.

SOURCES OF TIDAL INFORMATION

Always remember that all published information on tides provides only predictions and may not be exact for a given date and location. Actual tides often vary from predicted values because of unusual wind or barometric pressure conditions, or the runoff from heavy rains inland.

Since 1966, the federal government has not published *Tide and Tidal Current Tables.* It does, however, continue to make field measurements and calculations, and then furnishes the data to commercial publishers. The latter sell this tidal information in various formats such as books, stand-alone programs for personal computers, and for inclusion in electronic navigation programs.

Complete tidal predictions are prepared by the National

TIDES & CURRENTS

Ocean Service for a limited number of *reference stations*. Information is also available for thousands of *subordinate stations* in the form of time and height differences that can be applied to the data of a reference station to get local predictions. And don't forget "local knowledge," which can be better than formal predictions—when you are in unfamiliar waters, it never hurts to ask experienced local boaters.

Currents

Current is the horizontal motion of water. It may result from any one of several causes, or a combination of two or three. Although certain of these are of greater concern to boaters, a skipper should have a general understanding of all.

TYPES OF CURRENTS

Currents that affect boaters can be the result of several different natural causes or combinations of these causes. Currents may be categorized as tidal, river, or ocean. When there is a combination of causes, such as tidal action and normal river flow, usually only the predominant cause will be used in naming the current.

Tidal Currents

Boaters in coastal areas will be most affected by *tidal currents*—horizontal flows of water resulting from the rise and fall of tidal levels. The usual type of tidal current is a *reversing* current in which the flow alternates between two directions. Offshore, however, tidal currents may be *rotary,* flowing with little strength, but slowly changing in direction. A special type of tidal current, called a *hydraulic current,* occurs in sea-level canals or natural channels connecting two bodies of water with differences in the time and the height of their high and low waters. The flow from one body of water to the other and back again can result in currents of significant strength.

River Currents
Boaters on stretches of a river above the head of tidal action must consider the current that results from the natural flow of water toward the ocean. Such flows are often seasonal, varying widely with the amount of rainfall and snowmelt.

Below the head of tidal action, natural river flow and tidal effects merge together and are not considered separately.

Ocean Currents
Offshore piloting requires knowledge and consideration of *ocean currents*. These result from a number of causes, such as global wind patterns, warming and cooling areas, and the rotation of the earth.

The ocean currents of greatest interest are the Gulf Stream, which starts from the Gulf of Mexico and curves across the Atlantic Ocean, and the California Current, which flows along the Pacific Coast of North America. On the oceans and in large bays, there may also be local *wind-driven currents* caused by periods of sustained strong winds.

DEFINITION OF CURRENT TERMS
Currents have both direction and strength, and the proper terms should be used to describe each of these characteristics.

The *set* of a current is the direction *toward* which it is flowing. A current flowing from north to south has a set of 180 degrees and is described as a southerly current. Note that this is the exact opposite of the way in which winds are designated: a wind from north to south is a north wind.

The *drift* of a current is its strength or speed. This is normally measured in knots and tenths; non-tidal river currents may be stated in terms of miles per hour (mph).

A tidal current is said to *flood* when it flows in from the sea. It *ebbs* when it flows back toward the sea. (Tides do *not* "ebb" or "flood," only currents.) As a current changes from one direction to the other, there is a brief period of no detectable motion—this is termed *slack or slack water.* This is *not* the same as the time of *stand,* when the rise or fall of a tide changes. Due to the varying characteristics of bodies of water, the time of stand and the time of slack are almost always different. For example, at a given location on a tidal river, the tide may already have started to fall while the current is still flooding—consider each phenomenon separately.

CURRENT EFFECTS
The motion of a boat through water with respect to the bottom depends on whether or not the water itself is also moving. Currents may be a help or a hindrance, and may require a steering correction to make good a desired track.

Effects of Currents on Course and Speed Made Good
A current directly in line with a boat's motion through the water will have a maximum influence on her speed made good over the bottom, with no off-course effect. This will have a consequent effect on your arrival time and fuel consumption.

A current at a right angle to your course through the water will have a maximum influence on your course made good, plus a minor effect on your speed made good and on the time it will take to get to your destination.

Typical currents that are neither directly on your course or at right angles to it will affect both course and speed made good.

Critical Locations

There are locations where current conditions can be critical. Many ocean inlets are difficult or dangerous in certain combinations of current and onshore surf. The danger is greater if the current is ebbing.

In many narrow bodies of water, the strength of the current may be cause to limit or deny the use of the passageway for boats of insufficient power. There are also locations where riding a favorable current can significantly speed passage and reduce the amount of fuel used.

TIDAL CURRENT PREDICTIONS

As with tides, tidal current tables are now published by commercial entities, or included as part of computer software. However, the requisite data for reference stations and subordinate stations is still furnished by the National Ocean Service.

In most locations, as normal river flow adds to tidal current, the strength and duration of the ebb will be greater than that of the flood. The number of floods and ebbs per day will generally follow the pattern of tidal highs and lows described above.

CURRENTS AND PILOTING

The application of current information is essential to safe and efficient navigation. Failure to allow for offsetting influences may place a boat in dangerous waters, or cause it to miss its destination. Correction for current effects may be made graphically, or by use of a calculator or computer. Details on both methods will be found in *Chapman: Piloting, Seamanship and Boat Handling.*

TIDES &
CURRENTS

CHAPTER EIGHT

Weather

Weather is a vital factor in boating, affecting both your safety and enjoyment. You need not be a qualified weather forecaster, but you must be able to understand and use forecasts prepared by those who are experts. Know where to get forecasts and never start out without one. You should also be able to correctly interpret local weather signs, such as wind shifts and changes in cloud patterns. Keep a sharp lookout for any approaching hazardous conditions.

The Elements of Weather

Temperature, precipitation, and wind are the weather elements of greatest concern to boaters. Waves, of course, are a factor in boating, but they are primarily a consequence of wind.

Temperature is more related to comfort than safety, except when it plays a role in the formation of fog. Precipitation is of major concern only when it restricts visibility. Winds are thus the major worry—the direction from which they will blow, and how hard.

Clouds

Clouds are the most visible manifestation of weather; winds and temperature can be felt, but they cannot be seen. Clouds can also be meaningful indicators of weather conditions and trends.

HOW CLOUDS FORM

There is more water in the air than you might think. It evaporates from the oceans, lakes, and rivers, and can exist in the air in any of three physical states—vapor, liquid, or solid.

Relative humidity is the amount of water vapor in the air, stated as a *percentage* of the maximum possible amount at that temperature. Because this maximum amount decreases with decreasing temperature, relative humidity increases as temperature falls even though the actual amount of moisture is unchanged. When the relative humidity reaches 100%, and the air is further cooled, some moisture condenses into visible forms. The temperature at which this occurs is the *dew point.*

When warm, moist air rises from the earth's surface, it expands and cools. The relative humidity aloft increases, and when it reaches 100%, clouds are formed; there may also be precipitation in liquid form (rain or drizzle) or in solid form (snow, sleet, or hail). When moisture condenses into a visible form at or very near to the surface, the result is *fog.*

TYPES OF CLOUDS

According to an international system of classification, different cloud types have descriptive names based mainly on appearance, but also in some cases on their process of formation. Despite a near-infinite variety of shapes and forms, there are only 10 basic types, grouped according to the altitude at which they form.

High clouds usually form above 20,000 feet, and are composed of ice crystals. The types in this group are *cirrus, cirrocumulus,* and *cirrostratus.* In the *middle clouds* group are *altocumulus* and *altostratus,* formed between 10,000 and 20,000 feet. The *lower clouds* group consists of *nimbostratus, stratocumulus, cumulus,* and *stratus,* formed between 500 and 10,000 feet. (See Table 8-1.)

TABLE 8-1.

Cloud Formations

TYPE AND DESCRIPTION	APPROXIMATE HEIGHT (FEET)	WEATHER PORTENT
Cirrus—Very high white strands of cloud; commonly known as mares' tails.	25,000–35,000	Probably approach of a depression with wind and rain
Cirrostratus—Spreading white film or veil through which the sun can still be seen, probably with a halo effect.	Ditto.	More definite forecast of rain
Cirrocumulus—Compressed bunches of cloud forming a more clearly defined pattern; commonly known as a mackerel sky.	Ditto.	Changeable
Altostratus—Watery gray layer or heavy veil of cloud; sun usually just visible.	10,000–20,000	Almost certain rain
Altocumulus—An even layer of fairly dense cloud, often resembling the pattern of sand on the sea bed. Also sometimes called a mackerel sky.	Ditto.	Usually more settled weather; perhaps a chance of thunder
Stratocumulus—A lower version of altocumulus, with perhaps a more distinct definition.	5,000–10,000	Fairly settled conditions
Cumulus—Clearly defined fleecy clouds with a firm, dark base, often increasing in size and number during the day.	2,000–5,000	Fair conditions
Cumulonimbus—Larger, more menacing development of cumulus, with towering gray-and-white masses, often rising to an anvil-shaped plateau.	Rising from a fairly low based up to perhaps 25,000	Big air disturbances with possibility of thunder, heavy showers or hail
Nimbostratus—Heavy, dark, amorphous cloud, driving hard with the wind.	Mostly below 7,000	Prolonged rain likely; fresh or strong wind certain
Stratus—Blanket of fog or mist-like cloud suspended low in the sky.	500–20,000	Generally humid with prospect of rain or mist

Fog

Fog is merely a cloud whose base is on or very near the earth's land or water surface. It consists of water droplets suspended in the air, each so small that it cannot be seen individually, yet present in such tremendous numbers that objects close at hand cannot be seen.

TYPES OF FOG

There are several different types of fog, all of which can be a hazard to safe navigation.

Radiation fog occurs on cool clear nights with little or no wind, usually in late summer or early fall. The air near the ground is cooled as the temperature of the earth drops in the absence of solar energy; when it reaches the dew point, fog is formed. It can be patchy or uniformly dense, and in most areas it evaporates shortly after sunrise.

Advection fog is produced by winds carrying warm, moist air over a colder surface; coastal fogginess is often of this type. It dissipates less readily than radiation fog, not "burning off" from sunshine. A change in wind direction is usually needed to clear advection fog.

Precipitation fog results from rain descending from a warm layer of air aloft to a colder zone near the surface. Because this often happens during a frontal passage, this type of fog is sometimes called frontal fog.

The remaining type of fog of interest to boaters is steam fog. This occurs when cold air passes over much warmer water, resulting in a rapid transfer of heat and water vapor to the lowest layer of air. Because the water is much warmer, vertical air currents are formed and it appears that the water is steaming, much like a hot bath. Such fog in coastal areas, called sea fog, can be widespread and very thick.

WEATHER

Winds

Winds are the horizontal movement of air. They can vary from light, refreshing breezes to winds so strong that they threaten life and property. Winds are designated in degrees according to the direction *from* which they come. Strength is measured in knots or miles per hour.

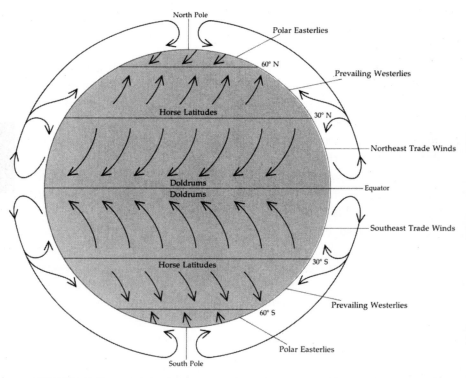

FIGURE 8-2. These idealized global air circulation patterns are based to a large extent on the heated air that rises along the equator and descends as cold air at the poles, and at latitudes approximately 30 degrees north and south of the equator.

CIRCULATION PATTERNS

When air is heated, it expands, becomes less dense, and rises. This air is replaced by colder air, which becomes warmer and rises. This process results in vertical currents over wide areas of the world.

The nearer the equator, the more surface heat there is to warm the air. Here the air rises and flows toward the poles. This air is replaced by colder air flowing down from the poles. This simple pattern, however, is modified by the earth's rotation.

In the Northern Hemisphere, the light, variable winds that circulate near the equator are called the *doldrums*. Moving north away from the equator, we come to the reliable *northeast trade winds* in the northern subtropical zone. Further to the north are the *prevailing westerlies*. Between the latter two zones are the *horse latitudes*, near 30° north latitude, where winds are weaker and less constant. This pattern is mirrored in the Southern Hemisphere.

Local Wind Patterns

The basic wind patterns described above are modified by local conditions generated by different patterns of heating and cooling. Land heats up more quickly than water areas during daylight. As a result, air that is rising over land is replaced by cooler air coming in from seaward—these are *sea breezes.*

At night, the land loses its heat more quickly, and the water becomes the warmer area. A reversal of flow occurs, creating *land breezes.* Both land and sea breezes are near-surface air patterns; at higher elevations, there are opposite air movements to complete the circulation pattern.

WIND MEASUREMENTS

With some experience, you can estimate wind speeds to an acceptable accuracy by observation of flags and pennants, or by its "feel on your face." More accurate estimations can be made using the *Beaufort Wind Scale* (see Table 8-4).

TABLE 8-4.
Beaufort Wind Scale

BEAUFORT NUMBER OR FORCE	WIND SPEED			WORLD METEOROLOGICAL ORGANIZATION DESCRIPTION
	KNOTS	MPH	KM/HR	
0	Under 1	Under 1	Under 1	Calm
1	1–3	1–3	1–5	Light Air
2	4–6	4–7	6–11	Light Breeze
3	7–10	8–12	12–9	Gentle Breeze
4	11–16	13–18	20–28	Moderate Breeze
5	17–21	19–24	29–38	Fresh Breeze
6	22–27	25–31	39–49	Strong Breeze
7	28–33	32–38	50–61	Near Gale
8	34–40	39–46	62–74	Gale
9	41–47	47–54	75–88	Strong Gale
10	48–55	55–63	89–102	Storm
11	56–63	64–72	103–117	Violent Storm
12	64 and over	73 and over	118 and over	Hurricane

ESTIMATING WIND SPEED

EFFECTS OBSERVED AT SEA	EFFECTED OBSERVED NEAR LAND	EFFECTS OBSERVED ON LAND
Sea like a mirror	Calm	Calm; smoke rises vertically
Ripples with appearance of scales; no foam crests	Small sailboat just has steerage way	Smoke drift indicates wind direction; vanes do not move
Small wavelets; crests of glassy appearance, not breaking	Wind fills the sails of small boats, which then travel at about 1 to 2 knots	Wind felt on face; leaves rustle; vanes begin to move
Large wavelets; crests begin to break, scattered whitecaps	Sailboats begin to heel and travel at about 3 to 4 knots	Leaves, small twigs in constant motion; light flags extended
Small waves 0.5 to 1.25 meters high, becoming longer; numerous whitecaps	Good working breeze, sailboats carry all sail with good heel	Dust, leaves, and loose paper raised up; small branches move
Moderate waves of 1.25 to 2.5 meters taking longer form; many whitecaps; some spray	Sailboats shorten sail	Small trees in leaf begin to sway
Larger waves 2.5 to 4 meters forming; whitecaps everywhere; more spray	Sailboats have double-reefed mainsails	Larger branches of trees in motion; whistling heard in wires
Sea heaps up, waves 4 to 6 meters; white foam from breaking waves begins to be blown in streaks	Boats remain in harbor; those at sea heave-to	Whole trees in motion; resistance felt in walking against wind
Moderately high (4 to 6 meter) waves of greater length; edges of crests begin to break into spindrift; foam is blown in well-marked streaks	All boats make for harbor, if near	Twigs and small branches broken off trees; progress generally impaired
High waves (6 meters); sea begins to roll; dense streaks of foam; spray may reduce visibility		Slight structural damage occurs; slate blown from roofs
Very high waves (6 to 9 meters) with overhanging crests; sea takes a white appearance as foam is blown in very dense streaks; rolling is heavy and visibility is reduced		Seldom experienced on land; trees broken or uprooted; considerable structural damage occurs
Exceptionally high (9 to 14 meters) waves; sea covered with white foam patches; visibility still more reduced		Very rarely experienced on land; usually accompanied by widespread damage
Air filled with foam; waves over 14 meters; sea completely white with driving spray; visibility greatly reduced		

WEATHER

Wind speeds are measured by a device called an *anemometer.* The instrument's sensor, usually small rotating cups, is located at a masthead or in the clear on a radar arch; the read-out is located near the helm or navigation station.

True and Apparent Wind

If your boat is moving, that motion must be taken into account in determining the actual wind. What you measure or estimate (except when using the Beaufort Wind Scale) is termed *apparent wind;* the vessel's speed and heading must be considered to determine *true wind.*

Wind Chill

The effect of air moving across the human body is to make the actual temperature feel colder than it really is—this is known as the *wind chill factor.* Table 8-5 gives the apparent temperature for various combinations of actual temperature and wind speeds.

TABLE 8-5.
Wind Chill Table
Prepared by the National Center for Atmospheric Research
Boulder, Colorado

LITTLE DANGER   INCREASING GREAT DANGER
DANGER THAT EXPOSED FLESH WILL FREEZE

WIND VELOCITY (MPH)

Temp °F	0	5	10	15	20	25	30	35	40	45	50
−10	−10	−15	−31	−45	−52	−58	−63	−67	−69	−70	−70
−5	−5	−11	−27	−40	−46	−52	−56	−60	−62	−63	−63
0	0	−6	−22	−33	−40	−45	−49	−52	−54	−54	−56
5	5	1	−15	−25	−32	−37	−41	−43	−45	−46	−47
10	10	7	−9	−18	−24	−29	−33	−35	−36	−38	−38
15	15	12	−2	−11	−17	−22	−26	−27	−29	−31	−31
20	20	16	2	−6	−9	−15	−18	−20	−22	−24	−24
25	25	21	9	1	−4	−7	−11	−13	−15	−17	−17
30	30	27	16	11	3	0	−2	−4	−4	−6	−7
35	35	33	21	16	12	7	5	3	1	1	0
40	40	37	28	22	18	16	13	11	10	9	8

Atmospheric Pressure

Familiarity with *atmospheric pressure,* also called *barometric pressure,* is essential to understanding weather. Atmospheric pressure at any given point is the weight of the air above that point on the earth's surface; it can vary as a result of many natural factors. It is measured by a *barometer,* and is stated in *inches* (of mercury) or in *millibars* (one-thousandth of a "bar," or standard metric sea-level pressure). The pressure distribution in the atmosphere controls the winds and, to a considerable extent, it also affects the occurrence of clouds and precipitation. To a boater watching the weather, it is important to understand how the winds and weather relate to the pressure distribution as shown on a weather map.

TABLE 8-6.
Conversion Table for Atmospheric Pressure

INCHES	MILLIBARS	INCHES	MILLIBARS
28.44	963	29.77	1009
28.53	966	29.86	1011
28.62	969	29.94	1014
28.70	972	30.03	1017
28.79	975	30.12	1020
28.88	978	30.21	1023
28.97	981	30.30	1026
29.06	984	30.39	1029
29.15	987	30.48	1032
29.24	990	30.56	1035
29.32	993	30.65	1038
29.41	996	30.74	1041
29.50	999	30.83	1044
29.59	1002	30.92	1047
29.68	1005	31.01	1050

WEATHER

HIGHS AND LOWS

The global circulation of the atmosphere fueled by uneven heating results in the build-up of areas of above-average barometric pressure along with corresponding areas of lower pressures. These are the *Highs* and *Lows* that are seen on weather maps, usually designated by large letters *"H"* and *"L."*

General Characteristics

Highs usually bring good weather; Lows bring bad or unsettled weather. In the Northern Hemisphere, circulation around a High is clockwise; around a Low, it is counterclockwise. Winds are generally weaker with Highs than they are with Lows.

Formation

Areas of high pressure are formed in polar regions and in the horse latitudes. Highs forming sequentially in north polar regions first move southward; then, as they reach the latitudes of the prevailing westerlies, the earth's rotation causes them to change direction to the southwest, then eastward, and often northeastward.

The formation of low pressure cells is quite different. On the boundary between warmer and cooler air, a horizontal wavelike situation develops. The boundary becomes more and more distinct, and may even curl and "break" like a wave on a beach.

The existence of continents and oceans somewhat distorts the theoretical patterns described above.

Air Masses and Fronts

A general knowledge of air masses and fronts will make weather forecasts more understandable and thus more useful.

AIR MASSES

Air mass is another term for a *high pressure cell,* a build-up of air descending from high-altitude global circulation. It is a huge "blob" of air that takes on the characteristics of the surface over which it forms. It may be an area as large as several hundred thousand square miles in which the conditions of temperature and moisture are the same horizontally. An air mass retains these characteristics even after it moves away and is over different surfaces. (There is no corresponding feature or name for the low pressure equivalent.)

WEATHER FRONTS

A *front* is the boundary between two different air masses, one cold and one warm. The two bodies do *not* tend to mix, but rather each moves with respect to the other. The passage of a front results in a change of weather conditions, frequently for the worse, and sometimes violent.

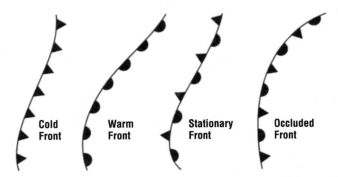

FIGURE 8-7. Fronts are shown as solid lines on weather maps, with triangles or half-circles used singly or in combination to indicate the type of front. These symbols face in the direction that the pressure system and its front are moving.

Cold Fronts

With a *cold front,* the oncoming cold air mass pushes under the warm air mass and forces it upward. In the Northern Hemisphere, such fronts generally lie along a SW–NE line and move eastward or southeastward at a rate of 400 to 500 miles per day (more in winter, less in summer).

A strong, rapidly moving cold front will bring weather changes that are quite intense, but relatively brief in duration. These active cold fronts often are preceded by a line of strong thunderstorms, called a *squall line,* that may produce more intense weather than the front itself.

The approach of a cold front is indicated by a shift of the wind in a clockwise direction towards south and then southwest, and by a fall in barometric pressure readings. Clouds lower and build up; rain starts slowly but increases rapidly. As the front passes, the wind continues to shift westward, then northwesterly, and even northerly. Skies clear and temperatures drop; pressure builds up and the wind may continue to shift to the northeast.

Warm Fronts

A *warm front* occurs when an advancing warm air mass reaches colder air and rides up over it. Warm fronts are generally oriented in a N–S, NW–SE, or E–W direction and move more slowly than cold fronts, 150 to 200 miles per day.

Weather along a warm front is usually less severe than that of a cold front and may extend several hundred miles in advance of the actual front. Clouds form at low levels and rainfall is more moderate but tends to last longer. The approach of a warm front is indicated by a falling barometer (but falling more slowly than for a cold front), a build-up of clouds, and the beginning of rain or drizzle. After the front passes, temperatures will go up and the barometer will slowly rise.

Other Fronts

Occasionally, a front will slow down to little or no forward movement. This *stationary front* will bring clouds and rain, much like a warm front.

An *occluded front* is a complex mix of warm air, cold air, and cool air. Its appearance on a weather map is that of a curled "tail" extending from the junction of a cold front and a warm front. This is a low pressure area with counterclockwise winds.

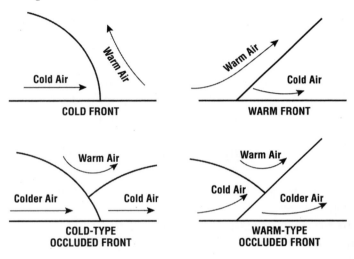

FIGURE 8-8. The above diagrams indicate the actions of warm and cold fronts, and show how their interaction forms occluded fronts.

Storms

Although a boater is generally interested in what the weather is now and what it is forecast to be, his or her main concern is the possibility of a *storm.*

EXTRA-TROPICAL CYCLONES
The technical name for the usual form of a storm is *extra-tropical cyclone.* Such a storm in the Northern Hemisphere is defined as a traveling system of winds rotating in a counterclockwise direction

around a center of low pressure and containing both a warm front and a cold front. These often occur in families of two, three, or four storms. At any given location it takes about 24 hours for a storm to reach maturity, and three or four days for complete dissipation.

THUNDERSTORMS

A *thunderstorm* is a powerful weather phenomenon characterized by lightning and strong, gusty winds that can be a serious threat to small craft. A thunderstorm can develop individually within a warm, moist air mass, or above a high mountain; or groups of them can form as part of a low pressure system or a squall line. They occur most frequently, and with the greatest intensity, in subtropical latitudes during summer. They may strike at any hour, but are most common in the late afternoon or early morning over land and coastal waters.

The prime danger signal alerting you to a thunderstorm is a cumulus cloud growing larger, with its top being blown off into an anvil shape. Lightning in the distance is a positive sign of such a storm even if no thunder has been heard yet.

TORNADOES AND WATERSPOUTS

Tornadoes are inland storms that may affect boaters on rivers and lakes. They can occur in any part of the continental United States, and most often are spawned by a squall line. They frequently appear in groups and move with the wind that prevails in the warm air ahead of a cold front.

A tornado is essentially a whirlpool of small horizontal extent that spirals down from a cumulonimbus cloud and has a funnel-like appearance. The average diameter of the visible funnel cloud is only about 250 yards, but the destructive effects may extend out as far as half a mile. The wind speed near the core is not measurable, but is undoubtedly as much as 200 knots or more.

A *waterspout* is essentially a tornado at sea, forming in much the same conditions, but more frequently in the tropics than in the mid-latitudes. A funnel shape forms at the base of a cumulonimbus cloud and spirals downward. Beneath it, the water surface is agitated and spray extends upward quite visibly. The funnel-shape cloud continues to descend until it merges with the spray; it then becomes a tube from the sea surface to the cloud. The diameter of a waterspout varies from 20 to 200 feet or more, while its length from the sea to the base of the cloud is usually between 1,000 and 2,000 feet. *Waterspouts* last from 10 minutes to a half-hour. Movement of the upper part of a waterspout may be in a different direction and at a different speed from that of its base, making the tube look stretched out. Finally, the tube breaks, and the lower portion quickly subsides.

HURRICANES

A tropical cyclone in the northern Western Hemisphere is known as a *hurricane;* different names are used in other areas of the world. A hurricane has a cyclone's characteristic counterclockwise winds, but is not associated with cold and warm fronts. It is the later development of a *tropical depression* that grows into a *tropical storm.* Tropical storms are given a name from a list that is established for each year, and become hurricanes when their winds reach 64 knots (75 mph).

In North American waters, the period from early December until mid-May is usually free of hurricanes. The months of August, September, and October are the times of peak activity. Spawning areas for hurricanes are the eastern tropical Atlantic off the west coast of Africa between 8°N and 20°N, the Caribbean Sea, the Gulf of Mexico, and off the east and west coasts of Central America. Modern satellite tracking systems ensure early detection, and advanced computer programs do much to provide reasonably accurate predictions of future track. While remaining in lower latitudes, hurricanes advance at about 15 knots, gradually picking up speed to about 25 knots, although in some cases they have reached forward speeds of 50 to 60 knots. Hurricanes decrease in intensity and tend to break up when they pass over land masses; they weaken after they reach higher latitudes with colder water.

ADVISORIES AND WARNINGS

The National Weather Service (NWS) issues advisories and warnings for specific weather threats.

Small Craft Advisories are issued when winds are expected to reach speeds of up to 33 knots (38 mph) and/or sea conditions are deemed dangerous for small craft in the forecast area. Small craft are defined by NWS as "small boats, yachts, tugs, barges with little freeboard, or other low-powered craft."

Gale Warnings are issued when winds are forecast to be between 34 and 47 knots (39 to 54 mph).

Storm Warnings are broadcast for winds greater than 48 knots (55 mph) with no upper limit on speed. A *Hurricane Warning* is issued only for hurricanes, with winds of 64 knots (75 mph) or more. A *Hurricane Watch* may be issued as an early alert to the possible arrival of a hurricane in the watch area. The watch will be changed to a *Hurricane Warning* when the storm is within 24 to 36 hours of arrival in the specified watch area.

Visual displays of flags by day and lights by night (white and/or red) are no longer officially used as weather warnings, but a single red pennant signifying that a Small Craft Advisory is in effect may sometimes still be seen at centers of boating activity.

Weather Prediction

The skipper of a small craft needs two kinds of weather information: what to expect in the next hour or two, and what the weather will be for the next two or three days.

SOURCES OF INFORMATION

For U.S. boating areas, *forecasts* are prepared by local offices of the National Weather Service (NWS), a component of the National Oceanic and Atmospheric Administration (NOAA). Specialized forecasts for severe types of weather are developed at facilities such as the National Hurricane Center. These are distributed electronically to the news media and are available directly to the public on the Internet.

Weather Maps

The old-fashioned daily weather maps, printed on paper and covered with many complex symbols for weather conditions of a previous day, are now things of the past in this era of modern electronic communications. Although some newspapers in larger cities print a daily weather map, it is usually a much-simplified *forecast map,* typically predicting conditions for the coming day.

Television Weather Broadcasts

The more common weather map today is the one you see on your TV screen during a local news broadcast. It usually shows both existing and anticipated conditions, frequently with animation. Many cable TV systems carry a channel of continuous weather information.

TV weather maps omit many technical details, but are useful in evaluating probable weather changes for your area. Satellite photos, still or time-lapse, are often used to explain patterns and trends.

Current weather radar scans show precipitation patterns out to about 125 miles.

Radio Weather Broadcasts

Almost all AM and FM radio stations broadcast weather information on regular schedules, with special bulletins when warranted. These are based on official information, but vary widely in level of detail—learn when and where to listen for the best weather reports in your area.

The best sources of marine weather information are the *continuous broadcasts* by NWS stations on frequencies that can be picked up by the VHF-FM transceivers used on boats, or on small, inexpensive "weather radios." Information can be obtained locally as to which channel covers that area.

Marine Weather Services Charts

The National Weather Service publishes a series of 16 *Marine Weather Services Charts* that cover U.S. coastal waters, the Great Lakes, the Hawaiian Islands, Alaska, and Guam and the Northern Mariana Islands. These contain detailed information on the location, frequencies, and coverage areas of NWS continuous FM broadcasts, plus some information on weather broadcasts from commercial stations.

WEATHER SIGNS

Weather forecasting is a science that has improved in recent years, but every skipper knows that it is not infallible. Get your forecasts by any and all available means, but keep an eye on present conditions, *and especially on changes in them.* A forecast of good, safe conditions for your general area does *not* preclude temporary local differences that could be hazardous. Keep alert for special warnings that are broadcast by the Coast Guard on VHF Channel 22A following an announcement on Channel 16.

TABLE 8-9
Wind and Barometer Indications

WIND DIRECTION	BAROMETER REDUCED TO SEA LEVEL	CHARACTER OF WEATHER INDICATED
SW. To NW.	30.10 to 30.20 and steady	Fair, with slight temperature changes, for one to two days.
SW. To NW.	30.10 to 30.20 and rising rapidly	Fair, followed within two days by rain.
SW. To NW.	30.20 an above and stationary	Continued fair, with no decided temperature change.
SW. To NW.	30.20 and above and falling slowly	Slowly rising temperature and fair for two days.
S. to SE.	30.10 to 30.20 and falling slowly	Rain within twenty-four hours.
S. to SE.	30.10 to 30.20 and falling rapidly	Wind increasing in force, with rain within twelve to twenty-four hours.
SE. To NE.	30.10 to 30.20 and falling slowly	Rain in twelve to eighteen hours.
SE. To NE.	30.10 to 30.20 and falling rapidly	Increasing wind, and rain within twelve hours.
E. to NE.	30.10 and above and falling slowly	In summer, with light winds, rain may not fall for several days. In winter, rain within twenty-four hours.
E. to NE.	30.10 and above and falling rapidly	In summer, rain probable within twelve to twenty-four hours. In winter, rain or snow, with increasing winds, will often set in when the barometer begins to fall and the winds set in from the NE.
SE. To NE.	30.00 or below and falling slowly	Rain will continue one to two days.
SE. To NE.	30.00 or below and falling rapidly	Rain with high wind, followed, within thirty-six hours, by clearing, and in winter by colder weather.
S. to SW.	30.00 or below and rising slowly	Clearing within a few hours, and fair for several days.
S. to E.	29.80or below and falling rapidly	Severe storm imminent, followed, within twenty-four hours, by clearing, and in winter by colder weather.
E. to N.	29.80 or below and falling rapidly	Severe northeast gale and heavy precipitation; in winter, heavy snow, followed by a cold wave.
Going to W.	29.80 or below and rising rapidly	Clearing and colder

WEATHER

Atmospheric pressure can be measured with a *barometer,* an instrument easily carried and used on a boat. It's possible to make broad forecasts of the weather for the next several days using pressure readings and wind directions (see Table 8-9). You can improve these predictions by systematically recording your data in a *weather log* that can be reviewed from time to time to detect trends.

Weather proverbs may be bits of timeworn folklore, but many of them have some scientific basis and are actually reasonably accurate. Perhaps the best known weather proverb is "Red sky at morning, sailor take warning; red sky at night, sailors' delight." Try to become familiar with weather proverbs that apply to your boating areas.

CHAPTER NINE

Electronic Communications and Navigation

The use of electronic equipment on boats has increased dramatically over the past decade, with new products being launched every year. Nearly all boats today have VHF radios, either installed or hand-held units. Digital Selective Calling (DSC) is on the horizon for more efficient and effective communications. Depth sounders are essential for safe navigation, and more and more of them also serve as fish finders. Radar can be used for collision avoidance and for navigation, especially at night or in reduced visibility. GPS receivers have become popular, while Loran sets are still widely used. The ways in which electronics can make your boating safer and more enjoyable are almost endless. And don't forget, all these "goodies" require basic electrical power, usually from the boat's 12-volt DC system.

Electrical Units

Volts, ohms, and amperes ("amps") are the terms used to describe, respectively, electromotive force ("voltage"), electrical resistance, and rate of current flow. One volt is the force that will produce a current of one ampere in a conductor that has a resistance of one ohm.

Two other important quantities are power and energy, and you should understand the difference between them. "Power" is defined as the rate at which energy is generated or consumed. For household or dockside electricity—usually 120 volts alternating current (AC)—power is measured in volt-amps or watts. For direct-current circuits on boats, power is measured in watts. Total energy consumed or generated is measured in units that factor in time, such as watt-hours, or amp-hours; a larger unit is kilowatt-hour, equal to 1,000 watt-hours.

Radio Terminology

Amplitude: The height of a radio wave.

Frequency: The number of times per second that a radio wave goes through its cycle. One cycle per second is one *Hertz (Hz)*. One thousand Hertz is one kilohertz (kHz). One million Hertz (one thousand kilohertz) is one megahertz (MHz). All radio waves travel at the speed of light. The shorter the wavelength, the more times per second it will go through its cycle, or the higher the frequency.

MF, HF, and *VHF* stand for Medium Frequency, High Frequency, and Very High Frequency radio bands. The *MF* band is 300 to 3,000 kilohertz (kHz); *HF* is 3,000 to 30,000 kHz (3 to 30 MHz); *VHF* is 30 to 300 *MHz.*

Carrier Wave: A radio wave of constant amplitude and constant frequency that is emitted by the transmitter when you press the button but do not speak into the microphone.

Modulation: The manner in which the carrier wave changes or varies when you speak into the microphone.

FM stands for Frequency Modulation, a process by which speech waves are impressed on the carrier wave by varying its frequency.

AM stands for Amplitude Modulation, a process by which speech waves are impressed on the carrier wave by varying its amplitude.

Side Bands are produced when speech frequencies are added to the carrier frequency. In conventional amplitude modulation (AM), two side bands are produced, an upper side band containing the carrier-wave frequency *plus* all the speech frequencies present, and a lower side band containing the carrier-wave frequency *minus* all the speech frequencies present.

SSB stands for Single Sideband, a newer method of radiotelephony. In SSB transmission, the carrier wave and one side band are suppressed, with only one side band being transmitted, but without eliminating the speech frequencies. All the power can then be put into this one side band, increasing the "speech power" by a factor of six as compared to the older double sideband AM transmissions.

DSC stands for Digital Selective Calling, a new high-tech, semi-automated method of establishing a contact between MF, HF, and VHF stations. Special channels are prescribed for DSC on the various marine radio channels. Eventually, DSC on VHF Channel 70 will replace voice calling on Channel 16.

ELECTRONICS

Radiotelephones

Three types of radio systems are used aboard boats; two of these are designed and licensed specifically for marine use. The third is the Citizens Band radio system.

VHF-FM marine radios are considered to be the prime system for marine communications over distances of up to about 30 miles. There are 50 channels in the VHF band dedicated to various marine uses in U.S. waters. Some are for communications between vessels, and these are divided between commercial and non-commercial (recreational) craft. Several are for special uses, such as navigational safety and direct bridge-to-bridge communications (see below). Some are for the exclusive use of the Coast Guard and other governmental entities. Others are for linkup with shoreside telephone systems. There also are channels for contact with shoreside facilities such as marinas and yacht clubs.

For long-distance communications, a Single Sideband (SSB) marine radio using designated frequencies in the MF and HF bands is required. Such a set can be installed only if the boat is already equipped with a VHF-FM radio, and the owner can certify a need for the long-range set. On this equipment, the international distress and calling frequency is 2182 kHz. Recreational boats can operate with sets having up to 150 watts output power; this will provide a range of hundreds to thousands of miles depending upon the frequency selected and the time of day.

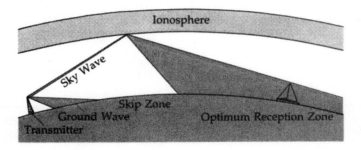

FIGURE 9-1. HF radio waves are transmitted both by groundwaves that extend out along the earth for a few hundred miles, and by skywaves that are reflected by the ionosphere and return to earth farther out. Between the reception for ground and sky waves is the "skip zone," an area of no signals.

Citizens Band radios can be used as an adjunct to the normal marine radios for informal, short-distance communications. There is no CB channel monitored by the U.S. Coast Guard, and there is no connection with the telephone system ashore. The range of CB radios is up to about 10 miles, but the distance may be greater to a base station ashore with a high antenna. A skipper may set up such a base operation at home or carry a hand-held set ashore for communicating back to his boat at anchor. While true marine radios must be used only for ship's business, there is no such restriction on CB sets. In areas where the Coast Guard is not operating, CB radios often provide the only means for calling for help in an emergency.

INSTALLATION AND MAINTENANCE

VHF radios may be physically installed and electrically connected by the boat owner or any person. An SSB set should be installed by a qualified technician and checked out by a person holding an FCC Commercial Operator License. Radio installations on gasoline-powered boats will generally require some form of ignition-noise suppression or shielding: this is a job for a technician. With regard to maintenance, an unlicensed person is limited to matters that will not affect the quality of the signal on the air. For example, he can replace a blown fuse, but cannot make internal repairs.

ELECTRONICS

Using Your Marine Radio

The operation of radio transmitters on boats in U.S. waters is governed by the rules and regulations of the Federal Communications Commission (FCC). This includes radiotelephones of all types, radars, emergency beacons, and all other devices that radiate a signal; receiving equipment is not regulated.

BASIC CONSIDERATIONS

The most important characteristic of marine radio communications is the fact that its primary function is *safety*—some other uses are permissible, but these are secondary, and there are some uses that are prohibited. Operational communications—those relating to the navigation, movement, or business of vessels—are legal; social communications are not. For example, making arrangements for dockage or fuel is permissible; making dinner reservations is not.

Safety communications take absolute priority over all other communications. If you hear a distress call, you must cease transmitting immediately, but should continue to listen to keep informed of the situation.

VHF radios for boats consist of a combined transmitter and receiver called a *transceiver.* It can perform both functions, but not at the same time. VHF radios on boats operate on a "one-way" basis—called "simplex" or "half-duplex." This means that you must stop transmitting (release the microphone button) in order to hear the other station; the other station cannot interrupt you while you are transmitting.

RADIO LICENSES

The FCC issues licenses for both stations and operators. These may be required in some instances, but not in others.

Station Licenses

For non-commercial boats used in United States waters, no station license is required for a VHF set; likewise, no license is needed for a radar or emergency beacon (but the latter should be properly registered; see below). If the craft is to cruise into international waters (except for a trip from and back into a United States port—such as an offshore fishing trip) or into the waters of another country, a station license must be obtained. There is one exception: Canada does not require a United States boat to have a VHF radio license if it is cruising in Canadian waters for less than 45 days.

A Single Sideband transceiver must be licensed regardless of where it is to be used. The license term is for ten years, and must be renewed.

Operator Licenses

Operator licenses may or may not be required depending on the equipment installed and the use of the craft. Use of a VHF radio in U.S. waters does not require any operator license. For operation of a Single Sideband radio, or any radio on a craft carrying six or fewer passengers for hire, the lowest grade of radio operator license—a Restricted Radiotelephone Operator Permit—is adequate. For vessels carrying more than six passengers in commercial service, the operator must have a Marine Radiotelephone Operator Permit. A higher class license is available for people with technical training and experience, but they are needed only for making tuning adjustments and repairs.

No technical knowledge is required to obtain a Restricted Permit, but the applicant must "certify" that he or she can speak and hear; is familiar with the treaties, laws, and regulations governing the use of the type of radio that he or she will be operating; and can keep at least a rough written log. The Permit can be obtained by mail and is valid for life without renewal.

For the Marine Radio Operator Permit, an examination is required; it is non-technical, covering only operating rules and procedures in a multiple-choice format.

Obtaining Licenses and Permits

Information on FCC forms, procedures, and fees can be found on the Internet at www.fcc.gov/resources.html.

ELECTRONICS

TABLE 9-2
SELECTED MARINE CHANNELS AND THEIR USES

This table lists channels used by recreational (non-commercial) boats. The channels designated with an "A" suffix are accessible only on U.S.—not international—frequencies.

CHANNEL NUMBER	FREQUENCY (MHZ) TRANSMIT	FREQUENCY (MHZ) RECEIVE	COMMUNICATIONS PURPOSE
06	156.300	156.300	Intership safety communications (mandatory).
09	156.450	156.450	Commercial and non-commercial intership and coast-to-coast (commercial docks, marinas and some clubs); also used by recreational boaters as alternate calling channel. This is also used at some locks and bridges.
12	156.600	156.600	Port Operations — traffic advisory — also USCG secondary working channel.
13	156.650	156.650	Navigational — ship's bridges to ship's bridges (1 watt only). Available to all vessels and is required on passenger and commercial vessels (including many tugs), as well as all power-driven vessels more than 20 meters (65.6 ft.) in length. Used at some bridges.
14	156.700	156.700	Port Operations (intership and ship-to-coast).
16	156.800	156.800	Distress Safety and Calling (mandatory). All distress calls should be made on Channel 16.
22A	157.100	157.100	Coast Guard Liaison and Maritime Safety Information Broadcasts; used for communications with USCG ship, coast and aircraft stations after first establishing communications on Channel 16.
24	157.250	161.850	Public telephone (Marine Operator); also Channels 25, 27, 84, 85, 86, 87, 88.
26	157.300	161.900	Public telephone (Marine Operator) (first priority).
28	157.400	162.00	Public telephone (Marine Operator) (first priority).
65A	156.275	156.275	Port Operations (intership and ship-to-coast); also Channels 20A*, 66A, 73, 74, 77* (* = intership only).
67	156.375	156.375	Commercial intership all areas, plus non-commercial intership (Pug Sound and Strait of Juan de Fuca). In the Lower Mississippi River, used limited to navigational bridge-to-bridge navigational purposes (1 watt).
68	156.425	156.425	Non-commercial intership and ship-to-coast (marinas, yacht clubs, etc.).
69	156.475	156.475	Non-commercial intership and ship-to-coast.

CHANNEL NUMBER	FREQUENCY (MHZ) TRANSMIT	FREQUENCY (MHZ) RECEIVE	COMMUNICATIONS PURPOSE
70	156.525	156.525	Distress and safety calling, and general purpose calling; may only be used by vessels equipped with Digital Selective Calling (DSC).
71	156.575	156.575	Non-commercial intership and ship-to-coast.
72	156.625	156.625	Non-commercial intership only.
78A	156.925	156.925	Non-commercial intership and ship-to-coast.
79A	156.975	156.975	Commercial intership and ship-to-coast. Non-commercial intership on Great Lakes only.
WX1		162.550	Weather broadcasts (receive only).
WX2		162.400	Weather broadcasts (receive only).
WX3		162.475	Weather broadcasts (receive only).

The Radio Log

A radio station log is not required for a station on a voluntarily equipped boat. You should, however, make notes of any distress communications that you hear. You should also keep a written record of any maintenance performed on your radio or radar set with the name and license number of the technician doing the work.

OPERATING PROCEDURES

There are only a few legally prescribed radio procedures, but there are operating practices that you must understand and follow for effective communications.

ELECTRONICS

Channels

Marine VHF radios operate on a number of frequencies designated by channel numbers; the actual frequency in megahertz (MHz) is seldom mentioned. Channels are allocated for one or more specific uses, and must not be used for other types of communications.

The most important channel is 16 (156.8 MHz), designated for distress communications, but also used for initial contacts. Voluntarily equipped boats are not required to maintain a continuous watch, but if their radio is turned on, it must be tuned to this channel when the set is not actively being used for communications on another channel.

For the channels and their authorized uses, see Table 9-2.

The Phonetic Alphabet

Many letters of the English language sound much alike—B, C, D, E, G, etc.—and can be misunderstood over a radio circuit if receiving conditions are less than good. Substituting words, called phonetic equivalents, for letters can greatly reduce misunderstanding and confusion, especially if the substituted words are standard ones that are widely understood. Figure 1-1 lists the standard phonetic equivalents used internationally by military and civilian authorities.

How to Make a Call

Listen carefully to make sure that the channel you want to use is not busy. If it is busy, you will hear voices, or from most public shore stations, an intermittent busy tone. Except for a safety emergency, don't interrupt. Wait until the channel clears.

When the conversation is to take place on a ship-to-ship frequency—unless you have reached an agreement in advance as to the time and frequency—establish contact on Channel 16 and then immediately shift to the agreed-upon inter-ship working channel. Do not use Channel 16 for even the briefest of non-emergency communications.

Use of the emergency channel for initial calls ensures that there are a maximum of vessels listening on that channel, increasing the chances that a distress call will be heard. Use of a working channel for the actual conversation ensures that Channel 16 is relatively free of talk so that a distress call will not be delayed or subjected to interference.

When the conversation is to take place through a commercial shore station, make your initial contact on a working frequency of that station; this will speed your call, and reduce traffic on Channel 16.

Steps to follow in making a Distress (or Urgent or Safety) Call
For an actual distress situation: Turn your radio dial to Channel 16, press the microphone button, and say, in the following order:

1. MAYDAY, MAYDAY, MAYDAY

2. THIS IS (boat name, boat name, boat name)

3. MAYDAY (boat name) POSITION (latitude and longitude, *or* distance and magnetic direction *from* a well-known landmark)

4. (nature of distress)

5. (type of assistance required)

6. (number of persons on board)

7. (description of boat—length, type, color, and any other distinguishing features)

8. I WILL BE LISTENING ON CHANNEL 16 (or other channel if for good reason 16 is not used)

9. THIS IS (boat name), OVER

ELECTRONICS

If the situation does not warrant a distress call, follow the same general procedure but rather than "MAYDAY," say "PAN PAN" (pronounced "pahn pahn") for an Urgent message, or "SECURITE" (pronounced "say-cur-i-tay") as appropriate, and change the text of the message to describe the situation.

Procedures for Making a Call (Other than a Distress, Urgency, or Safety Call)
Boat-to-boat calls. Make sure Channel 16 is not busy; recreational boats can alternatively use Channel 9. If, or when, the calling channel is free, press your microphone button and say:

"(Name of boat called), this is (name of your boat), over." To avoid confusion, always observe the proper sequence of call signs—state the name or call sign of the *other station first,* then give your own identification after saying "This is." (If necessary, the identification of the station called and your boat's name may each be given two or three times, but not more.) The entire calling transmission must not take longer than thirty seconds.

Listen for a reply. If no contact is made, repeat the above after an interval of at least two minutes. If no contact is made after three attempts, cease calling for 15 minutes. After establishing contact, immediately switch to the agreed-upon inter-ship working channel. One exchange of communications must not exceed three minutes after establishing contact on the working frequency. After the conversation is completed, say: "This is (name of your boat), out."

You must not establish contact again with the same boat until ten minutes have elapsed. Note: Call signs are not used in VHF communications, as a boat without a license does not have one. When good signals are being received, the procedure words "Over" and "Out" can be omitted.

Procedures for Ship-to-Shore Connections
Listen to make sure that the working channel you wish to use is not busy. If it is clear, put your transmitter on the air and say:

"(Location) Marine Operator, this is (name of your boat, and call sign if you have one) calling (telephone number desired), over." After the telephone conversation is completed say: "This is (name of your boat), out."

How to Receive a Call

Your boat can be reached only when your radio is turned on and tuned to the frequency over which you expect calls. Keeping the radio you use to maintain watch on Channel 16 (or 9) will ensure that you get calls addressed to you by other boats. For calls from public shore stations, you will generally need to keep a receiver turned to a working frequency of the station for that area, unless you are sure that the shore station makes preliminary calls on Channel 16. It is urged that you have one radio for keeping watch on Channel 16 and a second one to ensure that you can be reached by a public shore station over a working channel. A "dual-watch" or "triple watch" set can accomplish the same result.

Steps in Receiving a Call

Boat-to-boat calls. When you hear your boat called, put your transmitter on the air and say: "(Name of boat that called), this is (name of your boat), over." Switch to the agreed-upon inter-ship working channel. After the conversation is completed, say: "This is (name of your boat), out."

Shore-to-ship calls. When you hear the name of your boat called, put your transmitter on the air and say: "(Name of station that called), this is (name of your boat and call sign), over." After the conversation is completed, say: "This is (name of your boat), out."

SINGLE-SIDEBAND RADIO OPERATION

For marine SSB communications, there are various "bands" in the medium frequency (MF) and high frequency (HF) portions of the radio spectrum. In each band, there are calling and working channels; the procedures are generally the same, except that call signs issued by the FCC are used.

Digital Selective Calling

Digital Selective Calling (DSC) is a relatively new mode of operation for both VHF and single-sideband marine communications. It will permit the establishment of contact between two vessels, or a vessel and a shore station, without a voice transmission on a normal calling frequency. Each vessel and shore entity using this mode must have a Maritime Mobile Service Identity (MMSI) number, much like a telephone number. This is issued by the FCC as part of a station license; for vessels without a license, an MMSI can be assigned without charge upon request to the Boat Owners Association of the United States (BoatU.S.) or other source.

To establish contact with another station, a DSC set transmits a very brief burst of digital signals on Channel 70 for VHF, or on a designated MF or HF digital calling frequency. This will include the station's MMSI, the MMSI of the station called, and the proposed working channel. DSC receivers are totally silent until called, at which time an audible "ring" is heard, and the set shifts to the requested channel (or sends a digital message that it is unable to comply); voice communications are then carried on as in the present system. The MMSI of the called station can be keyed in manually or it can be stored in memory for frequently called stations. The proposed working channel is keyed in manually.

DSC is used only for establishing contact; once established, a working channel is used for voice communications in the usual manner. DSC can be used for ship-to-shore communications as well as boat-to-boat. DSC can also be used to transmit a distress call. This includes the MMSI of the vessel in distress, and will include its position (and time of last position determination) if the DSC set is connected to an electronic navigation system such as GPS. Distress calls may even indicate the nature of the distress, such as fire, taking on water, etc.

DSC sets can also transmit an "All Ships" call; this is useful if the individual identity of the vessel being called is not known. Calls can be made to DSC receivers in a specific geographic area, or to groups of stations, such as any or all Coast Guard units, or all boats in a cruising group.

DSC receivers are "selective" because calls can be addressed to a specific unit or group. Others do not know that the call is being made. When a DSC set "hears" a transmission, it looks at the address, geographic information, etc. The receiver is normally entirely silent; it alerts the operator only if the call is intended for that station.

U.S. Coast Guard implementation of DSC has been slow and spotty, but eventually it will be at all stations and on all craft, and will replace Mayday voice calls (but not subsequent distress communications).

Cellular Telephones

Never depend on a cellular telephone for distress and safety communications. There is no cellular service on the high seas and limited coverage in coastal areas. If there are system antennas near the coastline, cell phones may be operable out to about six or eight miles. Skippers with cell phones should make informal field checks in their boating areas to determine the extent of service. Another major difficulty is that other vessels will not hear the distress call if made on a cell phone; other boats in the area which might be able to render immediate assistance will not be aware of the situation.

A cell phone, however, can be very useful on board. In a safety or distress situation, after contact has been made with the Coast Guard, a shift of the working channel to cell phones may give you a much more "solid" and interference-free contact; indeed, the

ELECTRONICS

Coast Guard may ask if you have a cell phone available. Don't forget that the battery life of a cell phone may be quite limited if the phone is used frequently.

A cell phone can also be useful for calls to persons ashore, and for social communications between boats that cannot legally be conducted on marine VHF channels.

EPIRBs

An Electronic Position Indicating Radiobeacon (EPIRB) is a small device that can save your life! Any skipper operating well offshore out of reliable VHF range and away from other vessels should seriously consider equipping his boat with one. EPIRBs are not inexpensive, but are well worth the price. For occasional voyages, you can rent a unit from BoatU.S. at their local stores or by mail. Additional information can be found at their Web site, www.boatus.com.

EPIRBs can be started manually or activated automatically when immersed in water. The current models transmit a digital distress signal on 406 MHz, and are commonly referred to as "406 EPIRBs." (The older models that transmitted a tone on 121.5 and 243 MHz are being phased out.) The EPIRB signal is detected by one of several orbiting or geostationary satellites (these are satellites that maintain a position in space that is fixed relative to the earth, like those used for TV networking). The satellite transmits the signal to a ground station if one is within view; if one is not in view, the signal is stored and retransmitted at the earliest opportunity. The distress signal is then relayed to the appropriate search and rescue coordination center. The distress signal contains an identification number that will tell the rescue authorities the name and type of vessel, and the name and address of the owner.

A 406 EPIRB must be registered (at no cost) when it is purchased. The signal from some EPIRBs can also include the vessel's position if the unit has an internal GPS receiver or is connected to the vessel's GPS set. A 406 EPIRB transmits a signal as well on 121.5 MHz that can be used for direction finding by searching aircraft and vessels. It is also equipped with a flashing strobe light.

Depth Sounders

A depth sounder is a modern replacement for the hand-held lead line used for uncounted centuries to determine the depth of water beneath a ship. This electronic device furnishes a vastly greater amount of information and does it with much greater ease, especially in nasty weather. It provides safety as well as convenience in boating, and so is doubly advantageous to have on board.

HOW DEPTH IS MEASURED

A depth sounder determines depth by emitting a pulse of ultrasonic energy and measuring the time it takes for the pulse to travel from the boat to the bottom of the water and be reflected back to the point of origin (see Figure 9-3). The frequency of the audio pulses generally lies between 50,000 and 200,000 Hz (cycles per second), too high to be heard by human ears. Their average velocity through the water is approximately 4,800 feet per second; slight variations in speed will occur between salt and fresh water, and in different temperatures. The resulting small errors, however, can be safely ignored for the relatively shallow depths of interest to the operators of recreational boats.

Probably the greatest advantage of the electronic device over the hand-held line is the continuous nature of the information fur-

ELECTRONICS

nished. Depth sounders vary widely in the rate at which readings are taken, but in all cases many more soundings are taken than could be accomplished by hand. Current equipment takes readings at rates between one and thirty each *second*.

COMPONENTS OF A DEPTH SOUNDER

The primary components of a depth sounder are a source of energy (transmitter), a means of sending out the pulses and picking up the echoes (transducer), a receiver to amplify the weak echoes, and a visual presentation of the information. The transmitter, receiver, and display are housed in a small box that can easily be mounted near the helm. The transducer usually takes the form of a round

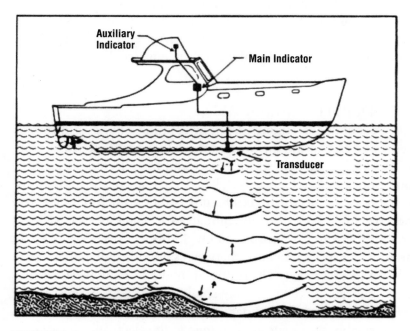

FIGURE 9-3. An electronic depth sounder measures depth by sending pulses of ultrasonic waves that are reflected back from the bottom. Distance is measured by the time taken by the pulses for the round trip.

block of hard ceramic material several inches in diameter and an inch or so thick mounted on the outside of the underwater hull, and is connected to the main unit with a cable. In many cases, the transducer is given an oblong, streamlined shape to reduce drag.

Information on the depth of the water is presented on a digital or video display, or is recorded on a moving paper strip. The display gives an easily read indication of the depth; the recorder provides a more permanent record.

The most sophisticated depth sounders are designed more for the serious fishing enthusiast than for actual depth measurement used in conjunction with piloting. Features include a white-line display to help separate low-lying fish from the bottom itself, the use of color in a video display to help identify types of fish, readouts of water temperature, and even the ship's position when hooked up to electronic navigation equipment.

USING YOUR DEPTH SOUNDER

Knowledge of the depth of the water under your boat not only contributes to its safe operation, but can also be used to help determine your position on a chart. A specific depth may not tell you where you are, but it will definitely tell you where you are not if the depth does not match the chart.

Fish Finders

Most electronic depth sounders with a video display can also be used for finding schools of fish or individual large fish. Indeed, many are designed and sold for this purpose, with depth-finding a secondary function.

ELECTRONICS

Radar

Radar is an excellent means of marine navigation and is used on vessels of all sizes, down to boats of about twenty feet in length. Although not installed on all recreational boats, its capabilities and limitations should be known to all boaters for their own safety when cruising on waters navigated by radar-equipped vessels.

RADAR PRINCIPLES

A radar set sends out brief pulses of super-high frequency radio waves that are reflected by objects at a distance. The time that it takes for the pulse to go out and the echo to return is a measure of the distance to the reflecting object. In broad terms, this is the same mechanism previously described for depth sounders, except that transmission is through air rather than water, and radio waves have been substituted for ultrasonic pulses. Another difference is that the radar pulses are sent out in a very narrow beam that can be pointed in any direction around the horizon and used to determine direction as well as distance.

COMPONENTS OF A RADAR SET

The major components of a radar set are:

1. The *transmitter,* which generates the radio waves; it includes the *modulator,* which causes the energy to be sent out in brief pulses.

2. The *antenna,* which radiates the pulses and collects the returning echoes. The antenna is highly directional in its horizontal characteristics, but eight to ten times wider vertically. The beam pattern can be thought of as being like a fan turned up on edge. The beam's narrow horizontal directivity gives it a fairly good angle-measuring capability, while its broadness in the vertical plane helps keep the beam on an object despite any rolling or pitching of the vessel.

3. The *receiver*, which detects the returned reflections and amplifies them to a usable strength.

4. The display, which provides a visual representation of objects sending back reflections.

Radars operate at frequencies far above the usual radio communications bands. At such super-high frequencies, radar pulses act much like light waves in that they travel in essentially straight lines at the speed of light, 186,000 miles per second. For each nautical mile of distance to the target, only a fraction more than twelve microseconds (one millionth of a second) are required for the round trip of the outgoing pulse and the returned echo. Pulses, each of which lasts for only a fraction of a microsecond, are sent out at a rate of from six hundred to four thousand each second depending upon the design of the equipment. The directional antenna rotates at a rate of one revolution in about four seconds. The round-trip time for a pulse is so short, however, that the antenna has not appreciably moved before the reflection is returned.

The Radar Display
The display of a radar is either a circular cathode ray tube (CRT) from five to twenty inches in diameter, or a rectangular "raster-scanned" view using a CRT or an LCD. The center of the face represents the position of the radar-equipped vessel and the presentation is roughly like that of a navigational chart. The presentation can be in color, or in several intensities of green (CRT) or shades of gray (LCD).

ELECTRONICS

A bright radial line on the face of the tube represents the radar beam; it rotates in synchronism with the antenna. Reflections show up as points or patches of light depending upon the size of the echo-producing object. The persistence of the screen is such that the points and patches of light do not completely fade out before the antenna has made another rotation and the lights are restored to brilliance. Thus the picture on the radarscope is repainted every few seconds.

The bearing of an object is indicated directly on the screen. A position corresponding to the 12 on a clock face is usually directly ahead. Some models can be programmed to have the display in a "North up" mode to match a chart. The direction of the object causing the echo can be read on a scale around the edge of the display. Some models have a moveable bearing cursor that when placed on the echo reads the bearing more exactly.

The distance to the object is proportional to the distance from the center of the screen to the point of light that is the source of the echo. On most radars, fixed concentric circles of light are used as range markers to make the estimation of distances both easier and more accurate. Some sets also have a moveable range ring that can be placed on the echo in order to read the distance exactly on a digital readout. All radar sets have multiple range scales that may be selected to suit the purpose for which the radar is being used. Longer range scales provide coverage of greater areas, but with less detail and poorer definition.

Maximum and Minimum Range

Radar sets have both a maximum and a minimum range, each of which is important to the operation of the equipment. The maximum range is determined by the transmitter power and the receiver sensitivity, provided, of course, that the antenna is at a sufficient height above water so that the range is not limited by the distance to the horizon. (The radar pulses normally travel with just a slight amount of bending; thus the radar horizon is about 15 percent farther away than the visual horizon.) Because a radar pulse has a definite duration, and therefore occupies a definite length in space as it moves outward from the antenna, there is a minimum range within which objects cannot be detected. This minimum range, usually between twenty and fifty yards, is important when navigating in close quarters, as when passing buoys at the side of a narrow channel.

RADARS FOR SMALL CRAFT

Radar sets for small craft usually consist of two units. Modern design of the components makes it possible to combine the antenna, transmitter, and a portion of the receiver into a single unit installed on a mast or radar arch, or on the pilothouse. This unit, usually weighing under 100 pounds, should be located as high as possible in order to avoid limiting the range of the set. The antenna should have as unobstructed a "look" in all directions as is possible. The remainder of the receiver and the display are located near the helmsman's position. Improved design techniques have resulted in indicator units so small that they may be fitted into a pilothouse in any number of positions.

Like VHF radios, radars must be licensed by the FCC if the craft is to operate in international or foreign waters, but this is not difficult to do. No license is required to operate a radar, but to install and maintain a unit, a technician must have a commercial radio operator's license with a special "ship radar" endorsement. The owner and station licensee of a marine radar installation is responsible only for making sure that all of the technical work on the equipment is done by a properly licensed technician.

ELECTRONICS

USING YOUR RADAR

Radars have two principal applications aboard ships and small craft. Although they are often thought of primarily as anti-collision devices, radars are used even more often to assist in the piloting of the vessel.

Radar was originally conceived for the detection and tracking of ships and aircraft. It offers an excellent means of extending the coverage of a visual lookout, especially at night and under conditions of reduced visibility. This greater range of detection affords more time for a ship to maneuver to avoid another craft or an obstacle.

Radar serves another valuable function in the piloting of a vessel when approaching a coastline or traveling in confined waters. Position can be determined by taking bearings on aids to navigation or landmarks. The ability of radar to measure distance as well as direction makes it possible to get a fix on a single object. Radar thus has significant usefulness even in daytime, but even more so, of course, at night or in fog.

PASSIVE RADAR REFLECTORS

The boat owner who does not have radar can still tap the power of other ships' radar to enhance the safety of his or her vessel. This is done by installing a *passive radar reflector*—a simple and inexpensive device consisting of thin, lightweight metal sheets arranged in mutually perpendicular planes. The sheets may fold for storage, but must remain rigid with respect to each other when opened for use. This relatively small reflector (each metal surface is only about a square foot in area) provides a radar reflection almost as strong as that from a medium-size steel ship. Without a reflector, the echo from the fiberglass (or wooden) hull of a small craft is so weak as to be easily overlooked among the echoes from the waves.

With a passive reflector hoisted as high as possible, the operator of a small craft can be sure that his boat will be detected on the radar screens of passing ships. Often Coast Guard or other res-cue craft searching for a boat in distress are radar-equipped; the use of a passive radar reflector greatly increases a small craft's chances of being quickly spotted.

Electronic Navigation Systems

There are two electronic navigation systems available to skippers of boats as well as to navigators of large ships. The cost, size, and power requirements of these systems have now been reduced to the point that they are feasible options for boats of almost any size.

The newer, and now the more widely used, system is the Global Positioning System (GPS). Also used by many boaters is Loran, an older system still in operation. Almost all new installa-tions, however, are GPS.

GLOBAL POSITIONING SYSTEM (GPS)

GPS provides world-wide continuous position information from a constellation of 24 satellites (plus some in-orbit spares) orbiting 10,900 miles above the earth. GPS satellites transmit their position in space and time to receivers on the earth. Receiver computers use the data from three satellites to determine a geographic position in two dimensions. Add signals from a fourth satellite, and a three-dimension position is determined (not needed by vessels, but use-ful to aircraft). Since signals from even more satellites increase the accuracy and reliability of the position, many receivers are designed to receive signals simultaneously from eight or more satellites.

ELECTRONICS

Accuracy

GPS was developed for military uses and is still operated by the Department of Defense. There are two modes of operation, the Precise Positioning Service (PPS) for the military and the Standard Positioning Service (SPS) for civilian users, who now outnumber military users by a wide margin.

Initially, the Defense Department intentionally degraded SPS for "national security reasons," using a technique called Selective Availability (SA). In May 2000, SA was effectively turned off, and a much more accurate SPS became available. (It remains less accurate than PPS, but is still very good.) The typical skipper can now consider that his or her GPS fixes are accurate within 30 meters (98 feet), 95% of the time; often the accuracy is better, but there is no way of knowing the actual error at any given moment. The use of Differential GPS (see below) will yield even better position accuracy.

GPS Equipment

GPS sets are receivers. As such, they do not transmit signals and do not require licenses. Some models are console-mounted, but more are "hand-held" units, usually used in a bracket. Some are small enough to be a part of a wristwatch! The use of GPS is not limited to boats and ships—the system can be used to find the position of aircraft, automobiles, buses and trucks, emergency vehicles, trains, many other means of transportation, and even wilderness hikers. It is widely used in land and marine surveying. New uses continue to be found almost every day. In the near future, cell phones will be GPS equipped so that the location of a 911 emergency call can be pinpointed.

GPS receivers are powered by internal dry-cell batteries or they can be connected to the boat's electrical system, using an adapter if necessary. Hand-held models have their own antenna, but operate more successfully if connected to a high, fixed antenna with a clear view of the sky in all directions. The display of a GPS receiver shows position in latitude and longitude; most sets can show either degrees, minutes, and fractions of minutes, or degrees, minutes, and seconds. GPS sets contain considerable computational capability—they can store waypoints and routes; compute speed and course made good, and estimated time of arrival at the next waypoint; and show the correct current time as well as the times of sunrise and sunset. There are many other "bells and whistles" depending upon the manufacturer and model—some models can show the location of a boat on its intended track (much like looking down the road ahead) or display a view of the sky showing the azimuth and elevation of the satellites within sight. Most sets will sound an alarm when a waypoint or destination is reached.

Differential GPS (DGPS)

When GPS became available for marine navigation, the imposition of Selective Availability limited its accuracy to 100 meters (328 feet). This was quite good enough for offshore navigation, but the Coast Guard considered it insufficient for harbor approach and entrance, and for proceeding down a channel. To provide greater accuracy, the Coast Guard developed *Differential GPS*. This is regular GPS plus an additional signal that increased the accuracy to not worse than 10 meters (33 feet) and typically to as good as 2 to 3 meters (7–10 feet).

Differential corrections are generated by placing one or more high-quality GPS receivers at a very precisely located position. The difference between the position reported by the GPS receivers and the true geographic position is thus determined, and correcting information is transmitted using transmitters and antennas from former marine radiobeacon stations (no longer used for their original purpose). The differential signals, near 300 kHz, are received on either a separate receiver or on a receiver integrated into the GPS set.

When SA was turned off, the accuracy of basic GPS improved significantly, but was still not considered to be good enough for close-in piloting. Thus the Coast Guard has continued the

Maritime DGPS system; the coasts and Great Lakes are covered to a distance of 50 to more than 200 miles offshore, and there are transmitters for portions of the Mississippi River System. GPS is so widely used for so many varied applications that a Nationwide DGPS System with more than 60 transmitters in the interior of the country is well on its way to implementation by the Coast Guard. Many countries have established DGPS systems using the same basic techniques as the USCG system.

Further Developments in DGPS

GPS has been widely adopted by civil aviation. As with ships, it is good enough for en route air navigation, but not for approaches and landings. The Federal Aviation Administration (FAA) is developing two differential methods to counter this deficiency: the Wide Area Augmentation System (WAAS) and the Local Area Augmentation System (LAAS). WAAS has applicability to boating and other marine interests.

WAAS generates differential corrections in much the same way as Maritime DGPS, but uses a quite different method of delivering them to the GPS receiver. Data is sent up to geostationary satellites, then relayed back to aircraft in flight and other users on the surface of the earth. The advantages of this technique include faster data transmission rates and a claimed higher degree of 3-D accuracy, required for landings in periods of limited visibility. GPS receivers for boats are now available with this type of differential correction, yielding position errors of less than 3 meters (7 feet).

The Future of GPS

Although the present Global Positioning System is fully operational, the technology continues to develop. The system will be expanded and improved by additional satellites and radio frequencies. As existing satellites die off and are replaced, enhancements to the system will be introduced, and GPS will steadily improve over time.

LORAN

LORAN—short for LOng RAnge Navigation—is an electronic system using shore-based radio transmitters and ship-board receivers to allow mariners to determine their position at sea. The type of Loran in use today is "Loran-C," but it is usually referred to simply as "Loran." The system works in all kinds of weather, twenty-four hours a day, but does not have worldwide coverage.

Loran-C principles

The transmitters of Loran-C all operate on 100 kHz in chains of a *master station* (M), plus two to four *secondary stations* designated as W, X, Y, and Z. Stations of a chain are located so as to provide signal coverage over a wide coastal area. Each station transmits groups of pulses on the same frequency; signals from secondary stations follow those from the master station at very precise time intervals. Chains are identified by their individual pulse group repetition intervals (GRI)—the time, in microseconds, between transmissions of the master signal. All Loran-C transmitters are frequency- and time-stabilized by atomic standards. If the signals of a pair should get out of tolerance, however, the chain will "blink" in a code that indicates the nature of the trouble.

The *difference* in the time of arrival at the receiver of pulse groups from the master and each secondary station is measured precisely by electronic circuitry, and this information is used to determine a line of position. The use of two or more master-secondary pairs of signals yields the same number of LOPs and thus a Loran-C fix.

Accuracy and Repeatability

Loran-C has a ground wave (most reliable) range of up to 1,200 nautical miles (2,200 km), with sky-wave reception out to as far as 3,000 miles (5,600 km). The accuracy of Loran-C positions from ground-wave signals varies from 0.1 to 0.25 nautical miles (0.2 to

0.5 km) depending upon where the receiver is in the coverage area; positional errors on sky-wave signals may be as much as eight times greater. A significant feature of Loran-C is the "repeatability" of positions obtained with this system. Ground-wave signals are very stable and a boat should be able to return to within 50 to 200 feet (15 to 60 m) down of a prior position.

Loran-C readings are highly accurate on or near the baseline between the master and secondary stations, but are subject to significant errors on or near the extensions of the baseline beyond each station. Using sky waves within 250 miles of a station being received is not recommended.

Loran-C Receivers

Loran-C receivers automatically acquire and track the signals from the chain to which the set is tuned. The system is complex, but such complexity is handled internally by advanced solid-state circuits—all the operator has to do is turn the set on and tune to the proper GRI. (The coverage area of a single chain is quite large and many boats will never need to change the GRI setting.) The Loran-C receiver may take several minutes to "settle down" and give steady readings. Position information can be displayed as measured time differences which the operator uses to plot his position on a chart that has been overprinted with Loran-C lines of position.

Most sets have two displays, allowing for a simultaneous readout of the two time differences required for a fix. Often a receiver will automatically make measurements on three or four station pairs and display these additional readings sequentially. Now, however, nearly all Loran receivers include a microprocessor that gives a direct readout in latitude and longitude. They will also provide additional information similar to that described above for GPS receivers.

Electronic Charts

An *electronic chart* is simply a digital computer file that contains all or part of the navigation information that appears on a conventional paper chart. These come in two different types, each with its advantages.

A *raster* chart is one that has been scanned from a paper chart—think of it as a digital photograph of a paper chart. A *vector* chart is one that has been drawn from charting information using computer technology. In both cases, the result is a digital file that can be stored in a small cartridge or on a CD-ROM. In most cases, the cartridge or CD will contain a number of charts of a rather wide region.

TYPES OF DISPLAYS

A number of different devices can be used to display both types of electronic charts. They are commonly shown on a stand-alone electronic device called a *chart plotter,* or on the screen of a personal computer—desktop or laptop/notebook—equipped with special navigation software programs. An electronic chart can also be shown as an overlay on the display of a radar, depth sounder, or some GPS receivers, even hand-held models.

A common problem, however, is that the display may not be bright enough to be seen properly in bright locations such as flybridges—the display that was so brilliant belowdecks becomes washed out to the point of not being readable. Sunlight-readable displays for PCs are available, but are very expensive.

ELECTRONICS

RASTER AND VECTOR CHARTS

Raster charts have the advantage of appearing essentially the same as a paper chart with which all skippers are familiar—a minimum of rethinking is required. A vector chart has the advantage of being constructed in a number of "layers," each of which has some different type of information, such as the shoreline and channels, aids to navigation, depth information, etc. All layers of a vector chart are usually viewed together at first, then any layers containing unnecessary information can be eliminated to reduce the level of complexity and make the chart easier to read and work with. The disadvantage is that the appearance of the chart—symbols used, etc.—is different from a paper chart and may take some getting used to. The big feature of both types is their ability to show on the chart display the present location of your boat as derived from GPS, DGPS, or other electronic navigation systems. Some electronic charts also have the capability of displaying "pop-up boxes" with information on aids to navigation and other landmarks. Techniques have been developed that will allow both types of charts to be updated as new information in published in *Notices to Mariners;* in some cases this can be received via the Internet.

A Caution on the Use of Electronic Charts

Electronic charts can greatly facilitate navigation by providing a constantly updated plot of your craft's position on a displayed chart. However, because electronic equipment can fail, or the supply of electrical power may be interrupted, electronic charts should not be the sole method of piloting—paper charts and pencil-plotted fixes are still a viable and important part of marine navigation.

CHAPTER TEN

Life on Board

This chapter covers many of the "little things" that are good to know, but perhaps not essential: How to fly your flags correctly, proper etiquette at meetings and rendezvous, how to be considerate of others as skipper of your boat, and how to be a good guest on some else's craft. Also included are proper pet care on board and some general housekeeping hints.

Customs and Etiquette

Modern boating is a relaxed, informal kind of recreation, no longer bound up in the ceremonial routines that once were considered essential elements of "yachting etiquette." However, there are still many occasions when proper observance and behavior are expected, even if only as a matter of common courtesy to your boating neighbors.

THE PROPER DISPLAY OF FLAGS

There is probably nothing that marks the knowledgeable skipper as much as the proper flying of flags on his or her boat. There are no laws or regulations governing the display of flags and pennants on a recreational craft, but there are well-established customs and procedures. These cover what flags are to be flown, what size they should be, and when and where on a boat they should be displayed.

The term "colors" properly applies only to the flag at the stern of a boat that denotes its nationality. In practice, however, it has come to be used to describe all the flags flown.

In general, only one flag should be flown from a single hoist. There are exceptions, as when a boat cannot fly all the flags desired at a single location on a single hoist and multiple hoists must be used. Where multiple flags are flown one above another, the proper order of precedence should be observed. In another exception to the formal rules, a boat that does not have a mast and spreaders can fly flags from a radio antenna.

The Various Flags

• *The United States Ensign* — 50 stars and 13 stripes — is proper for all U.S. craft without exception. It is normally flown from 0800 until sunset, but on the high seas, it need be displayed only when in the vicinity of other vessels.

On boats, power or sail, that have a mast with a gaff, the U.S. ensign should be flown at the peak of the gaff. On Marconi-rigged sailboats, it can be flown from the leech of the aftermost sail, two-thirds of the way up. It is never displayed on a sailboat while racing. On powerboats, and optionally on sailboats, the U.S. flag is flown at the stern. On sport-fishing boats, where it would obstruct normal fishing activity, the ensign can be flown from a halyard rigged on the centerline just aft of the tuna tower.

• *The Yacht Ensign* has the same 13 stripes, but with a fouled anchor in a circle of 13 stars in the union rather than 50 stars. Originally, it was to be flown in addition to the U.S. ensign to designate a yacht documented by the Coast Guard; now, however, it is seen on recreational craft of all types and sizes instead of the 50-star flag. It should not be flown in international or foreign waters where the national flag is required. The locations and hours are the same as for the 50-star flag.

• *The United States Power Squadrons Ensign* has 13 blue and white *vertical* stripes with a fouled anchor and circle of stars in a red union. It is flown to indicate that the boat is commanded by a USPS member. The preferred location is at the starboard spreader of the mast, the most forward mast if there is more than one. If there is no mast, it is often flown from a radio antenna on the starboard side. On smaller boats that have a location for only one flag, it can be flown at the stern in lieu of the national or yacht ensign. It is displayed during the same hours as the national ensign.

• *The U.S. Coast Guard Auxiliary Ensign* is blue with a wide white angled stripe running though the center; the Auxiliary's emblem is centered on this stripe. The "blue ensign" is flown, day and night, on a vessel that has been approved as a "Facility." On a boat without a mast, the Auxiliary ensign is flown at the bow. If there is a mast, it is flown at the masthead; if there is more than one mast, it is flown at the head of the most forward mast. It is never flown at the stern. It is improper to display a cocktail or other novelty flag when the Coast Guard Auxiliary ensign is being flown.

• *The USCG Auxiliary Operational Ensign* is flown when an Auxiliary "Operational Facility"—a boat with special standards of crew and equipment—is operating under Coast Guard orders. It is a white flag with the Coast Guard's red and blue "racing stripes" as seen on their vessels. This replaces the normal "blue ensign."

• *The yacht club burgee.* Usually triangular in shape, but sometimes swallow-tailed, a yacht club burgee is flown by day only, or by day and night, as set by a club's rules. It is flown from the bow of mastless and single-masted motorboats, and from the foremost masthead of vessels with two or more masts. The burgee may be flown while underway (but not racing) and while anchored or docked.

• *The Power Squadron pennant.* Each squadron has its own identifying pennant. This is always triangular in shape and is flown similarly to a yacht club burgee.

• *Owner's Private Signal.* This is normally swallow-tailed in shape, but may be rectangular or triangular (a pennant). It is flown from the masthead of a single-masted motorboat or sailboat. If there are two or more masts, it is flown from the aftermost masthead. It may be flown by day only, or by day and night. A mastless motorboat may fly this signal from the bow staff in lieu of a club burgee.

• *Officers' flags.* Flags designating yacht club or USPS officers are rectangular in shape. They are blue (with white designs) for the most senior officers, red (with white designs) for the next lower in rank, and white (with blue designs) for the lowest rank. Other officer's flags may be swallow-tailed or triangular in shape as provided for in local rules. An officer's flag is flown in lieu of his private signal on all rigs of sail and motor boats, except in the case of single-masted sailboats, where it is flown from the masthead in lieu of the club burgee.

Size of Flags

Although flags are made in standard sizes, there are guidelines to help you select the proper size for your boat. Keeping in mind that flags are more often too small than too large, follow these rules and round off upward.

The flag at the stern of your boat—U.S. ensign, yacht ensign, or USPS ensign—should be one foot on the fly (horizontal dimension) for each foot of overall boat length. The hoist (vertical dimension) is normally two-thirds of the fly, but a few flags have slightly different proportions.

Other flags, such as club burgees, officers' flags, and private signals on motorboats, should be approximately 5/8 of an inch for each foot of overall length. On sailboats, they should be approximately ½ inch on the fly for each foot that the highest masthead is above the water. The shape and proportions of pennants and burgees will be prescribed by the organization to which they relate.

Flying Flags in Foreign Waters

When in international waters, or those of a foreign nation, the U.S. ensign should be flown rather than the yacht ensign or USPS ensign. When in the waters of another country, it is proper to fly that country's flag as a "courtesy ensign." Many nations have different flag designs for various situations; the courtesy ensign is usually the one that vessels of the visited nation normally fly at their stern.

There being only a limited number of locations from which a flag can be flown on board a boat, the courtesy ensign will most likely displace a flag customarily flown at home. In general, on a mastless motorboat, the courtesy ensign is flown at the bow. If the motorboat has a mast, it is flown at the starboard spreader. On sailboats, it is flown from the starboard spreader of the most forward mast. There are a few exceptions for some countries, and it is advisable to ask or observe how other vessels are displaying the courtesy ensign. It is normally the size of an officer's flag or private signal.

Do *not* fly a foreign courtesy ensign after you have returned to the waters of your country. This may show that you have "been there," but it is not proper flag etiquette.

YACHTING ETIQUETTE

Etiquette in yachting takes many forms, but it essentially consists of showing consideration and courtesy to others. Correct yachting etiquette comprises simple everyday actions as well as formal daily routines and official ceremonies.

Daily Color Ceremonies

A boater at a yacht club, or at a military or naval base, where formal morning and evening color ceremonies are held should follow the actions of local personnel who are not in formation. If you are outdoors when the flag is being raised or lowered, and you're wearing a uniform or visored cap, face the flag and give a hand salute, and hold it until the ceremony is completed. A man wearing a civilian hat should remove it and hold it over his left breast. Men not wearing headgear and women should place their right hand over their left breast. This is called the "breast salute." Automobiles should stop and all personnel should remain inside.

The above rules do not apply, of course, if the boater is engaged in hoisting or lowering his own colors. He should complete his actions and then, if the official ceremonies have not ended, he should stand at attention, and salute if appropriate.

On official occasions, the same salutes described above are given for the playing of the *Star Spangled Banner* or the national anthem of another country.

Boarding or Leaving a Boat

The etiquette to be observed when coming on board another person's boat is derived from that of boarding a naval vessel. Salutes are seldom exchanged, but a simple request for permission to come aboard is always good taste. A salute might be in order if the individual boarding were wearing a uniform cap and the craft were that of the commodore of the yacht club or the commander of a U.S. Power Squadron or Coast Guard Auxiliary flotilla.

When leaving another's boat, the naval form of requesting permission is not used. A simple statement of thanks for the hospitality or best wishes for a pleasant cruise is sufficient.

Salutes Between Vessels

In formal ceremonies, such as the rendezvous of a yacht club or Power Squadron, the fleet of boats present may pass in review before the flagship of the commodore or other unit commander. In such cases, each craft will salute as it passes. Vessels may also exchange salutes when joining a club cruise, for example, or when passing a ship with a high public official on board.

Dipping the Ensign in Salute

Federal law prohibits dipping the flag of the United States (the 50-star flag) to any person or thing, and only government vessels are permitted to dip the national ensign in reply to a dip.

The status of the yacht ensign (13 stars in a circle around an anchor on a blue field) is not spelled out clearly, but since the law specifically covers only the flag of the United States, the assumption has been made that the yacht ensign may be dipped.

In a fleet review of a unit of the Power Squadron, the USPS ensign should be flown from the stern or gaff if a suitable-size flag is available. In this way, the flag dipped would be that of the organization holding the review.

All vessels in any review flying either the USPS or yacht ensign at the stern or gaff should dip that flag when their bow comes abreast of the stern of the flagship and return it to full height when their stern clears the bow of the flagship. On such an occasion, the flag of the United States should *not* be flown, but if it is, *do not dip it* and use only the hand salute described below. Do not dip any flag other than the flag being flown at the stern staff or gaff, including the equivalent position on a Marconi (three-sided) sail.

Hand Saluting

When a vessel is officially reviewing a parade of other vessels, the senior officer present stands on the deck of the reviewing ship with his staff in formation behind him. Only he gives the hand salute in return to the salute rendered him.

On a boat passing in review, if the skipper has his crew and guests in formation behind him, only he gives the hand salute. If the crew and guests are in uniform and standing at attention at the rail facing the reviewing boas as they pass, they all give the hand salute. The criterion is whether or not the other persons aboard are in formation. If in formation, only the skipper salutes; but if not in formation, all salute. In both situations, the hand salute is given as the flag is dipped and is held until it is raised again.

Yacht Routines

The following regulations are taken from that portion of the New York Yacht Club code entitled *Yacht Routine*. These deal with salutes, boats (meaning tenders and dinghies), and general courtesies. Other sections of the code, not given here, relate primarily to the display of flags, signaling, and lights.

The routines of other yacht clubs may be considerably less formal and detailed than those that follow, but whatever routines are used, they are likely to have been derived from the procedures of the New York Yacht Club.

• *Salutes.* All salutes shall be made by dipping the yacht ensign once, lowering the ensign to the dip, and hoisting it when the salute is returned. All salutes shall be returned. Whistles shall never be used in saluting.

Vessels of the United States and foreign navies shall be saluted.

When a flag officer of the club comes to anchor, he shall be saluted by all yachts present, except where there is a senior flag officer present.

When a yacht comes to anchor where a flag officer is present, such officer shall be saluted. A junior flag officer anchoring in the presence of a senior shall salute.

Yachts passing shall salute, the junior saluting first.

All salutes shall be answered in kind.

A yacht acting as race committee boat should neither salute nor be saluted while displaying the committee flag.

• *Boats.* Upon entering and leaving boats, deference is shown seniors by juniors' entering first and leaving last.

When aboard boats, flag officers display their flags, captains (owners) their private signals, and members (non-owners) the club burgee. When on duty, the fleet captain and race committee display their distinctive flags. The flag of the senior officer aboard takes precedence. A flag officer aboard a boat not displaying his distinctive flag should be considered as present in an unofficial capacity.

When two boats are approaching the same gangway or land-ing stage, flag officers shall have the right-of-way in order of seniority.

Courtesies

When a flag officer makes an official visit, his flag, if senior to that of the yacht visited, shall be displayed in place of the burgee while he is on board. A yacht may display the personal flag of a national, state, or local official when such an individual is on board, or the national ensign of a distinguished foreign visitor. This flag should be displayed in place of the private signal or officer's flag for the President of the United States, and in place of the burgee for all other officials and visitors.

On Independence Day, and when ordered on other occasions, a yacht shall, when at anchor and the weather permits, *dress ship* from morning to evening colors.

Cruising

When cruising away from home waters, the wise skipper keeps a sharp eye out for local customs. It is a mark of courtesy to conform to local procedures and practices. While visiting at a yacht club of which you are not a member, observe the actions and routines of the local owner-members, and particularly the club officers. This is especially important with respect to evening colors. Not all clubs strictly calculate the daily time of sunset, and some may be earlier than you would normally expect. If you will be off your boat at the time of evening colors—in the clubhouse for dinner, for example—be sure to take down your flags before you leave your craft.

Be a Good Neighbor

Consideration of the other skipper is an important element of yachting etiquette. Don't anchor too closely to another boat so as to give cause for concern for the safety of both craft; consider the state of the tide and the effect of its range on the radius about which you will swing. Use a guest mooring only with permission; make fast to a fuel pier only briefly.

In the evening hours at an anchorage, don't disturb your neighbors on other boats. Sound travels exceptionally well across water and many cruising boaters turn in early for dawn departures. Keep voices down and play radios only at low levels. If you should be one of the early departees, leave with an absolute minimum of noise.

Be a good neighbor in other ways, too. Don't ever throw trash and garbage overboard. Secure flapping halyards; they can be a most annoying source of noise for some distance. When coming into or leaving an anchorage area, do so at a dead slow speed to keep your wake and wash at an absolute minimum.

Passing Other Boats

A faster boat overtaking and passing a slower one in a narrow channel should slow down *sufficiently* to cause no damage or discomfort. Often overlooked is the fact that it may be necessary for the *slower* boat itself to reduce its speed. For example, if the overtaken vessel is making 8 knots, the faster boat can only slow down to about 10 knots in order to have enough speed differential to get past. At this speed, the passing boat may unavoidably make a wake that is uncomfortable to the other craft. In such cases, the overtaken boat should slow to 4 or 5 knots to allow herself to be passed at 6 or 7 knots with little wake. (This is technically a violation of the Navigation Rules requirement that a stand-on vessel must keep her course and speed, but it is a logical action.)

If adequate depths of water extend outward on one or both sides of the course, it is the courteous thing for the passing boat to swing well out to a safe side to minimize the discomfort of the overtaken boat.

Proper etiquette calls for powerboats to pass sailing craft astern or well to leeward.

Guests on Board

If you are invited to go cruising for a day, a weekend, or a more extended period, there are many things you need to consider—clothes, promptness, gifts, aid, noise, smoking, privacy, and time.

Take a minimum of *clothes,* packed in collapsible containers, or at least in suitcases that will nest inside each other when empty—storage space is severely limited aboard boats. Bring one outfit of "city clothes" for use at those places ashore that require such dress. Bring two bathing suits if you plan to do much swimming—things dry slowly around a boat.

For the *stowage of clothing* you bring aboard, the skipper may assign you a special locker, which has been cleared for your convenience. Don't scatter gear and clothing all over the boat. Use the locker provided, keep it orderly, and thus help the skipper keep things shipshape.

When a *sailing time* is given, be there ahead of time. The skipper generally chooses a time with a purpose in mind—the tides and current, normal weather patterns, the length of the planned run, etc. Meal times are set for the convenience of the galley hand. It is inconsiderate for a tardy guest to delay meals. In any event, it is bad manners to be late for a meal.

Since washing and toilet facilities are generally limited on board, follow the skipper's lead regarding *rising* and *bedtimes.* Get up promptly when the skipper or crew are heard moving about. Use the head as expeditiously as possible, make up your bunk, stow any loose gear about the cabin, and appear on deck. When the skipper suggests that it is time to retire for the evening, take the hint and bed down.

Noise on a boat seems to be amplified, so walk and speak softly and your shipmates will be glad you're aboard.

Smoking should stop, of course, when gasoline is to be taken aboard, but care is the order of the day even when smoking is permissible. A carelessly flicked cigarette ash or butt has started many a fire in a chair, awning, or compartment. Cigars leave a particularly unpleasant after-odor on boats and should be enjoyed only in the open air.

Small particles—pipe tobacco and ashes, peanut shells, bits of potato chip, crumbs, etc.—have a way of getting into cracks, crevices, and corners, thereby defying the ordinary cleaning facilities found on a boat. Pay attention to what you leave behind you, and make sure to pick up after yourself.

Privacy becomes a valuable commodity on a protracted cruise. Part of every day should be set aside for getting away from everyone else aboard. Your cruise mates will appreciate your company all the more if it is not constant.

Should occasions arise when you board the boat from a *dinghy,* or have an opportunity to use the skipper's dinghy (with his permission, of course), use care in coming alongside.

Gifts are certainly not expected, but they are always acceptable. Be sure, however, that they are appropriate for boating—if in doubt, make it liquid and consumable. When invited on board for a day or a week, ask what you can bring. If the owner wants to provide all of the food and drink, the guest might take the cruising party ashore for a good dinner at the first port of call.

Assistance on board a boat can be useful, or it can do more harm than good. If you don't know what to do, sit down, stay out of the way, and keep quiet. Always keep out of the line of vision of the helmsman and be particularly quiet and unobtrusive when the craft is being docked or undocked.

If being on board is not a new experience, or you wish to learn how to be more useful, you may ask what you can do to help. Ask, however, when things are calm and uneventful; don't ask in the midst of getting under way or coming alongside a pier.

Above all, if you are assigned to do something, do exactly that. If you think that the instructions were wrong, say so, but don't go off on your own when the skipper thinks that you are doing what he asked.

Pets and Boats

Some dog breeds take to boating readily. Retrievers, spaniels, poodles, beagles, and dachshunds seem to be natural sailors. Short-haired breeds seem to do better than those with long hair, and most puppies can usually acclimate themselves to the water. Old dogs who have a violent dislike of the water should not be forced to go along on boats. Many boaters find that a cat is less trouble to have on board and fits in better with a cruising life style.

DOGS AND WATER

If your dog swims in salt water as part of his boating experience, wash him off with fresh water at least once a day, dry him well, and keep him away from drafts. Salt water, if left on the dog, can cause skin problems.

Some pets will drink excessive amounts of salt water, causing them to become nauseous. If that happens, give a small amount of Pepto-Bismol and do not feed the animal for a while. Fresh water should be available to your dog at all times; renew it four or five times a day, if necessary, to make sure it is fresh and pure. Excessive ice water, however, can lead to diarrhea.

Feeding your Dog

Canned dog foods are ideal for the boat; dry foods tend to pick up dampness and become soggy. Most table scraps are all right, but avoid all bones, and double-check the condition of leftovers from the ice box or refrigerator.

Onboard Dog Care

Dogs need plenty of exercise and should have it, ashore, three or four times a day. Make sure there's a total of at least an hour a day for exercise. Dogs find it necessary to relieve themselves with some degree of regularity, and scheduled times should be provided. Most of them prefer to have this opportunity after they've eaten, so a good walk on shore following the evening meal is recommended, if possible.

Don't allow your pet on deck when coming in alongside a pier or another boat. Most dogs regard the boat as family property to be guarded and may try to bite anyone who reaches aboard to take a line or steps aboard for any reason. A dog or cat moving about on a deck could also be a tripping hazard.

Don't go off from the boat at night and leave a noisy dog in the cabin, and don't allow your dog to run loose in a marina.

CATS

Cats make excellent cruising companions, and are really more practical than dogs. They do not need trips ashore for exercise, and an on-board kitty litter pan serves them very well. They can swim, too, in case they fall overboard. At anchor, it is a good idea to have a piece of carpeting rigged from the stern down into the water, so that the cat can get itself back on board.

Housekeeping Hints

Space on any boat is limited, and good housekeeping practices are a must. Much can be learned from those who have cruised for many years. The items below are derived from Ruth Lundgren Williamson's column, "The Companionway," which appeared for several years in *Motor Boating* magazine.

Mark your Food Containers

The tops of all cans on board should be marked with a water-proof pen. Moisture can cause labels to fall off and "pot luck" ceases to be fun after a day or two. Any kind of paper packaging is not for boats. Transfer things like flour and sugar to airtight plastic containers, and mark their tops. Or put the paper package into a tightly tied plastic bag. If you've got some heavy-duty plastic bags, incidentally, you can stuff them with canned foods, seal them, and drop them into the bilge for storage. In that way, you'll never be without variety for your menus.

When It Comes to Pots and Pans

It is generally felt that rust-resistant stainless steel or enamel cookware is best for the boat. Many experienced galley hands favor high, fairly narrow cookware. It saves space in a galley and prevents liquids from sloshing over when the going gets rough. However, water boils faster in a wide pot (the same amount, of course) and, with the pot covered, one-dish meals simmer in absolutely no time. Wide pots save both cooking time and stove fuel.

Pressure Cookers

Some boat cooks seem to feel that for cooking in a hurry, pressure cookers are great, but they must be used with care. They reduce cooking time for just about everything by two-thirds or more. Sometimes this is important. Sometimes, it's not, especially if you're looking forward to a long, beautiful cruising day and have plenty of time to spare. At any rate, you can use a pressure cooker as long as there's a steady source of heat and cold water. (Some recipes call for running the cooker under a faucet or pouring cold water over it to reduce the pressure. In most cases, however, you can just let the pressure drop of its own accord.)

LIFE ON BOARD

Mildew Control

A useful little pamphlet, *Mold and Mildew,* is available from the Office of Information, U.S. Department of Agriculture in Washington, DC. Mildew is caused by molds that grow on anything from which they can get enough food. Boaters do not need to be told that as the molds grow they cause damage and leave a musty odor. Obviously, it's pretty hard to get rid of the dampness that encourages the mildew, but there are some actions you can take to protect your property. Providing ventilation is the first rule. Boat sheets, pillowcases, towels, and extra blankets should always be stored in plastic bags when they're on the boat. These bags also keep leather and canvas shoes dry and mildew-free. And plastic covers are a must for cotton mattresses—they are nice on foam, too, but are essential on cotton. There are now mildew-resistant finishes that can be put on some surfaces to protect them. Here are two helpful hints from *Mold and Mildew:* To remove mildew already present on fabrics, use lemon juice and salt in solution, perborate bleach, or chlorine bleach. To remove mildew from books, apply talcum powder.

Rust-proof Hangers

A good coat of colorless nail polish on a regular wire hanger will keep it from rusting. This type of rust-free hanger takes up much less room than plastic or wooden ones. Bear in mind that the metal hanging hook of a plastic or wooden hanger can also leave a rust mark on a garment, and should also be coated with nail polish. Coat hooks, if not plastic or plastic-covered, can be given the same rust-proofing treatment.

Bedding

Bed sheets and pillowcases are now available that can be slept on for up to a week and then thrown away. Not only do they stay soft and cozy the whole week long, with nary a rip or tear, they also store in about a quarter of the space taken up by ordinary bed linen.

A Boat Bucket with a Lid

Rubbermaid's rectangular, 14-quart-capacity boat bucket is handy for dozens of things aboard. It can be used to hold bait one day, for icing beverages the next, and for mopping the deck after that—it's that easy to keep clean. The lid makes it even handier.

CHAPTER ELEVEN

Government Requirements

Although you don't need a license (in most cases) to operate your boat, there are certain federal and state laws that govern its registration, equipment, and use. The major federal legislation is the Federal Boat Safety Act of 1971. It incorporates many provisions of the Motorboat Act of 1940 and the registration provisions of the Federal Boating Act of 1958. This chapter will summarize the major requirements of these laws.

The equipment that you *must* have on board, and the extra items you *should* have, will vary depending on the size and use of your craft. Read this chapter, and get a Vessel Safety Check from your local Coast Guard flotilla or Power Squadron to learn exactly what you should have on board.

Federal Equipment Requirements

The Motorboat Act of 1940 established four size categories for boats—A, 1, 2, and 3—and set minimum equipment requirements for boats in each category; these are summarized in Table 11-1. (See Table 11-2 for a listing of the various sizes and types of fire extinguishers.) The 1971 act permits the Commandant of the Coast Guard to modify these or make additions that he deems necessary to promote safe boating. In any case, the requirements listed in Table 11-1 should be regarded as an absolute minimum. You should carry at least all the items necessary to earn the sticker of the Vessel Safety Check program, described on page 222.

TABLE 11-1
Required Equipment

EQUIPMENT	CLASS A LESS THAN 16 FEET (4.9M)	CLASS 1 16 FEET TO LESS THAN 26 FEET (4.9–7.9M)
Personal flotation devices	One Type I, II, III, or IV for each person.	One Type I, II, or III for each person on board or being towed on water skis, etc., plus one Type IV available to be thrown.
Fire extinguishers		
When no fixed fire-extinguishing system is installed in machines space(s)	At least one B-I type approved hand portable fire extinguisher. Not required on outboard motorboats less than 26 feet (7.9 m) in length and not carrying passengers for hire if the construction of such motorboats will not permit the entrapment of flammable gases or vapors.*	
When fixed fire-extinguishing system is installed in machine space(s)	None.	
Ventilation	At least two ventilator ducts fitted with cowls or their equivalent for the purpose of properly and efficiently ventilating the bilges of every engine and fuel-tank compartment of boats constructed or decked over after April 25, 1940, using gasoline or other fuel having a flashpoint less than 110°F (43°C). Boats built after July 31, 1981 must have operable power blowers.	
Whistle	Boats up to 39.4 feet (12 m) — any device capable of making an "efficient sound signal" audible ½ mile.	
Bell	Boats up to 39.4 feet (12 m) — any device capable of making an "efficient sound signal."	
Backfire flame arrester	One approved device on each carburetor of all gasoline engines installed after April 25, 1940, except outboard motors.	
Visual distress signals	Required only when operating at night or carrying six or few passengers for hire. Same equipment as for larger boats.	Orange flag with black square-and-disc (D); and an S-O-S electric light (N); or three orange smoke signals, hand-held or floating (D); or three red flares of hand-held, meteor, or parachute type (D/N).

*Dry chemical and carbon dioxide (CO_2) or the most widely used types, in that order. Other approved types are acceptable. Toxic vaporizing-liquid type fire extinguishers, such as those containing tetrachloride or chlorobromomethane, are not acceptable. Fire extinguishers manufactured after January 1, 1965 will be marked "Marine Type___Size___Approval No. 162.028/EX__"

TABLE 11-1 (continued)
Required Equipment

EQUIPMENT	CLASS 2 26 FEET TO LESS THAN 40 FEET (7.9–12.2M)	CLASS 3 40 FEET TO NOT MORE THAN 65 FEET (12.2–19.8M)
Personal flotation devices	One Type I, II, or III for each person on board or being towed on water, skis, etc., plus one Type IV available to be thrown.	
Fire extinguishers		
When no fixed fire-extinguishing system is installed in machinery space(s)	At least two B-I type approved hand portable fire extinguishers, or at least one B-II type approved hand portable fire extinguisher.	At least three B-I type approved hand portable fire extinguishers, or at least one B-I type plus one B-II type approved hand portable fire extinguisher.
When fixed fire-extinguishing system is installed in machinery space(s)	At least one B-I type approved hand portable fire extinguisher.	At least two B-I type approved hand portable fire extinguishers, or at least one B-II approved unit.
Ventilation	At least two ventilator ducts fitted with cowls or their equivalent for the purpose of properly and efficiently ventilating the bilges of every engine and fuel-tank compartment of boats constructed or decked over after April 25, 1940, using gasoline or other fuel having a flashpoint less than 110°F. (43°C). Boats built after July 31, 1981 must have operable power blowers.	
Whistle	Boats up to 39.4 feet (12 m)—any device capable of making an "efficient sound signal" audible ½ mile.	Boats 39.4 to 65.7 feet (12–20 m)—device meeting technical specifications of Inland Rules Annex III, audible ½ mile.
Bell	Boats up to 39.4 feet (12 m)—any device capable of making an "efficient sound signal."	Boats 39.4 to 65.7 feet (12–20)—bell meeting technical specifications of Inland Rules Annex II; mouth diameter of at least 7.9 inches (200 m).
Backfire flame arrester	One approved device on each carburetor of all gasoline engines installed after April 25, 1940, except outboard motors.	
Visual distress signals	Orange flag with black square-and-disc (D); and an S-O-S electric light (N); or three orange smoke signals, hand-held or floating (D); or three red flares of hand-held, meteor, or parachute type (D/N) on specified waters.	

*Dry chemical and carbon dioxide (CO_2) or the most widely used types, in that order. Other approved types are acceptable. Toxic vaporizing-liquid type fire extinguishers, such as those containing tetrachloride or chlorobromomethane, are not acceptable. Fire extinguishers manufactured after January 1, 1965 will be marked "Marine Type___Size___Approval No. 162.028/EX__"

TABLE 11-2
Fire Extinguishers

CLASSIFICATION (TYPE SIZE)	FOAM (MINIMUM GALLONS)	CARBON DIOXIDE (MINIMUM POUNDS)	DRY CHEMICAL (MINIMUM POUNDS)	FREON (MINIMUM POUNDS)
B-I	1¼	4	2	2½
B II	2½	15	10	10

NAVIGATION LIGHTS AND DAY SHAPES
The requirements for navigation lights and day shapes for all sizes of vessels are contained in the *Navigation Rules, International–Inland*. There are slight differences between these two sets of Rules, but a boat having lights in compliance with the International Rules is deemed to be in compliance with the Inland Rules. See Tables 11-3 and 11-4.

NAVIGATION RULES
The Inland Navigation Rules require that all boats 12 meters (39.4 feet) or longer must have on board a copy of the Inland Rules. It also makes sense to carry a copy of the International Navigation Rules if you operate in waters where they apply. Both sets of Rules are included in the Coast Guard publication *Navigation Rules, International–Inland,* available from many dealers in nautical charts and books.

TABLE 11-3

Lights for Various Types of Vessels — 1980 Inland Rules

VESSEL	MASTHEAD (FORWARD)	SIDE
Power-driven vessel less than 12 m in length	Can be less than 2.5 m above gunwale, but at least 1 m above side lights[1],[2]	Separate red and green, 112½°, or combination, vis. 1 mi. Above hull at least 1 m below masthead light[1],[3]
Power-driven vessel 12 m but less than 20 m in length	White, 225°, vis. 3 mi. At least 2.5 m above gunwale[1]	Separate red and green, 112½°, or combination, vis. 2 mi. Above hull at least 1 m below masthead light[3]
Power-driven vessel 20 m but less than 50 m in length	White, 225°, vis. 5 mi. Not more than ½ of length aft from stem; 6 m or beam (up to 10 m) above hull	Red and green, 112½°, vis. 3 mi. At or near sides of vessel; above hull at least 1 m below masthead light
Power-driven vessel 50 m or more in length	Not more than ½ of length aft from stern; 6 m or beam (up to 10 m) above hull	Red and green, 112½°, vis. 3 mi. At or near sides of vessel; above hull at least 1 m below masthead light
Sailing vessel under 12 m in length	None	Separate red and green, 112½°, or combination, vis. 1 mi.[3],[4],[5]
Sailing vessel under 20 m in length	None	Separate red and green, 112½°, or combination, vis. 2 mi.[3],[4]
Vessel propelled by oars	None	May show separate red and green, 112½°, or combination, vis. 1 mi.[6]
Vessel towing; tow less than 200 m overall from stern of towing vessel. (Also towing alongside or pushing ahead)	Two white, arranged vertically, 225°, vis. determined by length of vessel (not required pushing ahead or towing alongside on Western rivers)	Normal for size of vessel
Vessel towing; tow 200 m or more overall length	Three white, arranged vertically, 225°, vis. determined by length of vessel	Normal for size of vessel
Vessel being towed astern, if manned	None	Normal for size of vessel

Equivalent measures in customary units
1 m = 3.3 ft; 2 m = 6.6 ft; 2.5 m = 8.2 ft; 4.5 m = 14.8 ft; 6 m = 19.7 ft; 7 m = 23.0 ft; 12 m = 39.4 ft; 20 m = 65.6 ft; 50 m = 164 ft; 100 m = 328 ft; 200 m = 656 ft

STERN	ADDITIONAL LIGHTS OR REMARKS
White, 135°, vis. 2 mi.	[1]May substitute all-round white light, vis. 2 mi., for masthead and stern lights
White, 135°, vis. 2 mi.	[2]After masthead light may be shown but not required. (Exception allowed on Great Lakes.) [3]Fitted with inboard screens if necessary to prevent being seen across bow
White, 135°, vis. 2 mi.	After masthead light may be shown; at least 2 m higher than forward masthead light
White, 135°, vis. 3 mi.	After masthead light required; at least 2 m higher and ¼ of vessel length (but need not be more than 50 m) aft of forward masthead light. Forward masthead light must be not more than ½ of the vessel length from the stem
White, 135°, vis. 2 mi.[4], [5]	[4]May be combined into triple combination light at masthead. [5]Less than 7 m, need only have flashlight or lantern to show
White, 135°, vis. 2 mi.	Optional—two all-round lights at or near top of mast, red over green, separated at least 1 m, vis. 2 mi.
May show white, 135°, vis 2 mi.[6]	[6]Need only have flashlight or lantern to show white light
Normal for size of vessel	Towing astern: towing light[7] over stern light. Pushing ahead or towing alongside. Two towing lights[7] vertically. [7]Vis. 3 mi. for vessels 50 m or more in length. 2 mi. for shorter vessels.
Normal for size of vessel	Towing light: yellow, 135°, above sternlight[7]
Normal for size of vessel	

TABLE 11-3 (continued)
Lights for Various Types of Vessels — 1980 Inland Rules

VESSEL	MASTHEAD (FORWARD)	SIDE
Vessel being towed alongside or pushed ahead	None	Normal for size of vessel; at forward end
Vessel engaged in trawling or other types of fishing	When not engaged in fishing, show only normal lights of power-driven or sailing vessel for size of vessel	
Vessel engaged in trawling	None [12]	When making way through water, normal for size of vessel
Vessel engaged in fishing, other than trawling	None [12]	When making way through the water, normal for size of vessel
Vessel at anchor, less than 50 m in length	None	None
Vessel at anchor; 50 m or more in length	None	None
Vessel aground	None	None
Pilot vessel	None if on pilot duty; normal if under way and not on pilot duty	When under way, normal for size of vessel
Vessel not under command	None	If making way through the water, normal for size of vessel
Vessel restricted in ability to maneuver	None	When making way through the water, normal for size of vessel

Equivalent measures in customary units
1 m = 3.3 ft; 2 m = 6.6 ft; 2.5 m = 8.2 ft; 4.5 m = 14.8 ft; 6 m = 19.7 ft; 7 m = 23.0 ft; 12 m = 39.4 ft; 20 m = 65.6 ft; 50 m = 164 ft; 100 m = 328 ft; 200 m = 656 ft

STERN	ADDITIONAL LIGHTS OR REMARKS
Normal for size of vessel (not used for pushed ahead)	Also "special flashing light" at center or forward end. A group of vessels is lighted as a single vessel
When not engaged in fishing, show only normal lights of power-driven or sailing vessel for size of vessel	
When making way through water, normal for size of vessel	Under way or at anchor, two all-round lights, green over white[7,9,10,11] [9]Vertical spacing not less than 1 m [10]Lower light not less than 4 m (2 m if under 20 m in length) above hull [11]Lower light above sidelights at least twice vertical spacing
When making way through water, normal for size of vessel	Under way or at anchor, two all-round lights, red over white[7,9,10,11] [12]When not actually fishing, show normal masthead lights for vessel its size
None	White, all-round light where can best be seen. Vis. 2 mi. (not required if less than 7 m in length and not anchored in a narrow channel or where vessels normally navigate)
None	White, all-round light in fore part of vessel not less than 6 m above hull. A second white, all-round light in after part, not less than 4.5 m lower than forward anchor light. Vis. 3 mi.
None	Anchor light(s) as for vessels at anchor, plus two red all-round lights of same visibility range[7,9,10] (not required if less than 12 m in length)
When under way, normal for size of vessel	Two all-round lights, white over red, at masthead[7, 9,10] If at anchor, normal anchor light(s); line 15 or 16
If making way through the way, normal for size of vessel	Two red all-round lights, vertically where best can be seen[7,9,10]
When making way through the water, normal for size of vessel	Three all-round lights vertically, red-white-red[7,9] If at anchor, normal anchor light(s)

TABLE 11-4
Lights for Various Types of Vessels — 1972 International Rules

VESSEL	MASTHEAD (FORWARD)	SIDE
Power-driven vessel less than 12 m in length	White, 225°, vis. 2 mi. Can be less than 2.5 m above gunwale, but at least 1 m above side lights [1]	Separate red and green, 112½°, or combination, vis. 1 mi. Above hull at least 1 m below masthead light [3]
Power-driven vessel 12 m but less than 20 m in length	White, 225°, vis. 3 mi. At least 2.5 m above gunwale [1]	Separate red and green, 112½°, or combination, vis. 2 mi. Above hull at least 1 m below masthead light [3]
Power-driven vessel 20 m but less than 50 m in length	White, 225°, vis. 5 mi. Not more than ¼ of length aft from stem; 6 m or beam (up to 12 m) above hull	Red and green, 112 ½°, vis. 2 mi. At or near sides of vessel; not more than ¾ height of masthead light
Power-driven vessel 50 m or more in length	White, 225°, vis. 6 mi. Not more than ¼ of length aft from stem; 6 m or beam (up to 12 m) above hull	Red and green, 112½°, vis. 3 mi. At or near sides of vessel; not more than ¾ height of forward masthead light
Sailing vessel under 12 m in length	None	Separate red and green, 112½°, or combination, vis. 1 mi. [3],[4]
Sailing vessel under 20 m in length	None	Separate red and green, 112½°, or combination, vis. 2 mi.
Vessel propelled by oars	None	May show separate red and green, 112½°, or combination, vis. 1 mi. [6]
Vessel towing; tow less than 200 m overall vessel. (Also towing alongside or pushing ahead)	Two white, arranged vertically, 225°, vis. determined by length of vessel	Normal for size of vessel
Vessel towing; tow 200 m or more overall length	Three white, arranged vertically, 225°, vis. determined by length of vessel	Normal for size of vessel
Vessel being towed astern, if manned	None	Normal for size of vessel

Equivalent measures in customary units
1 m = 3.3 ft; 2 m = 6.6 ft; 2.5 m = 8.2 ft; 4.5 m = 14.8 ft; 6 m = 19.7 ft; 7 m = 23.0 ft; 12 m = 39.4 ft;
20 m = 65.6 ft; 50 m = 164 ft; 100 m = 328 ft; 200 m = 656 ft

STERN	ADDITIONAL LIGHTS OR REMARKS
White, 135°, vis. 2 mi.	[1]Can substitute all-round white light for separate masthead and stern lights, vis. 2 mi. Less than 7 m and less than 7 kt max speed need only have all-round white light, vis. 2 mi. but should have sidelights
White, 135°, vis. 2 mi.	[2]After masthead light may be shown but not required [3]Fitted with inboard screens if necessary to prevent being seen across bow
White, 135°, vis. 2 mi.	After masthead light may be shown; at least 4.5 m higher than forward masthead light
White, 135°, vis. 3 mi.	After masthead light required; at least 4.5 m higher and half of vessel length (up to 100 m) aft of forward masthead light
White, 135°, vis. 2 mi.[4,5]	[4]May be combined into triple combination light at masthead. [5]Less than 7 m, need only have flashlight or lantern to show
White, 135°, vis. 2 mi.	Optional—two all-round lights at or near top of mast, red over green, separated at least 1 m, vis. 2 mi.
May show white, 135°, vis. 2 mi.[6]	[6]Need only have flashlight or lantern to show white light
Normal for size of vessel	Towing light[7] over stern light (not shown when towing alongside or pushing ahead) [7]Vis. 3 mi. For vessels 50 m or more in length; 2 mi. for shorter vessels
Normal for size of vessel	Towing light over stern light[7]
Normal for size of vessel	

TABLE 11-4 (continued)

Lights for Various Types of Vessels — 1972 International Rules

VESSEL	MASTHEAD (FORWARD)	SIDE
Vessel being towed along-side or pushed ahead	None	Normal for size of vessel; at forward end
Vessel engaged in trawling or drift fishing	When not engaged in fishing, show only normal lights of power-driven or sailing vessel for size of vessel	
Vessel engaged in trawling	None [12]	When making way through water, normal for size of vessel
Vessel engaged in fishing, other than trawling	None [12]	When making way through water, normal for size of vessel
Vessel at anchor; less than 50 m or more in length	None	None
Vessel at anchor; 50m or more in length	None	None
Vessel aground	None	None
Pilot vessel	None if on pilot duty; normal if under way and not on pilot duty	When under way, normal for size of vessel
Vessel not under command	None	If making way through the water, normal for size of vessel
Vessel constrained by her draft	Normal for size of vessel	Normal for size of vessel

Equivalent measures in customary units
1 m = 3.3 ft; 2 m = 6.6 ft; 2.5 m = 8.2 ft; 4.5 m = 14.8 ft; 6 m = 19.7 ft; 7 m = 23.0 ft; 12 m = 39.4 ft; 20 m = 65.6 ft; 50 m = 164.0 ft; 100 m = 328.1 ft; 200 m = 656 .2ft

STERN	ADDITIONAL LIGHTS OR REMARKS
Normal for size of vessel (not used for pushed ahead)	A group of vessels is lighted as a single vessel
When not engaged in fishing, show only normal lights of power-driven or sailing vessel for size of vessel	
When making way through water, normal for size of vessel	Under way or at anchor, two all-round lights, green over white[7,9,10,11] [9]Vertical spacing not less than 2 m for vessels 20 m or more in length; not less than 1 m for shorter vessels [10]Lower light not less than 4 m (2 m if under 20 m in length) above hull [11]Lower light above sidelights at least twice vertical spacing
When making way through water, normal for size of vessel	Under way at anchor, two all-round lights, red over white[7,9,10,11] [12]When not actually fishing, show normal masthead lights for vessel its size
None	White, all-round light where can best be seen. Vis. 2 mi. (not required if less than 7m in length and not enclosed in a narrow channel or where vessels normally navigate)
None	White, all-round light in fore part of vessel not less than 6 m above hull. A second white, all-round light in after part, not less than 4.5 m lower than forward anchor light. Vis. 3 mi.
None	Normal anchor light(s) plus two red all-round lights of same visibility range[7,9,10]
When under way, normal for size of vessel	Two all-round lights, white over red, at masthead[7,9,10] If at anchor, normal anchor light(s) as for vessels at anchor
If making way through the water, normal for size of vessel	Two red all-round lights, vertically where best can be seen[7,9,10]
Normal for size of vessel	Three red all-round lights, arrange vertically and equally spaced[7,9,10]

GOVERNMENT

ADDITIONAL STATE AND LOCAL REQUIREMENTS

Individual states, and some local jurisdictions, often have equipment and operation requirements that supplement federal requirements. Typically, these include an anchor and line; paddles or oars are often required for smaller craft. In many states, children under a specified age—6, 9, or 12—must wear life preservers when above deck on a boat underway.

State laws also apply to waters that are not covered by federal regulations. Table 11-5 lists the offices from which this type of information can be obtained, but always inquire locally when venturing into a new boating area.

Registration

Boat registration is required by the Federal Boating Act of 1958. The types of boats required to be registered, and the state offices that handle the registration, are shown in Table 11-5.

TABLE 11-5
STATE REGISTRATION REQUIREMENTS

All watercraft must be registered in the "state of principal use." Listed below are the states and other political subdivisions with specific information on the types of watercraft that must be registered and where to inquire regarding forms and fees.

STATE	BOATS AFFECTED	WHERE TO GET INFORMATION & APPLY
ALABAMA	All motorboats, sailboats, boats for hire	Local County Probate and License Commission Office www.state.al.us
ALASKA	All motorized vessels on waters under federal jurisdiction	Boat Registration, 17th Coast Guard District P.O. Box 25517, Juneau, AK 99802-5517 www.uscg.mil/d17
ARIZONA	All watercraft except non-motorized	Game & Fish Department, 2221 W. Greenway Rd., Phoenix, AZ 85023-4312 www.state.az.us
ARKANSAS	Vessels propelled by sail or machinery of any type	Licensing Division, Department of Finance & Administration, P.O. Box 1272, Little Rock, AR 72203-1272 www.state.ar.us
CALIFORNIA	All motorboats; sailboats over 8 ft.	Division of Motor Vehicles, Vessels Section, Mail Stop E-272 P.O. Box 825341, Sacramento, CA 94232-5341 www.dmv.ca.gov
COLORADO	All vessels powered by motor or sail	Division of Parks & Outdoor Recreation, 13787 S. Highway 85, Littleton, CO 80125-9721 www.parks.state.co.us/boating
CONNECTICUT	All motorboats; any vessel 19 ft or larger, with or without a motor	Marine Vessel Section, Department of Motor Vehicles, 60 State Street, Wethersfield, CT 06161-3032 Or any branch office of the DMV dmvct.org/boatdocs.httm
DELAWARE	All motorboats	Boat Registration, Division of Fish & Wildlife 89 Kings Hwy., Dover, DE 19901-7305 www.dnrec.state.de.us
DISTRICT OF COLUMBIA	All watercraft	Harbor Patrol, Metropolitan Police Department, 550 Water Street, S.W., Washington, DC 20024-2399 www.dc.gov
FLORIDA	All vessels, except non-motorized and those used exclusively on private lakes and ponds	County Revenue Collector www.hsmv.state.fl.us

GOVERNMENT

STATE	BOATS AFFECTED	WHERE TO GET INFORMATION & APPLY
GEORGIA	All motorized vessels; all sailboats over 12 ft.	Department of Natural Resources 2189 Northlake Pkwy, Suite 108 Bldg., 10 Tucker, GA 30084-4111 www.ganet.org/dnr/wild
HAWAII	All motorboats; sailboats over 8 ft.	Division of Boating and Ocean Recreation, 333 Queen St., Suite 300, Honolulu, HI 96813-4726 boating@hula.net
IDAHO	All motorboats and sailboats	Idaho State Parks and Recreation P.O. Box 83720, Boise, ID 83720-0065 www.idahoparks.org/rec/boating.html
ILLINOIS	All watercraft	Department of Natural Resources 524 S. Second Street, Springfield, IL 62701-1787 dnr.state.il.us/boatreg
INDIANA	All motorized watercraft	Bureau of Motor Vehicles, 100 N. Senate Ave., Indianapolis, IN 46204-2214 www.state.in.us/bmv/watercraft
IOWA	All boats, except non-powered canoes and kayaks 13 ft. or less in length	Division of Law Enforcement, Department of Natural Resources, Wallace Office Building E. Ninth and Grand Avenue, Des Moines, IA 50319-0034 www.state.ia.us/government/dnr
KANSAS	All boats powered by machinery or sail if used on public waters of Kansas	Department of Wildlife and Parks 512 SE 25th Avenue, Pratt, KS 67124-8174 www.kdwp.state.ks.us/boating
LOUISIANA	Any boat with a motor, including a trolling motor; any sailboat 12 ft. in length or greater	Department of Wildlife & Fisheries P.O. Box 98000, 2000 Quail Drive, Suite 130, Baton Rouge, LA 70898-9000 www.wlf.state.la.us
MAINE	All watercraft, except vessels required to be documented and those used exclusively for racing	Licensing Division, Department of Inland Fisheries & Wildlife, 284 State Street, Augusta, ME 04333-0041 Or local offices and agents www.state.me.us/ifw
MARYLAND	All vessels with mechanical propulsion (except documented vessels)	Any Department of Natural Resources Service Center www.dnr.state.md.us/boating/registration
MASSACHUSETTS	All propelled vessels	DFWELE SPORT Licensing, 251 Causeway Street, Boston, MA 02114-2152 www.state.ma.us/dfwele

STATE	BOATS AFFECTED	WHERE TO GET INFORMATION & APPLY
MICHIGAN	All motorboats; all other vessels over 12 ft. except those 16 ft. or less powered by oars or paddles, and canoes	Local Branch offices of Secretary of State www.dnr.mi.us
MINNESOTA	All watercraft except those 9 ft. or less non-motorized	Registration and Titling Unit, Bureau of Information, Education, and Licensing, Department of Natural Resources 500 Lafayette Rd., St. Paul, MN 55155-4026 www.dnr.state.mn.us/information_and_education
MISSISSIPPI	All boats with any type of motor; all sailboats	Department of Wildlife, Fisheries & Parks 2906 N. State St., Jackson, MS 39216-4290 www.mdwfp.com/lawenforcement_boating.asp
MONTANA	All motorized water-craft, plus sailboats over 12 ft.	Title & Registration Bureau, Motor Vehicle Division, 1032 Buckskin Drive, Deer Lodge, MT 59722-2375 www.doj.state.mt.us
NEBRASKA	All boats powered by any mechanical device	Registration Supervisor, Game & Parks Commission, 2200 N.E. 33rd Street, Lincoln, NE 68503-0370 www.ngpc.state.ne.us/boating
NEVADA	All watercraft with motors	Regional offices, Division of Wildlife, Department of Conservation and Natural Resources www.nevadedivisionofwildlife.org/license/how2.htm
NEW HAMPSHIRE	All motorboats; sail-boats over 12 ft.	Boat Registrations, Motor Vehicle Division 10 Hazen Drive, Concord, NH 03305-0002 www.state.nh.us
NEW JERSEY	All powered vessels; all other vessels over 12 ft.	Division of Motor Vehicles P.O. Box 0403, Trenton, NJ 08666-0403 www.state.nj.us/mvs/boats.htm
NEW MEXICO	All motorboats propelled by machinery or sail	Motor Vehicle Division, Taxation & Revenue Department, P.O. Box 1028, Santa Fe, NM 87504-1028 www.state.nm.us/tax/trd_form.htm
NEW YORK	All boats powered by a motor	Local offices, Department of Motor Vehicles nydmv@dmv.state.ny.us
NORTH CAROLINA	All motorized vessels, including PWC; all sailboats longer than 14 ft. (documented vessels exempt)	Wildlife Resources Commission 322 Chapanoke Road, Raleigh, NC 27603 Or local Wildlife Service Agent www.ncwildlife.org

GOVERNMENT

STATE	BOATS AFFECTED	WHERE TO GET INFORMATION & APPLY
NORTH DAKOTA	All boats powered by a motor	Game & Fish Department, 100 North Bismarck Expressway, Bismarck, ND 58501-5095 www.state.nd.ud/gnf
OHIO	All watercraft (including documented vessels)	Division of Watercraft, Department of Natural Resources ,1952 Belcher Drive, Columbus, OH 43224-1386 www.dnr.state.oh.us/odnr/watercraft
OKLAHOMA	All watercraft; outboard motors over 10 hp	Boat & Motor Section, Motor Vehicle Division, Oklahoma Tax Commission, 2501 Lincoln Blvd., Oklahoma City, OK 73194-1000 www.oktax.state.ok.us
OREGON	All motorboats and sailboats 12 ft. or more	State Marine Board, P.O. Box 14145 Salem, OR 97309-5065 www.boatoregon.com/LawEnforcement/ Regulations.htm
PENNSYLVANIA	All motorboats and all boats launched on Fish and Boat Commission-owned lakes or at Commission-owned access areas	Licensing and Registration Section, Fish and Boat Commission, P.O. Box 68900, Harrisburg, PA 17106-8900 www.fish.state.pa.us
RHODE ISLAND	All boats 14 ft. and longer; motorized boats of any length; outboard motors	Boat Registration & Licensing, Department of Environmental Management, 235 Promenade St., Providence, RI 02908-5767
SOUTH CAROLINA	All motorboats and sailboats with propulsion devices (except documented vessels)	Dept. of Natural Resources, P.O. Box 167, Columbia, SC 29202-0167 www.dnr.state.sc.us/etc/boating.html
SOUTH DAKOTA	Motorboats of any length; other boats over 12 ft.	Applicant's county treasurer www.state.sd.us/revenue/forms.htm
TENNESSEE	All mechanically powered vessels; all sailboats (documented vessels included)	Wildlife Resources Agency P.O. Box 40747, Nashville, TN 37204-0747 www.state.tn.us/twra/boatmain.html
TEXAS	All motorboats; sailboats 14 ft. or longer	Texas Parks & Wildlife, 4200 Smith School Road, Austin, TX 78744-3291 www.tpwd.state.tx.us/boat/boat.htm

Government Requirements ⚓ *221*

STATE	BOATS AFFECTED	WHERE TO GET INFORMATION & APPLY
UTAH	All motorboats and sailboats	Motor Vehicle Division, Utah State Tax Commission, 210 North 1950 West, Salt Lake City, UT 84134-0001 parks.state.ut.us/parks
VERMONT	All motorboats	Marine Division, Dept. of Motor Vehicles 120 State Street, Montpelier, VT 05602-2703 www.state.vt.us
VIRGINIA	All watercraft propelled by machinery, including gasoline, diesel, and electric motors	Boat Section, Department of Game & Inland Fisheries, P.O. Box 11104, Richmond, VA 23230-1104 www.dgif.state.va.us
WASHINGTON	All boats, except less than 10 hp or less than 16 ft. length, and used solely on non-federal waters	Vessel Licensing, Department of Licensing P.O. Box 9909, Olympia, WA 98507-8500 www.wa.gov/dol
WEST VIRGINIA	All motorized boats	Department of Motor Vehicles, Capitol Complex Building 3, Charleston, WV 25317-0001 www.dot.state.wv.us
WISCONSIN	All motorboats; all sailboats over 12 ft.	Boat Registration, Department of Natural Resources, P.O. Box 7236, Madison, WI 53707-7236 www.dnr.state.wi.us
WYOMING	Boats with over 5 hp	Fish & Game Department, 5400 Bishop Blvd., Cheyenne, WY 82006-0001 gf.state.wy.us/HTML/fish/boating.htm
VIRGIN ISLANDS	All vessels up to 150 ft. in length	Division of Environmental Enforcement, Department of Planning and Natural Resources, Cyril E. King Airport, 2nd Floor, St. Thomas, VI 00802

GOVERNMENT

Vessel Safety Check Requirements

The long-time "Courtesy Motorboat Examination" program of the U.S. Coast Guard Auxiliary has now been expanded, revised, and renamed. The new "Vessel Safety Check" (VSC) program now includes checks by members of the United States Power Squadrons as well as members of the USCG Auxiliary.

A Vessel Safety Check is a courtesy examination of your boat to verify the presence and condition of safety equipment required by federal regulations, plus certain additional requirements. A boat must also meet any requirements of the state in which it is being examined.

Following the examination, the specially trained examiner will also make recommendations and discuss safety issues that may make you a safer boater. This is not a law enforcement action; no citations will be issued as a result of the examination. You will receive a copy of the evaluation of your boat so that you may follow the suggestions given. Boats that pass the examination will be able to display the distinctive VSC decal. This does not exempt your boat from law enforcement boarding.

In most boating areas, a skipper can obtain a Vessel Safety Check for his boat and receive a decal for the current year. The examination is free, and the decal indicates that the boat meets equipment and safety standards beyond those legally required. The requirements for the decal, listed below, make a good checklist for any well-equipped boat.

NUMBERING AND PAPERWORK

The boat must be properly registered by a state or documented by the Coast Guard; the paperwork must be on board.

For state registered boats, the registration numbers must be permanently displayed on each side of the forward half of the boat;

they must be plain, vertical, block characters not less than three inches high, and in a color contrasting with the background. A dash or a space equal in width to a letter must separate the numerals from the letters that precede and follow them; for example, **FL-1235-AB** or **FL 1234 AB**. Any state sticker should be placed in accordance with the state's requirements.

For a documented boat, the documentation number must be permanently marked on a visible part of the *interior* structure. The craft's name and hailing port must be displayed on the *exterior* hull in letters not less than four inches in height.

PERSONAL FLOTATION DEVICES (PFDS)

An approved personal flotation device in good serviceable condition, and of a suitable size, is required for each person on the boat, with a minimum of two (one wearable and one throwable) for boats 16 feet and over. Children must have properly fitted child PFDs, which come in various sizes marked for the user's weight.

Wearable PFDs must be *readily accessible;* throwable devices must be *immediately available.* PFDs must not be stored in unopened plastic packaging.

For inflatable PFDs to count toward the legal requirements, you have to be wearing them at the time of inspection or boarding.

For personal watercraft riders, the PFD must be worn and have an impact rating.

FIRE EXTINGUISHERS

The Vessel Safety Check standards for fire extinguishers on smaller boats are likewise more demanding than the legal requirements. Although a boat of open construction under 26 feet, or one which has a built-in fire extinguisher system, need not carry an additional hand-portable extinguisher to meet the legal minimum, it must have one B-I extinguisher for a VSC decal. Only

GOVERNMENT

rowboats and sailboats less than 16 feet with no mechanical propulsion are exempt. The letter "B" designates the type of fires on which the extinguisher can be used (see Tables 11-1 and 11-2); the Roman numeral designates the extinguisher's capacity. Size I is the smallest; size V is the largest.

Sailboats of 16 feet or more in length, even without any auxiliary power or fuel tanks, must have at least one B-I extinguisher. (For more on onboard fire safety, see Chapter 2, "Safety," pages 23-25.)

NAVIGATION LIGHTS

The law does not require that a boat operated only in the daylight have navigation lights, but in order to meet the VSC standards for all craft 16 feet or more in length, a boat must have properly mounted and functioning lights. Proper lights for use both under way and at anchor must be shown. The decal will not be awarded if lights are grossly misplaced, even if they are operable.

A sailboat with an auxiliary engine must be capable of showing the lights of both a sailboat and a power boat; the lights must be wired so that they can be changed from one display to the other.

VISUAL DISTRESS SIGNALS

To receive VSC approval, all recreational boats used on coastal waters or the Great Lakes must have a minimum of three Coast Guard-approved day and night visual distress signals that have not reached their expiration dates. Some signals, such as red flares, can serve for both day and night requirements. Boats operating on inland waters should have some means of making a suitable day and night distress signals.

PLACARDS

A boat 26 feet or more in length with a machinery compartment must have an "oily waste pollution" placard posted in the machinery space or where the bilge pump switch is located. Boats of this length must also display a "MARPOL" trash placard "in a prominent location." Craft 40 feet and over must have a written trash disposal plan.

MARINE SANITATION DEVICE

Any installed toilet must be a Coast Guard approved device. Overboard discharge outlets must be capable of being sealed. Special local or state restrictions may apply.

OVERALL BOAT CONDITION

The boat must be free from fire hazards and in good overall condition, with bilges reasonably clean and visible hull structure generally sound. The use of automobile parts such as carburetors, alternators, and starters on boat engines is not acceptable. The engine horsepower must not exceed that shown on any capacity plate.

The electrical system must be protected by fuses or trip-free circuit breakers. Wiring must be in good condition, properly installed, with no exposed areas or deteriorated insulation. Batteries must be firmly secured with terminals covered.

Any self-circling or kill-switch mechanisms must be in proper working order. All personal watercraft must have a self-circling or kill-switch mechanism.

Portable fuel tanks (normally 7 gallons or less) must be of non-breakable material and be free of corrosion and leaks. All vents must be capable of being closed. The tank must be secured and have a vapor-tight, leak-proof cap. Each permanent fuel tank must be properly vented.

GOVERNMENT

Galley stoves and heating systems must have fuel tanks that are properly secured with no flammable material nearby.

VSC Recommendations

The VSC program also recommends a number of items for the safety and proper operation of a boat—items beyond those required for award of the decal. The actual selection of items from this list will depend on the size and use of the boat involved; the VSC examiner will make recommendations and suggestions. The VSC list includes the following items:

Marine radio

Dewatering device and backup (scoop or bilge pump)

Mounted fire extinguishers in appropriate locations

Anchor and line, suitable for area

First-aid kit

Person-in-the-water kit (one extra wearable PFD and a throwable device with line attached)

Visual distress signals for inland boating

VSC examiners may also discuss operational and educational matters in the interest of increased safety. These topics might include:

Accident reporting/operator responsibilities

Offshore operations

Charts and aids to navigation

First aid and survival tips

Fueling and fuel management

Float plans

Insurance considerations

Boating checklists

Safe boating classes

Additional information on the Vessel Safety Check program is available on the Internet at www.safetyseal.net.

A FINAL WORD ON FIRE EXTINGUISHERS
When it comes to equipping your boat with fire extinguishers, it is prudent to go beyond even the Vessel Safety Check requirements. Consider installing extinguishers in the following locations, or wherever else you deem necessary to meet the needs of your own boat:

The helm, where there is always someone when underway

The engine compartment

The galley

Adjacent to the skipper's bunk, for quick reach at night

GOVERNMENT

CHAPTER TWELVE

Maintenance

A properly maintained boat is a safer craft and a more enjoyable one to use.

Some skippers find that part of the enjoyment of boating is the work they put into their boats. Whether they must clean, paint, or make engine adjustments, hands-on skippers take pride in their ability to do the job and have confidence in the results of their efforts.

Whether you find it a pleasure or not, maintenance is as much a part of boat ownership as is the operation of the boat. Whether for spring fitting out, or for upkeep of a vessel that's in use all year long, there are tasks that should be part of your yachting routine. Carry the proper tools and spare parts so that you won't get caught short if you are away from your home dock.

Here is the basic information you need on cleaning and painting, engine maintenance, care of electrical systems, plumbing, trailers, and tools.

Tools

BASIC ON-BOARD TOOL KIT

Screwdrivers
Straight-blade and Phillips in various sizes to fit your needs; larger sizes should have square shafts.

Wrenches
Open-end and box (or combination wrenches) in various sizes to meet your needs
Adjustable open-end (crescent)

Pliers
  Regular, locking (Vise
  Grips®), and needle-nose
Knife
Drill and bits
Hammer

Chisel
Assorted files
Flashlight or electric lantern
Any special tools specific to
  the equipment on your boat

DESIRABLE ADDITIONS TO BASIC ON-BOARD KIT

Depending on the size, construction, and use of your boat, you may want to add the following items to your basic tool kit:

Hack saw
Wood saws, crosscut and rip
Brace with bits up to 1 inch in
  diameter
Oval rasp
Pipe wrench
Snub-nose pliers

Soldering gun or iron
  Soldering-gun tip for cutting
  line
Metal snips
Disc, belt, and orbital sanders
Shop vacuum cleaner
Circular and saber saws
Plus your own favorite tools

NON-TOOLS FOR YOUR TOOL BOX

Pencils
Pad
Tape measure
Roll of paper towels
Rags
Can of silicone lubricant
Oil can
Tape, various types

Can of bedding and sealing
  compound
Epoxy putty and glue
Fiberglass repair kit
Whetstone
Magnet
Plastic drop cloth
Staple gun and Monel staples
Fid

Assortment of stainless-steel
   hardware:
Wood and machine screws,
   with nuts and washers
Hose clamps
Shackles and thimbles

Plastic cable ties
Work light and extension cord
Electric multimeter

Cleaning Materials and Procedures

BASIC CLEANUP GEAR
Depending upon the size of your boat, these items may be carried on board or kept in a "dock box" near your slip. If all are not carried on board, a small kit of selected items should be on your boat.

Fifty feet of hose
Soap and scouring cleanser
Rust remover and old rags
Large sponge and long-
   handled mop

Bilge-cleaner compound
Metal polish and wax
Scouring pads or bronze wool
Wet or dry sandpaper
Rubber gloves

TOPSIDES
Topsides may be cleaned on either a scheduled or as-required basis. Boats in covered slips or dry storage buildings will require less cleaning than those in open slips. With all covers and bracing removed, first hose down to wash off all traces of salt, dust, and loose grime. Scrub with a trisodium-phosphate–based cleaner, available from paint, hardware, and building-supply outlets. Stubborn spots can be treated with scouring powder, though this may remove gloss. Areas dulled by scouring should be buffed to renew gloss.

BOTTOM

Growth, scum, and waterline weeds along the boot topping that are not removed when the boat is hauled will harden and become twice as hard to get off. Many launching ramps provide hoses at a nearby location. Clear the ramp area so that others can use it, but don't fail to take advantage of the wash-down facility.

Local marine stores may stock compounds particularly suitable for loosening the barnacles or pollutants that attack boats secured afloat all season. The most effective mix of bottom cleaner will vary from harbor to harbor, and may be determined by the type of bottom paint you use; make sure to choose the best antifouling bottom paint and the correct cleaning compound for the waters you're in. Follow these steps to clean and maintain the bottom of your boat:

• Hose the bottom to wash off or soften any growths.

• Attack barnacles with a metal scraper.

• Use a power sander on stubborn spots.

• Keep wetting the bottom to avoid breathing toxic dust if antifouling paint has been used.

• Note any seams or gouges that will require sealant or pointing up before painting.

• Recall and note down, if possible, the brand of bottom paint previously used. A different type or brand may not bond to the old paint. If in doubt, cleaning down to the bare hull may be necessary.

MAINTENANCE

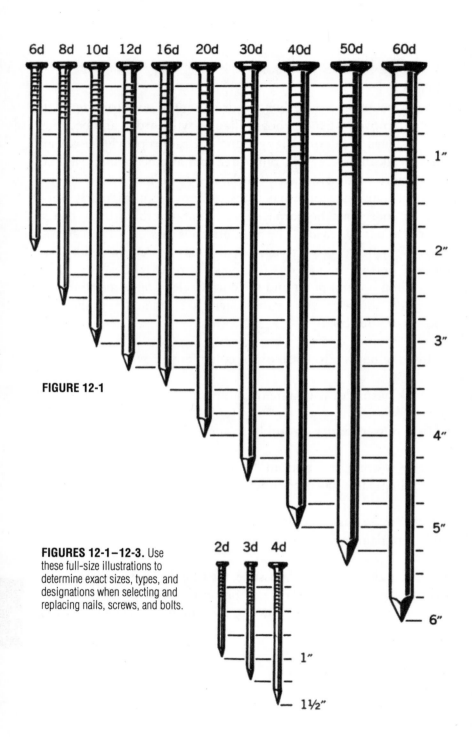

6d 8d 10d 12d 16d 20d 30d 40d 50d 60d

1"

2"

3"

FIGURE 12-1

4"

5"

2d 3d 4d

FIGURES 12-1–12-3. Use these full-size illustrations to determine exact sizes, types, and designations when selecting and replacing nails, screws, and bolts.

1"

1½"

6"

FIGURE 12-2

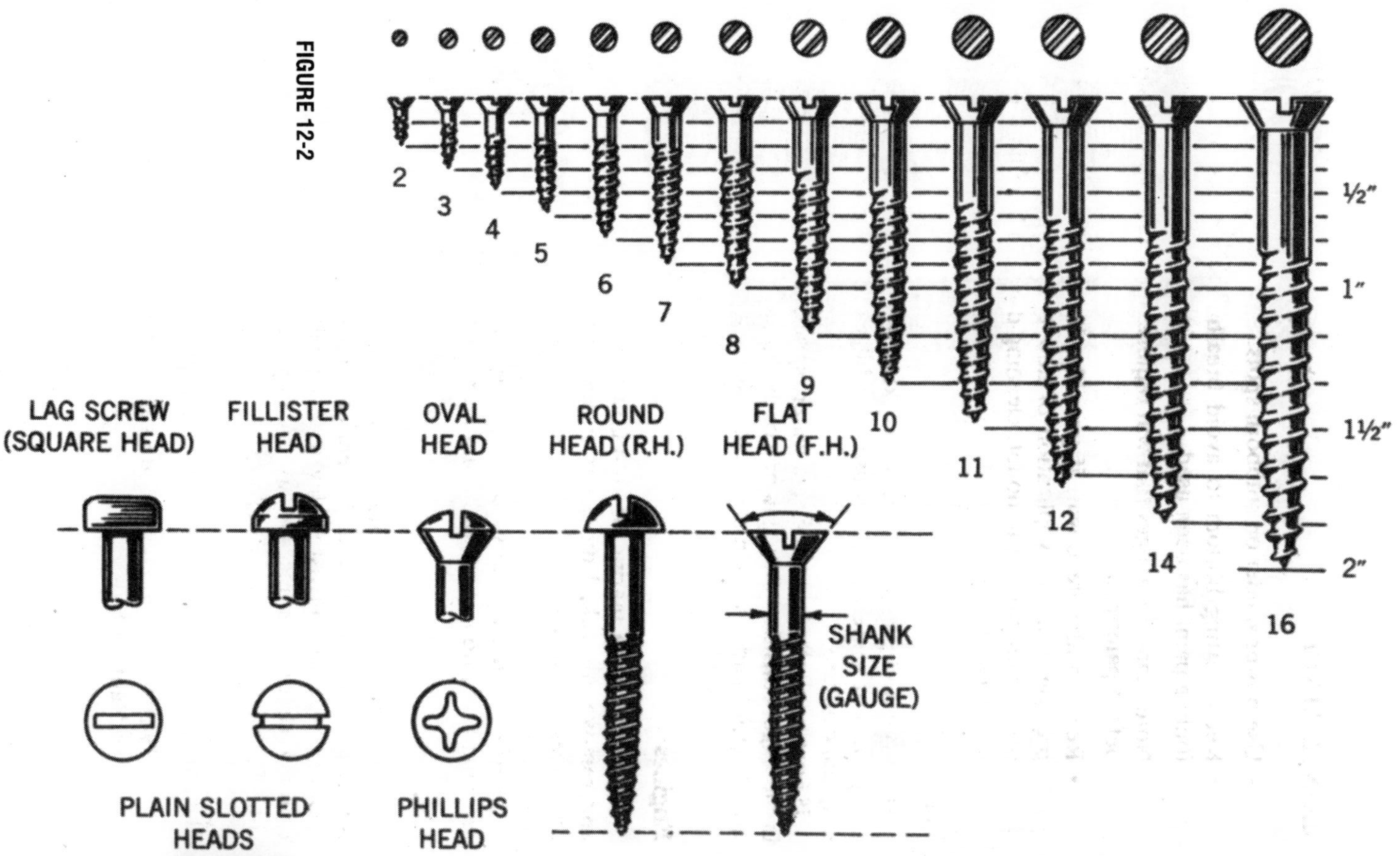
2
3
4
5
6
7
8
9
10
11
12
14
16
½"
1"
1½"
2"
LAG SCREW (SQUARE HEAD)
FILLISTER HEAD
OVAL HEAD
ROUND HEAD (R.H.)
FLAT HEAD (F.H.)
SHANK SIZE (GAUGE)
PLAIN SLOTTED HEADS
PHILLIPS HEAD

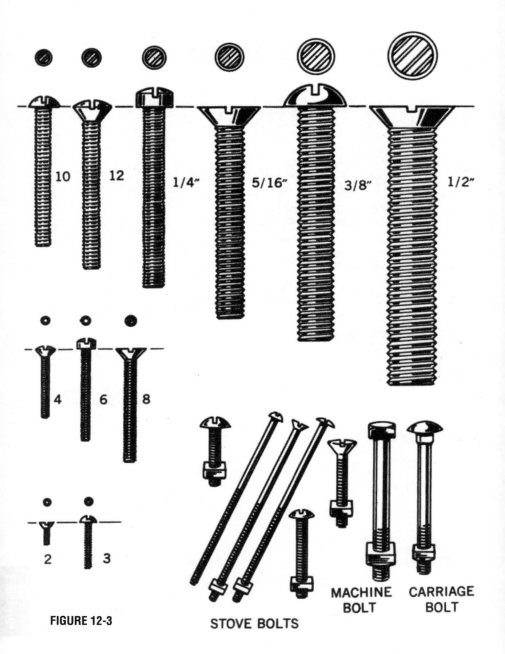

10 12 1/4" 5/16" 3/8" 1/2"

4 6 8

2 3

FIGURE 12-3

STOVE BOLTS

MACHINE BOLT

CARRIAGE BOLT

BILGE

Hose out and pump out bilges, checking freedom of limber holes and pumps at the same time. Rewash with bilge-cleaner compound or soap concentrate. Do not pump out any oil and water mixture that would violate pollution regulations. Pump it out internally and dispose of it properly on shore.

If your boat normally has some rain water, spray, or leakage collecting in the bilge, consider putting in one of the bilge-cleaner additives that slosh around and maintain clean conditions while the boat is under way.

ENGINES

Exterior: Use a marine or automotive cleaner that can degrease and remove any caked dirt from the engine so that you can observe the condition of the paint and detect excessive rusting, chafing hoses, or loose control linkages.

Interior: Run automotive solvent through the carburetor to dissolve any gum formation. Add water inhibitor to the gas tank as needed.

LINES

Give all cordage a freshwater washing while you check for chafes. Turn cordage end-for-end to equalize wear; replace any lines of doubtful strength.

Spot check by untwisting the lay to examine for interior sand that could be chafing the line. Do not use a pressure hose for washing since that might force in cutting grit.

MAINTENANCE

INTERIORS

Wash down bulkheads with soap and water or a multipurpose cleaner. On wooden boats, treat forepeak and cuddy corners that get little ventilation with anti-dryrot compounds.

After washing and airing, use a fungus-control treatment to inhibit mold and mustiness in cabinets and lockers.

METALS

Aluminum: Remove oil and grease with cleaning fluid. Use a cleaner-wax-polish combination to treat bare aluminum. For painted aluminum, use mild soap and water or auto-body polish-cleaner.

Brass, Bronze, Chrome: Regular metal cleaners and polishes will remove tarnish. Use a heavy-duty compound for tougher corrosion. Spray coatings or waxes will help metals keep their shine.

Stainless, Iron, Monel: Scouring pads and powder can remove surface rust. Use products such as Rust Eater® or Naval Jelly for extensive rust. Polish with wire brush. Rinse down.

PLASTICS

Fiberglass, Formica: Various products are sold specifically for fiberglass cleaning, or you may use mild detergent and water. Gel coat stains can be scoured, though buffing afterward with a suitable compound may be necessary to renew gloss and match the color. Wax for fiberglass can help protect surfaces. Mild soap and water is suitable for Formica.

Vinyl: A detergent will remove dirt; special vinyl cleaners and protectors are also available.

Plexiglas: Clean with mild soap and water, but don't use scouring powder. Salt crystals can be washed off with special fluids formulated for this purpose (these also work as a wash fluid for windshield wipers). Scratches can be removed with special Plexiglas buffing compounds.

PVC (Polyvinyl Chloride): Use wood alcohol sparingly; overuse will soften surfaces.

WOOD

Painted Surfaces: Washing down with multipurpose boat soap is sufficient. For cabinets, mix in an antifungus additive.

Varnished Surfaces: Wash down with fresh water; note that breaks in a varnished surface may have allowed discoloration to start—these will require bleaching before re-varnishing.

Teak: Use one of several special teak cleaners available. Then restore color with a teak oil/sealer.

SAILS

Day sailors should wash off salt when a sailboat is docked or hauled. Mild sudsing with soap (no detergents) plus freshwater rinse is the best springtime treatment.

Paints and Painting Procedures

PAINTING BASICS

• Read and heed the instructions on the paint can.

• Clean and prepare the surface carefully.

• Remove loose flakes of previous coats; remove all previous paint if you have doubts about its compatibility with the new paint.

• Use the same brand, if possible, for each coat.

• Observe specified temperature and humidity requirements.

• Note whether the boat should be launched while the bottom paint is still wet.

• Clean brushes before they dry.

Wood

Suitable for application on wood are alkyd, alkyd acrylic, alkyd polyurethane, polyurethane, polyester silicone, epoxy, latex liquid rubber, and vinyl paints. Success, however, will depend on how well the wood surface has been cleaned, sanded, and prepared. Primers and fillers should usually be of the non-oily type and preferably of the same brand as the final paint. A wood bottom may be treated with any of the antifouling paints or with a hard non-toxic racing surface if the boat will not be left in the water between uses.

Varnishes, whether tung oil and phenolic resin types or the newer synthetics and two-part epoxy systems, require careful application. Follow instructions as to surface sanding and bleaching if brightwork has weathered. Then, on a nearly windless day with the right temperature, apply the needed number of coats.

Fiberglass

First wash unpainted surfaces with solvent to remove any wax or mold-release substance. Fill cracks, dents, or hairlines with the surfacing compound recommended by the manufacturer of the paint you are using. Alkyd acrylic, alkyd polyurethane, polyurethane, polyester silicone, epoxy, and vinyl paints are all suitable for fiberglass. Tinted epoxy and polyester are now available with pigments to match breaks in the gel coat or areas that have weathered and changed color so that a molded-in hue can be matched.

Bottom Antifouling

Boats that are hauled out after every use may not need bottom paint, but could use a hard gloss (containing no antifouling properties) for speed.

Aluminum

Your boatyard can probably recommend the proper paints and tell you which brands work best. Vinyl-based paints are usually satisfactory. Prepare previously unpainted aluminum by washing with an etching cleaner. Then rinse and let dry before applying a vinyl-based primer.

Before applying antifouling bottom paint, start with a vinyl primer-undercoat. For aluminum hulls, use paints specifically recommended for such applications.

Engines

Use only paints that resist high heat. To paint the engine compartment, you'll need fire-retardant paints or additives.

Lower Drive Units

Stern drive and outboard motor shafts that project down into the water may be treated with anticorrosive enamels and, in some cases, antifouling compounds. Engine builders and paint manufacturers can make recommendations. Original colors can usually be matched.

Steel

Once the metal has been properly prepared, you can apply paints suitable for wood, fiberglass, or aluminum surfaces, as well as those with special rust inhibitors. First sandblast the surface or apply an etching-type wash. Prime with zinc chromate, red lead, or other rust inhibitor.

Before applying antifouling on the bottom of a steel hull, you need to apply two coats of barrier nonmetallic paint over the primer beneath the final antifouling. Galvanic corrosion could result if copper-bearing paint came in contact with the steel. Some paint producers provide a system of compatible paints for steel hull use.

Vinyl

Cushions, seat covers, and curtains made of vinyl, as well as vinyl tops and cockpit covers, can be renewed with liquid vinyl coatings available in many colors.

HOW MUCH PAINT DO YOU NEED?

The following guidelines for calculating paint quantities are from a booklet published by Woolsey Marine Industries, Inc., entitled *How to Paint Your Boat* (©1967 by Woolsey Marine Industries, Inc., reprinted by permission).

In estimating the amount of material needed for a specific job, you may assume that one gallon of paint or enamel will cover 500 square feet for one coat on the average painted surface. Over new wood, use the figure of 325 square feet per gallon. One gallon of varnish will cover 750 square feet on average for re-coat work, and 500 square feet on new wood. Paint and varnish remover may take several applications and consequently can be expected to soften only about 200 to 250 square feet per gallon.

Some Useful Formulas
Here are some formulas based on practical experience. They should help you in determining how much paint you will need. The results given will be in gallons.

Spars (Varnished)
Multiply the greatest diameter (in feet) by the length (in feet) and multiply the result by 2.5. For new wood, divide the result by 500; for previously finished wood, divide by 750 to obtain the gallonage required.

For example, suppose you have a new spar 8" in diameter and 40' long. Then (8/12 x 40 x 2.5) ÷ 500 = 67/500 or approximately ⅛ gallon (1 pint) for the priming coat. For refinishing work, a pint is enough for about 1½ coats. To determine the requirements for painted spars, change the coverage factor to 325 for new work and to 500 for previously painted wood.

Cabins or Deckhouses
Multiply the height of the deckhouse (in feet) by the girth (in feet). Deduct the area of any large areas such as windows and doors. If the deckhouse is to be painted, divide the result by 325 for the priming coat and 500 for each finishing coat. If it is to be varnished, divide by 500 for the first coat and 750 for the following coats.

Decks
Multiply the length of the boat (in feet) by its greatest beam (in feet) and then multiply the result by 0.75. From this deduct the area of cabin houses, hatches, etc. Divide the remainder by 325 to obtain

MAINTENANCE

gallons required for priming coat and by 500 for each finishing coat of color.

If the deck is to be coated with varnish, divide the figures by 500 and 750, respectively.

TOPSIDES

Multiply the length over all (in feet) by the greatest freeboard (in feet). Multiply the result by 1.5. Divide by 325 for new work and by 500 for old work to obtain the gallonage.

BOTTOM

Multiply the waterline length (in feet) by the draft (in feet). For a keel boat, multiply by 3.5 and for a centerboard boat multiply by 3.0 Divide the result by 300 for priming new work, and by 400 for subsequent coats, to get the required gallonage.

Sealants and Bedding Compounds

Before fiberglass became the hull material of choice, a boat's seams were caulked in the springtime and then the boat would be launched and watched carefully to see if the seams would swell shut before the boat took on too much water and started to sink. Fortunately, raking out old dried compound and refilling the seams of wooden boats is no longer a major part of fitting-out. But keeping water outside the boat where it belongs is still the job of a variety of sealants.

BEDDING COMPOUNDS

The old bedding compound—used under deck fittings to keep water from leaking through the bolt holes and moisture from starting rot in the wood—tends to dry out and harden in a year or so. It is still used to bed through-hull fittings below the waterline when a toxic mixture is needed to repel barnacles. But now, most bedding and sealing chores are handled by the rubber-type products that keep their elasticity indefinitely, do not dry out or harden, and do not use an oil that keeps paint from bonding. Only in the bilge around the engine, where gasoline and oil can get at them, are the rubber-base types less than ideal.

The new synthetic rubbers can be divided into polysulfide (Thiokol), polyurethane, and silicone compounds. They are available in two-part systems that combine the sealant with a catalyst to cure it, or one-part products that take moisture from the air to cause the curing; the latter are usually slower acting. All are available in a variety of colors and are suitable for bonding a fitting that is being bolted to the deck, repairing a leak around a windshield gasket, or stopping a dribble of water seeping from a through-hull fitting. Seams, of course, are usually sealed once and for all, since the synthetic rubber material has great adhesion as well as stretch and sheer strength.

ELECTRICAL CONNECTIONS

The new silicones also make it easy to insulate electrical connections and protect them from corrosion. Some of the compounds are transparent so that terminals and wiring remain visible, but are protected from vibration and corrosion. Crimp-type butt-connectors and terminals are available with plastic sleeves that shrink when heat is applied, thereby sealing the connections.

NEW BOATS

Fortunately, boatbuilders are using these same new sealants in quantity as well, so that a new boat is less likely to require much corrective treatment at fitting-out time. But when a new fitting or locker is installed, a through-hull fitting added, or a leak noted around an engine connection, chances are one of the new polysulfide, polyurethane, or silicone compounds, under a variety of trade names, can seal the area quickly and permanently with the squeeze of a tube. Read the label directions on each product to make the most suitable choice.

Outboard Motor Maintenance

Spark plugs: Replace with fresh, correctly gapped ones.

Ignition wiring: Inspect. Replace tired-looking or cracked high-voltage wires. Tighten all connections.

Fuel tank: Empty out stale gas. Flush.

Fuel line: Inspect for tightness. Replace any in-line filter if dirt is detected.

Fuel filter: Drain. Clean. Replace element.

Carburetor: Send it to the shop if it gave trouble last season. Otherwise, tighten hold-down nuts; check control linkages and lubricate them.

Grease fittings: Locate all grease fittings and apply grease as needed.

Lower unit: Drain all oil from the lower unit. Refill with fresh lubricant of specified grade and viscosity.

Cooling system: Flush out the cooling system with clean fresh water. Alternatively, run the motor in a tank or barrel of fresh water in order to purge it while allowing you to watch the water pump operate.

Propeller: Inspect the propeller critically. If it's nicked or dented, replace it. Keep it for a spare.

Anticorrosion: Install new sacrificial anodes on the lower unit. Sometimes these are combined with a trim tab.

Exterior cleaning: Wipe down the entire power head and lower unit with an oily cloth. Alternatively, spray with rustproofing compound.

TABLE 12-4
Oil-Fuel Mixtures—Mixing Procedure

Correct mixture ratios for engines using oil-fuel blends are very important to assure proper engine operation and protection along with maximum economy of both fuel and oil. The ratios of oil to gasoline shown in the accompanying table are those recommended by the various manufacturers for their individual makes and models. They are for average conditions of use, and it is recommended for special situations (racing, for example) that the engineering department of the outboard engine manufacturer be consulted.

Outboard engine manufacturers caution against adding any special chemicals or compounds to gasoline in an attempt to secure greater power output.

Correct mixture ratios also depend on thorough blending of the oil and gasoline portions. First, measure the ingredients accurately; next, put a small amount of the fuel in the mixing can or tank, and then add the lubricating oil and the remainder of the gasoline. Shake well, or otherwise agitate to assure thorough mixing.

Gasoline-to-Oil Ratio Table

PINTS OF OIL PER GAL.	ACTUAL RATIO	PINTS WHEN APPLIED TO				
		2 GALLON	3 GALLON	4 GALLON	5 GALLON	6 GALLON
$\frac{1}{12}$	96:1	$\frac{1}{6}$	$\frac{1}{4}$	$\frac{1}{3}$	$\frac{5}{12}$	$\frac{1}{2}$
$\frac{1}{6}$	48:1	$\frac{1}{3}$	$\frac{1}{2}$	$\frac{2}{3}$	$\frac{5}{6}$	1
$\frac{1}{5}$	40:1	$\frac{2}{5}$	$\frac{3}{5}$	$\frac{4}{5}$	1	$1\frac{1}{5}$
$\frac{1}{3}$	24:1	$\frac{2}{3}$	1	$1\frac{1}{3}$	$1\frac{2}{3}$	2
$\frac{3}{8}$	21:1	$\frac{3}{4}$	$1\frac{1}{8}$	$1\frac{1}{2}$	$1\frac{7}{8}$	$2\frac{1}{4}$
$\frac{1}{2}$	16:1	1	$1\frac{1}{2}$	2	$2\frac{1}{2}$	3
$\frac{3}{4}$	11:1	$1\frac{1}{2}$	$2\frac{1}{4}$	3	$3\frac{3}{4}$	$4\frac{1}{2}$

NOTE: In some cases, it may be more convenient to mix by the ounce rather than by the pint. Graduations on the containers are given in both pints and ounces. There are sixteen fluid ounces to the pint.

MAINTENANCE

Inboard Motor Maintenance

Spark plugs: Remove. Clean and gap plugs or, preferably, replace them.

Ignition wiring: Inspect. Replace if insulation is cracked or chafed. Tighten all connections. Wipe with anti-moisture dielectric spray.

Distributor cap: Remove, clean, and inspect for chips or cracks. Replace unless perfect, unblemished. Wipe with dielectric spray.

Distributor rotor: Remove and inspect for cracks or burning. Replace unless perfect. Wipe with dielectric spray.

Distributor points: Inspect. Replace if pitted. Adjust to specification using a dwell meter if possible. Readjust after first ten hours.

Ignition timing: Adjust to spec after points are properly set. Use a timing light if possible.

Coil: Snug up mounting hardware and connections. Wipe down with dielectric spray.

Ignition switch: Test all connections. Looseness here is a frequent cause of unexplained engine miss.

Condenser: Check connections and mounting hardware.

Fuel tank: Inspect mountings for security. Pour in several cans of gum-dissolving solvent to fight tar, which may have formed.

Fuel lines: Inspect all connections for leaks. Be sure lines are secure and tight.

Fuel pump: Snug up mounting-cap screws. Drain and clean filter if pump has one. Replace the pump (or rebuild) if it's four seasons old or older.

Fuel filter: Drain; replace the element.

Flame arrester: Remove and clean thoroughly; reinstall.

Carburetor: Send it to the shop if it gave trouble last season. Otherwise, tighten hold-down nuts; check connections, and, if possible, pour a few ounces of gasoline into the float bowl vent tube as a pre-start prime. Be careful with the gas!

Distributor: Put a few drops of oil on the felt under the rotor. If there's an oil cup on the distributor body, squirt in a few drops of engine oil.

Grease fittings: Look for all grease fittings; apply suitable grease as needed.

Alternator: Check for proper belt tension.

Crankcase: Warm the engine, change the oil.

Oil filter: Replace with fresh element.

Block and head: Wipe the entire engine down with rustproofing oil. Tighten valve cover.

Hoses: Carefully inspect. Replace cracked and rotten-looking hoses.

Hose clamps: Look for rusty clamps. Replace "tired" ones with good stainless-steel ones. Tighten all.

MAINTENANCE

Water pump: Install a new drive V-belt. Readjust this belt after first hour or two of operation. If possible, hand prime pump before first start-up.

Seacocks: Ensure that handles will turn; leave in open or closed position as appropriate. Lubricate if applicable. Check hose connections.

Cooling: Immediately after the first start-up, see that the cooling water pump is functioning.

Engine zincs: Locate all zinc electrodes in cooling water system. Remove and inspect; replace if more than half-worn.

Instruments: Watch the needles to see that there is oil pressure, that the alternator is charging, and that engine temperature settles at the correct point.

Transmission: Warm the transmission by running the engine; then change the lubricant. Follow manufacturer's specs as to grade of oil.

Alignment: Align the engine/transmission assembly exactly with the propeller shaft after the boat has been afloat for several days.

Outdrive: Service and lubricate the outdrive lower unit according to specs.

Propeller: Inspect the prop minutely. If it is even slightly nicked or dented, send it to the shop for rework and balancing.

Prop shaft: Inspect the shaft, looking for bends or scoring. Check zincs and replace if necessary.

Struts: Physically shake the prop-shaft struts to make sure they are secure and tight to the hull.

Strut bearings: Shake the prop shaft in the strut bearings, seeking excess looseness. Slight clearance is OK; if you're in doubt, get an expert opinion.

Prop replacement: Mount prop hub on taper snugly; don't let it ride up on the key and get off center.

Shaft log: Be sure the shaft log is well bedded to the hull and secured to the boat's bottom. Tighten the fastenings; they may loosen as the bedding compresses.

Stuffing box: If the box dribbles, tighten the gland nuts slightly. Don't over-tighten.

Zincs: Install fresh new protective zinc anodes on the struts, prop shaft, and rudder.

TABLE 12-5
Inboard Engine Troubleshooting

How to use this chart: (1) find situation below that matches the problem; (2) note the solution key letter or letters; (3) refer to solutions in Table 12-6 in order listed.

SYMPTOM	SOLUTION
Motor stops suddenly after period of proper operation.	A, E, B, C, D, K, F
Motor stops suddenly, no spark to spark plugs.	A, E, G
Motors stops, has good spark, won't restart.	A, D, J, K, S

MAINTENANCE

TABLE 12-5 (continued)
Inboard Engine Troubleshooting

SYMPTOM	SOLUTION
Motor stops, restarts when cool, stops again when hot.	F
Motor stops suddenly, will not turn through full revolution. (Do not restart until after inspection and repair.)	Q
Motor stops "frying hot," won't turn over when cool.	OVERHAUL
Motor stops after period of rough, uneven operation.	A, B, C, D, E, G, H, I, S
Motor overheads before stopping, coolant OK. (Restart only when it has cooled.)	H, L, I
Motor stops hot, low coolant or no coolant flow. (Restart only when it has cooled)	A, C, LL, L, M
Motor runs by spurts, stops, fuel filters clean.	D, E, H, I, J
Motor runs by spurts, stops, water in fuel filters.	S, R
*Motor stops with heavy black smoke from exhaust pipe.	O
*Motors stops with loud clatter	A, Z, ZZ, P, Q
Motor misses, gallops, spits, backfires, loses power	A, R, E, I, S, J
Motor runs rough, idles poorly, overheats. (Do not run at full power until overheating is corrected.)	L, H, I, J
Motor starts hard, especially in cold weather.	G, I, E, Y, GG
Motor "pops" and "pings" in exhaust pipe at all speeds, loss of power and compression, hard starting.	Y, Z

SYMPTOM	SOLUTION
**Lube oil level rises, oil looks and feels gummy.	M
**Lube oil level rises, oil feel very thin.	N
Motor idles poorly, indicates ice in carburetor throat, loses to rpm's after a change in brand or type o fuel.	V
Motor "pings" at full load, starts hard.	H, V
Starter motor spins without engaging flywheel gear.	T
Starter motor turns engine, engine won't operate.	D, E, F, H, I, K
Starter motor jams against flywheel gear, won't turn.	U
Stolenoid clicks when starter button is pushed. Battery up.	
**Motor runs rough, noisy, one or more cylinders not giving power as shown by shorting spark plugs with insulated screwdriver.	P
**Motor runs rough, loses power, water on spark plug electrodes.	W
**Hot water in the bilges.	X
Motor "eats" lube oil, low compression and power.	Z, B
**Motor runs with thumping or knocking noise.	ZZ

*Restart and operate motor before prescribed repairs only in an emergency.

**Continue to operate motor at low power only in emergency before correcting condition.

IMPORTANT! Always check your engine manual for proper repair and adjustment procedures!

DANGER! Always mop up spilled fuel and ventilate engine compartment before restarting a marine engine!

SAFETY FIRST! Disconnect and cover batteries before working on starter, generator, or where tools can fall on terminals, causing electrical short!

TABLE 12-6
Inboard Engine Solutions

KEY		KEY	
A	Inspect motor for obvious damage, excessive heat, leaking fuel, oil or coolant, loose or disconnected wires, control parts, fuel and water lines.	H	*Spark timing incorrect; have readjusted with timing light.
		I	*Ignition points burned and/or spark plug electrodes eroded. Replace, adjust. Inspect high-tension ignition wires for insulation breaks.
B	Check lube oil level and quality on dip stick, add oil if needed. If level too high, refer to treatments M and N.	J	*Look for and repair break or leak in fuel line.
C	Check for leaks in coolant system, leaky pump shaft seal, defective circulating pump. Check exhaust cooling water.	K	*Replace fuel pump and/or pump diaphragm.
		L	*Replace worn or broken circulating pump impellers, check thermostat.
D	Check to see if fuel tank is empty or shut off.	LL	Raw (sea) water suction plugged or shut off. Remove obstruction.
E	Check ignition system for: loose, broken or disconnected wires; cracked distributor cap; broken breaker-point string; shorted condenser, disconnected battery "hot" line; broken rotor; ignition switch "off."	M	*Coolant leaking into lube oil in base. Check for internal gasket leaks, cracked head or block; do not operate until overhauled.
		N	*Fuel leaking into oil in crank case. Use solution K.
F	Replace defective ignition coil that shots out when hot.	O	Carburetor needle valve stuck open. STOP MOTOR INSTANTLY if still running. Drain raw gas from carburetor throat, mop up spilled fuel. Ventilate motor compartment thoroughly. Reseat valve by tapping carburetor lightly on side with hammer. Have mechanic replace valve as soon as possible.
G	Battery voltage low. Bad cell, generator not charging, generator not big enough to carry electrical load, poor battery hot and ground connections.		
GG	Change to lighter lubrication oil for cold weather operation.		

*Should be done by a competent mechanic familiar with your model of motor.

KEY

KEY

P *Valve springs broken, motor probably running too cold. Overhaul.

V Fuel octane rating wrong for your
motor. Change to proper fuel.

Q *Broken-off valve head is on top of
piston, hits cylinder head at top of
piston stroke. Remove cylinder
head, replace broken valve, look for
further internal damage.

W *Coolant is leaking into intake manifold or cylinders. Remove head,
look for leaky gasket or crack in
head or motor block. Have repaired
before operating.

R *Dirt or water in carburetor jets and
bowl. Remove, clean, readjust.

X Exhaust pipe or hot raw water discharge is leaking into bilges.
Repair.

S Clean fuel filter more often.
Remove water and dirt from fuel
tank.

Y *Exhaust valves burned. Motor
needs overhaul.

T *Disconnect battery, remove starter,
clean drive shaft with kerosene and
steel wool, look for and replace broken Bendix spring.

Z *Worn or broken piston rings
and/or worn valve guides.
Overhaul.

ZZ *Burned main or connecting rod
bearings. Overhaul.

U Starter gear is jammed against
flywheel gear teeth. Disconnect
battery, loosen starter holding bolts
until starter is free from block,
turn motor over in reverse rotation
with wrench applied to V-belt
wheel or shaft at front end to
unjam gears. Tighten starter
bolts, reconnect battery.

*Should be done by a competent mechanic familiar with your model of motor.

MAINTENANCE

TABLE 12-6 (continued)
Basic Repair Tools

IGNITION	MECHANICAL	SPECIAL
Ignition wrench set	Combination box, end	Ratchet sockets,
Ignition point file	wrenches	extension bar
Feeler gauge	Stillson and monkey wrenches	Oil squirt gun
Low-voltage test bulb	Set of Allen wrenches	Hand oil-pan pump
Neon test bulb	Vise Grip® and regular pliers	Hydrometer
Spark plug wrench	Machinist's hammer	Flashlight, troublelight
Timing light	Hack saw and blades	
	Screwdriver set	
	Jackknife	

Inboard Engine Solutions
Basic Spare Parts

IGNITION	MECHANICAL	FLUID, ETC.
2 sets breaker points	Pump impellers, shaft seals	Extra lubricating oil
2 sets point condensers	Fuel pump or diaphragm	Pump and gear grease
1 set of spark plugs	Head valve cover gaskets	Hydraulic clutch fluid
Distributor cap, rotor	Thermostat	Penetrating oil
Ignition coil	V-belts to fit	Gasket shellac
	Flexible hose to fit	
	Assorted hose clamps	
	Mixed bolts, nuts, washers	
	Plastic and common tape	
	Sheet gasket material	
	Fuel and lube filter elements	

Controls Maintenance

Steering gear: Test the control for full starboard and port rudder (or outboard motor swing). Clear possible obstructions.

Steering lubrication: Oil or grease all working parts of the steering mechanism.

Throttle adjustment: Definitely see that when the hand lever is closed (idle) the throttle stop is against the adjusting screw on the carburetor. Also see that the throttle opens wide as required for full-bore operation.

Throttle lubrication: Work oil or thin grease through the throttle linkage and cable until action is smooth and free.

Throttle friction: Adjust the friction device in the throttle quadrant, if necessary, to prevent the throttle from creeping.

Manual choke (if applicable): Lubricate the choke control and adjust as described for the throttle. Be sure choke opens wide.

Clutch: Disconnect the clutch lever on transmission. Work the control, making sure there is adequate travel for forward and reverse. Lubricate.

Trim tabs: If the boat has trim tabs, lubricate and adjust the controls according to specs.

Electrical System Maintenance

Wiring: Inspect all visible wires. Watch for frayed insulation, poor connections. Repair or replace as required.

Main switchboard: Check every connection for tightness. Do the same for distribution panels.

Bonding: Make sure that tanks, engine, all electrical accessories are bonded together with heavy wire.

Battery: Charge the battery(s) fully. Clean the posts and terminals. Observe polarity and connect securely.

Battery mounting: Fasten down the battery securely so pitching and rolling will not move it.

Battery cables: Provide the heaviest possible gauge battery cables to assure minimum voltage drop. Replace worn, acid-eaten cables. Replace weak clamps.

Alternator: Install a fresh V-belt and retighten this belt after an hour of operation. Check electrical connections.

Starter: Tighten cable connection and mounting-cap screws or bolts.

Lights: Check every light on the boat. Be sure to have on board a stock of replacement bulbs.

Fuses: Test every fuse on the boat. Be sure to have on board a stock of replacement fuses.

Bilge pump: Test. Be sure that the switch and fuse are in the "hot" ungrounded side of the line.

Voltage: Measure voltage drop at the terminals of accessories such as blowers. When motor is energized, voltage must not drop more than 10 percent (only 3 percent for electronic gear).

Auxiliary AC generator: Give its engine same check as inboard engine. Tighten all connections.

AC electrical system: As far as practical, inspect the wiring. See that all white wires tie to other white, blacks to blacks, and green to green.

Electronics: Perform voltage drop checks as described above. Increase wire conductor size where voltage sags.

Sails and Rigging Maintenance

SAILS

Wash sails in mild detergent and cool water by hand and with a soft scrubbing brush. After washing sails, inspect them thoroughly for rips or tears. The stitching in Dacron sails is their weakest point, so inspect each seam carefully. Most experienced sailors make a practice of having their sailmaker examine and restitch each sail as needed every year. It is not excessively expensive and worth every penny. Home repairs are possible but usually not as satisfactory.

SPARS

Anodized spars can be merely washed. Non-anodized spars should be cleaned up with an abrasive (scouring powder, scouring pads, or fine wet sandpaper) and then coated with one of the clear coatings formulated for this purpose. If you want a really shiny spar, buff with rubbing compound before coating. While you're cleaning, check spars for straightness, check fittings for looseness and defects (cracks in castings), and oil all sheaves.

Noise Abatement

Aluminum spars are noisy, particularly those with internal halyards and wiring. Wiring can be enclosed in a plastic tube(s) or it can be seized to the after side of the spar. To do this, lay the spar aft side down, drill pairs of holes about six feet apart on each side of the sail track, and seize the wires through the holes with stainless seizing wire. Finish holes with epoxy.

Lights and Instruments

Test all circuits and replace components as needed. Consider replacing all bulbs.

STANDING RIGGING

Examine all standing rigging with great care. Pay particular attention to all swage fittings. Examine these with a magnifying device that will show any hairline cracks present. Cracked swage fittings are unreliable and should be discarded. Examine all hardware with a sharp eye. Clevis pins in particular should be replaced if they show wear; replace all cotter pins as a matter of course. Lock nuts aloft should be drilled and pinned if they haven't been already.

Tape

White rigging tape is a rigger's best friend. Everything that can possibly get near a sail should be taped to eliminate tearing. Additionally, when a wire is to be seized to another wire or to a piece of hardware (spreaders), tape the wire first, then seize it and follow with more tape. The first taping will effectively prevent slipping.

RUNNING RIGGING

Check for wear and chafe. Replace as indicated. Sometimes sheet life can be extended by turning it end-for-end. Additionally, a long sheet with one worn section may be useful in another function requiring a shorter length. Finally, fenders always need lines. Wire running rigging should also be examined for wear, indicated by short barbs sticking out at the point of chafe or wear. Remove damaged section, then turn the wire end-for-end or replace entire wire if needed. If flexible wire running rigging is fitted with swage fittings, pay special attention to junctions that are points of particular sensitivity. Consider replacing swage fittings with more flexible splices or Nicopress fittings.

OIL

Be liberal with the oil can throughout the rig. Shackles should snap, pole fittings should open easily, sheaves should revolve without strain, and track cars should move without having to be forced.

MAINTENANCE

Plumbing Maintenance

FUEL SYSTEM

Filler: Make sure cap assembly is secure to deck. Inspect hose and the ground wire from filler cap to tank. Tighten or replace hose clamps as necessary.

Tank vent: Inspect and clean.

Tank: Inspect for leaks. Make sure hold-downs or straps are tight and secure. Check operation of tank shut-off valve. Drain and refill with fresh gasoline or diesel fuel.

Fuel lines: Inspect for cracks, abrasions, and leaks at fittings.

COOLING SYSTEM

Intakes: Check, tighten, and replace clamshell fastenings as required. Clean clamshells and sediment screens.

Through-hull fittings, valves: Check operation. These should open and close with hand pressure alone. Clean and lubricate; replace units as necessary. Check bedding blocks and caulking.

Pumps: Clean. Check packing and washers.

Hoses: Inspect and replace any that are worn, abraded, or weak. Tighten or replace clamps as necessary.

Raw (sea) water cooling: Drain and flush. Inspect for leaks.

Freshwater cooling: Drain and flush raw water side of system. Drain, flush, and refill freshwater side. Use rust inhibitor and other additives as specified by engine or cooling system manufacturer. Check intake, screens of keel coolers; disassemble if necessary to clear obstructions in keel cooler unit.

EXHAUST SYSTEM

Transom flanges: Inspect fastenings; replace as necessary.

Hoses, piping: Inspect and replace if necessary; tighten or replace clamps.

Manifold water jackets: Inspect for leaks. Drain and flush.

Wet mufflers: Check thermostat operation, if one is present, at engine side of feed to muffler. Clean and inspect muffler. Paint with heat-resistant finish, if necessary.

POTABLE WATER SYSTEM

Tanks: Drain and refill. Add purifying tablets as required. Check and adjust tank hold-downs.

Hoses: Inspect and replace as required. Tighten or replace clamps as necessary.

Pumps: Inspect packing and washers. Clean screens. Check float valves and polarity of connections to electrical pumps. Switches must be in "hot" wire from battery.

Heater: Clean. Check operation and thermostat settings.

MAINTENANCE

Vents, drains: Clean and inspect. Check through-hull fittings and valves. Seacocks and valves should open and close by hand pressure alone. Lubricate or replace units as necessary.

SEWAGE SYSTEM

Pumps: Inspect and clear joker or check valves of hand pumps. Check connections and operation of electrical units.

Hoses: Clean inside and out. Inspect and replace as necessary. Tighten or replace hose clamps as required.

Bowl: Clean. Inspect for cracks and chips. Check hold-down fastenings. Lubricate lid hinges.

Chlorinators, other chemical units: Clean and inspect; replace chlorine or other chemicals according to manufacturer's specifications.

Holding tanks: Should be drained when boat is hauled. Clean and inspect for cracks and leaks; also check hoses and pump-out fittings.

Through-hull fittings, seacocks, valves: Check bedding blocks and caulking. Seacocks and valves should open and close with hand pressure alone. Lubricate or replace units as required.

MISCELLANEOUS
Clear dirt and debris from scuppers, self-bailing ducts, limber holes, and similar passages through which water must pass.

Trailer Maintenance

A well-built boat trailer should remain in excellent condition indefinitely with a minimum of maintenance. In addition to periodic inspections and lubrication, the most important ingredient is a thorough wash down after each use. Wash with soap and water, just like your car, to remove water residue, road tars, and dirt.

TRAILER FRAME

Use a stiff wire brush to remove rust scale. Paint as necessary with a rust-inhibiting coating. Inspect and lubricate tilt lock and hinge mechanism, if trailer is so equipped. Lubricate rollers several times each season and use strips of old carpeting to replace torn or rotted bunker covers.

SPRINGS

Wash well after each trip. Use a paint brush to coat springs with motor oil, or spray on a commercial rust preventive.

WHEEL BEARINGS

Remove hub and grease seals and wipe axle spindle clean. Inspect bearings and bearing cups for pitting, then check grease seals for undue wear. Coat inside bearing with grease and put it in position. Press on the grease seal. Put additional grease on the open area of the hub and install the hub on the spindle. Grease the outer bearing and install it. Reinstall the nut on the spindle and tighten as far as it will go. Then back it off until the wheel spins freely. Reinstall or replace the cotter pin to hold the nut in place. Reinstall the hubcaps.

MAINTENANCE

TABLE 12-7
Load Capacity of Trailer Tires

TIRE SIZE	PLY RATING	POUNDS OF THE PRESSURE (MEASURED COLD)												
		30	35	40	45	50	55	60	65	70	75	80	85
4.80/4.00 x 8	2	**380**											
4.80/4.00 x 8	4	380	420	450	485	515	545	575	**600**				
5.70/5.00 x 8	4		575	625	665	**710**							
6.9/6.00 x 9	6		785	850	915	970	1030	**1080**					
6.90/6.00 x 9	8		785	850	915	970	1030	1080	1125	1175	1225	**1270**	
20 x 8.00–10	4	825	**900**										
20 x 8.00–10	6	825	900	965	1030	**1100**							
20 x 8.00–10	8	825	900	965	1030	1100	1155	1210	1270	**1325**			
20 x 8.00–10	10	825	900	965	1030	1100	1155	1210	1270	1325	1370	1420	**1475**
4.80/4.00 x 12	4	545	550	595	635	680	715	755	**790**				
5.30/4.50 x 12	4	640	700	760	810	865	**915**						
5.30/4.50 x 12	6	640	700	760	810	865	915	960	1005	1045	1090	**1135**	
6.00 x 12	4	855	935	**1010**									
6.00 x 12	6	855	935	1010	1090	1160	1230	**1290**					
6.50 x 13	6	895	980	1060	1130	1200	**1275**						

NOTE: Figures in bold represent maximum permissible pressure

LIGHTS AND WIRING

If the lights have been submerged, remove the glass or plastic cover, drain water, and dry the interior with cloth or paper towels. If you can't remove the lights and it's necessary to submerge them, cover the entire light housing with a plastic bag secured with rubber bands—this is better than no protection at all. Check wiring for cracks and breaks; replace as necessary. Be sure connectors are clean.

WINCH

Inspect and lubricate winch gears, handle, and lock mechanism. Wipe the metal cable with an oil rag to prevent rust. If the cable is worn or frayed, replace it with new cable. If a fiber winch line is used, inspect and replace it if necessary.

FIGURE 12-8

STOWAGE PLAN

Sketch location of lockers and cabinets. Label "A," "B," "C," etc., and list contents below.

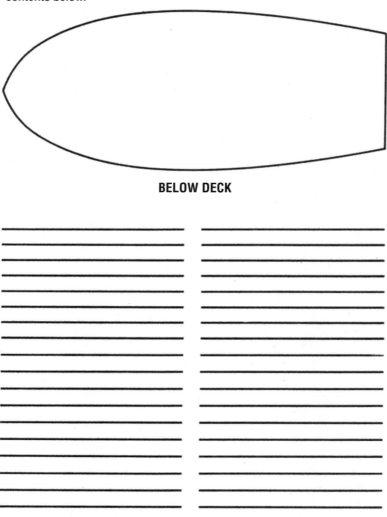

BELOW DECK

FIGURE 12-9

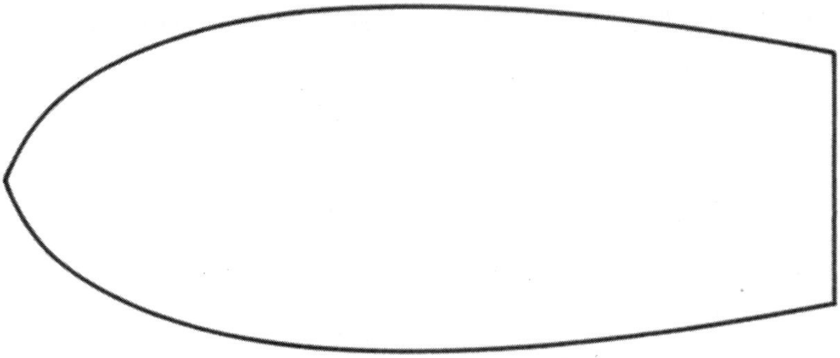

ABOVE DECK

FIGURE 12-10

WIRING DIAGRAMS

Sketch in location of battery, running lights, other electrical accessories, and the run of the wiring to each. Note wiring color code, and other distinguishing characteristics.

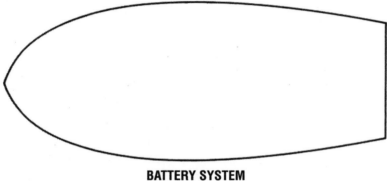

BATTERY SYSTEM

Sketch location of items served by the 110 volt AC system, location of generator, service panel, shore connectors, and run of the wiring.

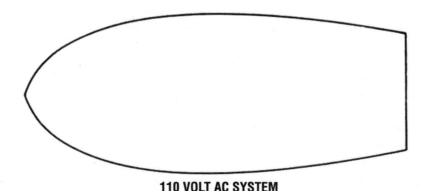

110 VOLT AC SYSTEM

TABLE 12-11
General Information

Boat Name_____ Manufacturer_____

Year Built _____ Designer_____

Length Overall_____ Waterline Length _____ Beam_____

Draft _____ Sail Area_____ Displacement _____

State Registration Number_____

Engine(s) Make_____ Horsepower_____ Year_____

INSURANCE

Firm Name_____ Agent Name _____

Address _____ Address _____

_____ _____

Phone _____ Phone, Office _____ Home_____

BOATYARD   MECHANIC

Name_____ Name _____

Address _____ Address _____

_____ _____

Phone _____ Phone, Office _____ Home_____

Manager's Home Phone _____

Licensed Radio Technician _____ Radio Call Sign _____

Name_____ Frequencies _____

Address _____

Phone, Office _____ Home_____

NUMBERS AND SIZES

Engine(s) Make _____ Serial Number(s) _____

Spark Plug Size _____ Gap_____ Firing Order _____

Distributor Point Gap _____

Timing Mark Location _____ Setting_____

Oil Grade _____ Oil Capacity_____

Transmission Lube Grade_____ Capacity_____

ELECTRONIC EQUIPMENT

Radiotelephone Make _____ Serial Number(s) _____

Depth Indicator Make _____ Serial Number(s) _____

Other Electronic Gear _____

    Make — Item _____ Serial Number(s) _____

    Make — Item _____ Serial Number(s) _____

    Make — Item _____ Serial Number(s) _____

FRESHWATER COOLING SYSTEM CAPACITY _____

SAIL INVENTORY

SAIL	MAKER	YEAR	REMARKS

BULB SIZES

Running Lights _____ Masthead _____

    Starboard* _____ Stern _____

    Port _____ Others _____

Cabin Light(s) _____ _____

Searchlight _____ _____

Instrument Panel _____

Others _____

FUSES, CIRCUIT BREAKER SIZES (Amps)

Main _____ Radiotelephone _____

Running Lights _____ Appliances _____

General Lighting _____ _____

Receptacle Outlets _____ _____

Bilge Pump _____ Other Electronic Gear _____

_____

_____

*Starboard light usually requires brighter bulb than port light
to meet United States Coast Guard visibility requirements.

CHAPTER THIRTEEN

Information Sources

This book doesn't have all the boating information you might need—if it tried to deliver that, it would fill a bookshelf. For the nuggets of wisdom that are not included within these covers, you can turn to the organizations, publications, and other sources of information listed in this chapter. Included are names and postal addresses, telephone numbers and Web addresses, and basic information about the organization, publication, or other source.

Organizations

One way to get more pleasure from your boating is to join others with similar boating interests. And if you need special information, or want your voice as a boater heard in legislative councils, there are organizations that can provide the help you need.

Listed here are major national organizations and a brief statement of purpose for each. For complete details, write to the group's headquarters.

GENERAL ORGANIZATIONS

United States Coast Guard Auxiliary, c/o Commandant (G-OCX), U.S. Coast Guard, Washington, DC 20593-0001; www.uscg.mil. This civilian volunteer arm of the Coast Guard provides boating classes and courtesy safety-related examinations of pleasure boats. It also assists in search and rescue operations under Coast Guard orders.

United States Power Squadrons, P.O. Box 30423, Raleigh, NC 27622; 888-367-8777; www.usps.org. A fraternal organization of boating men and women that provides free basic boating classes (there is a nominal charge for course materials) to the public. For its members, it provides advanced courses in seamanship and navigation, along with courses covering such topics as sailing, weather, engine maintenance, and marine electronics. The USPS also sponsors other civic programs and social activities.

Boat Owners Association of the United States (BoatU.S.), 880 S. Pickett St., Alexandria, VA 22304-4695; www.boatus.com. A full-service representational membership organization of recreational boaters, offering group-rate marine insurance, a boating-equipment savings program, charts, books, cruise planning, consumer-complaint bureau, theft protection, correspondence courses, and other services for members. It is active in legislative and conservation programs related to boating and waterways.

National Boating Federation, P.O. Box 4111, Annapolis, MD 21403-6111; 410-626-8566; rpdavid@capecod.net. A federation of national, state, and regional boating organizations, yacht clubs, and individuals that keeps members informed of news on boating legislation, etc., and provides an elected, responsible voice for the boating public nationally.

RACING ORGANIZATIONS, POWER

American Power Boat Association, P.O. Box 377, Eastpointe, MI 48021-0377; 810-773-970; apbahq@aol.com. This organization sanctions all major powerboat races in the United States.

Union Internationale Motonautique, 1, Avenue des Castelans, Stade Louis II – Entrée H, MC 98000, Monaco. The Union of International Motorboating sanctions all major international powerboat races. It is represented in the United States by the American Power Boat Association.

RACING ORGANIZATIONS, SAIL

Cruising Club of America, P.O. Box 4024, Boston, MA 02101-4024; www.cruisingclub.org. CCA uses the collective knowledge and experience of its members to influence "the adventurous use of the sea" through its efforts to improve seamanship, the design of seaworthy yachts, safe yachting procedures, and environmental awareness.

Slocum Society International, 15 Codfish Hill Road Extension, Bethel, CT 06801-3208; 203-790-6616. An organization established in 1955 to record, encourage, and support long-distance passages in small boats. Publishes a periodic journal, *The Spray,* and monthly newsletters. Dues: $30 per year. Awards are made for outstanding seamanship and maritime literature.

United States Sailing Association (US SAILING), P.O. Box 1260, Portsmouth, RI 02871-0907; 401-683-0800; www.ussailing.org. The national governing body for the sport of sailing, whose mission is to encourage participation and excellence in sailing and racing in the United States. Its goals are achieved through member organizations and volunteers, supported by an administrative staff at the US SAIL Headquarters.

United States Olympic Sailing Committee, 15 Maritime Drive, Portsmouth, RI 02871-6145; 401-683-0800; www.ussailing.org. This organization helps to raise funds to facilitate U.S. participation in Olympic yachting competition.

GOVERNMENT AGENCIES
National Oceanic and Atmospheric Administration, Room 6013, 14th St and Constitution Ave, N.W., Washington, DC 20230; www.noaa.gov. This branch of the Department of Commerce includes the National Weather Service and the National Ocean Service, among other services. It publishes nautical charts and a wealth of other material useful in piloting and seamanship (see the listings of available publications and chart sources in this chapter).

Corps of Engineers, Department of the Army, 441 G St. N.W., Washington, DC 20002-4301; www.usace.army.mil. This branch of the U.S. Army is charged with the maintenance of all federal navigation projects within the United States.

National Association for State Boating Law Administrators, P.O. Box 11099, Lexington, KY 40512-1099; www.nasbla.org. This organization plays a key role in the development of uniform boating legislation at the state level.

United States Coast Guard, Coast Guard Headquarters, 400 7th Street, N.W., Washington, DC 20591; www.uscg.mil.This is the government organization charged with responsibility for recreational boating safety and regulation on a national level.

INDUSTRY ASSOCIATIONS

American Boat and Yacht Council, Inc., 3069 Solomons Island Road, Edgewater, MD 21037-1416; www.abycinc.org. This non-profit technical society develops and publishes voluntary safety standards and recommended practices for design, construction, equipment, and maintenance of all types of recreational boats.

American Boat Builders and Repairers Association, 345 Pier One Road, Suite 106, Stevensville, MD 21666-2610; 410-604-0060; www.abbra.org. A professional organization of the marine service industry.

National Marine Electronics Association (NMEA), P.O. Box 3435, New Bern, NC 28564-3435; www.nmea.org. A non-profit trade association of manufacturers, distributors, dealers, technicians, consultants, boat builders, and others interested in marine electronics. NMEA sponsors certification programs and standards for data exchange, NMEA 0183 and NMEA 2000.

National Marine Manufacturers Association (NMMA), 200 E. Randolph Dr., Chicago, IL 60601-6528; 312-946-6200; www.nmma.org. NMMA represents the North American recreational boating industry, with membership that includes manufacturers of boats, marine engines and outboard motors, and boating accessories; publishers; original equipment manufacture (OEM) suppliers; and local and regional trade associations. Provides services and benefits to improve the profitability of members through government relations activities, standards and engineering programs, group insurance plans, marketing statistics, market promotions, public relations, and management education. It owns and produces trade and consumer boat shows across the United States.

INFORMATION

Underwriters Laboratories, Marine Department, 12 Laboratory Dr., P.O. Box 13995, Research Triangle Park, NC 27709-3995; 919-549-1534; www.ul.com/marine. This facility evaluates products or systems intended for marine use with respect to safety. For products found to comply with the Laboratories' requirements, manufacturers are authorized to use an appropriate listing mark on or in conjunction with such products, contingent upon the establishment of UL's Follow-Up Service, which is designed to check on manufacturer compliance on a continuing basis.

Publications

GENERAL REFERENCE

Elbert S. Maloney. *Chapman Piloting: Seamanship and Boat Handling, 63rd edition.* New York: Hearst Marine Books, 1999. 656 pages, illustrated. A complete compendium of boating information, frequently called "The Boater's Bible." Revised at frequent intervals.

NOTICES TO MARINERS

Notice to Mariners. Marine Safety Information Center, National Imagery and Mapping Agency, Bethesda, MD 20816-5003; www.nima.mi. Published weekly in conjunction with the National Ocean Service and the U.S. Coast Guard. (There are also Notices to Mariners published by the Canadian Coast Guard and marine safety organizations of other maritime nations.)

Local Notice to Mariners. Each Guard District Headquarters; www.navcen.uscg.mil/lnm. Published weekly, except for 9th District (Great Lakes), which publishes seasonally.

COAST PILOTS

U.S. Waters: Nine volumes covering the U.S. Atlantic, Gulf, and Pacific Coasts; Atlantic and Gulf Intracoastal Waterways; the Great Lakes. Published by NOS and sold by the FAA Distribution Division AVN-530, Riverdale, MD 20737-1199 (VISA or MasterCard accepted); 800-638-8972; http://acc.nos.noaa.gov/; also available from local sales agents listed in NOS Chart Catalogs.

Canadian Waters: Canadian Sailing Directions: Chart Sales & Distribution Office, Canadian Hydrographic Services, Department of Fisheries & Oceans, P.O. Box 8080, 1675 Russell Rd., Ottawa, Ont. K1G 3H6, Canada; 613-998-4931; www.chs-shc. dfo-mpogc.ca/chs_hq/purchase_chs.html.

LIGHT LISTS

Light List. Seven volumes covering the U.S. coastal waters, the Great Lakes, and the Mississippi River system. Published annually by the U.S. Coast Guard, except for Volume V (Mississippi River system), which is updated every two years; sold by the Superintendent of Documents, P.O. Box 371954, Pittsburgh, PA 15250-1954; http://bookstore.gpo.gov. Phone 202-512-1800 from 0730 until 1630 ET Monday through Friday; fax 202-512-2250, 24 hours daily (VISA, MasterCard, or Discover/NOVUS accepted); also available from many of the sales agents listed in NOS Chart Catalogs.

U.S. COAST GUARD PUBLICATIONS

Navigation Rules, International–Inland. COMDTINST 16672.2. This small book contains the full text of the 1972 International Rules of the Road and the 1980 U.S. Inland Navigation Rules, and all Annexes; illustrated. Also contains information on Demarcation Lines separating the two sets of Rules, and the text of the Bridge-to-Bridge Radiotelephone Act. Sold by the Superintendent of Documents, P.O. Box 371954, Pittsburgh, PA 15250-1954; http://bookstore.gpo.gov. Phone 202-512-1800 from 0730 until 1630 ET Monday through Friday; fax 202-512-2250, 24 hours daily (VISA, MasterCard, or Discover/NOVUS accepted); also available from many of the sales agents listed in NOS Chart Catalogs.

Federal Requirements for Recreational Boats. Digest of boating laws and regulations covering numbering, accidents, sales to aliens, law enforcement, documentation, and equipment requirements, plus safety suggestions. Available at all Coast Guard offices.

Visual Distress Signals. CG-152. Illustrated booklet provides description and guidance for use of distress signals suitable for boats. Free from Coast Guard district offices, or Headquarters. U.S. Coast Guard, Washington, DC 20593-0001.

Light List. Seven volumes, COMDTPUB P16502.n. Sold by the Superintendent of Documents, P.O. Box 371954, Pittsburgh, PA 15250-1954; http://bookstore.gpo.gov. Phone 202-512-1800 from 0730 until 1630 ET Monday through Friday; fax 202-512-2250, 24 hours daily (VISA, MasterCard, or Discover/NOVUS accepted); also available from many of the sales agents listed in NOS Chart Catalogs.

PUBLICATIONS OF THE NATIONAL IMAGERY AND MAPPING AGENCY

NIMA publications are sold by the Superintendent of Documents, P.O. Box 371954, Pittsburgh, PA 15250-1954; http://book-store.gpo.gov. Phone 202-512-1800 from 0730 until 1630 ET Monday through Friday; fax 202-512-2250, 24 hours daily (VISA, MasterCard or Discover/NOVUS accepted); also available from authorized sales agents.

NIMA Catalog of Nautical Charts and Publications. Published for nine world regions. Region 1 covers the United States and Canada. Region 2 covers Central and South America.

Sailing Directions. Books supplementing NIMA charts contain descriptions of coastlines, harbors, dangers, aids, port facilities, and other data that cannot be shown conveniently on charts.

Pilot Charts published by NIMA

Pub 105. Atlas of Pilot Charts–South Atlantic Ocean

Pub 106. Atlas of Pilot Charts–North Atlantic Ocean

Pub 107. Atlas of Pilot Charts–South Pacific Ocean

Pub 108. Atlas of Pilot Charts–North Pacific Ocean

Pub 109. Atlas of Pilot Charts–Indian Ocean

INFORMATION

Lists of Lights and Fog Signals

Pub 110. Greenland, east coasts of North and South America (excluding continental U.S. except for east coast of Florida), and the West Indies.

Pub 111. West coasts of North and South America (excluding continental U.S. and Hawaii), Australia, Tasmania, New Zealand, and the islands of North and South Pacific Ocean.

Pub 112. Western Pacific and Indian Oceans including the Persian Gulf and Red Sea.

Pub 113. West coasts of Europe and Africa, the Mediterranean Sea, Black Sea, and the Sea of Azov.

Pub 114. British Isles, English Channel, and North Sea.

Pub 115. Norway, Iceland, and Arctic Ocean.

Pub 116. Baltic Seas with Kattegat, Belts and Sound, and Gulf of Bosnia.

Miscellaneous NIMA Publications

Chart No. 1. Nautical Chart Symbols and Abbreviations.

Pub 9. American Practical Navigator, originally by Nathaniel Bowditch.

Pub 102. International Code of Signals.

Pub 117A and 117B. Radio Navigation Aids, Marine Direction-finder and radar stations; time signals; navigational warnings; distress, emergency, and safety traffic; medical advice; long range navigational aids; Automated Mutual-assistance Vessel Rescue System (AMVER); emergency procedures and communication instructions for U.S. Merchant Ships.

Pub 150. World Port Index.

Pub 151. Distances Between Ports.

Pub 217. Maneuvering Board Manual.

Pub 226. Handbook of Magnetic Compass Adjustment and Compensation.

Pub 1312. Radar Navigation Manual.

WEATHER PUBLICATIONS

Marine Weather Service Charts. A series of 16 charts containing coverage diagrams for NOS. VHF-FM weather stations, broadcast schedules of commercial radio stations, and National Weather Service telephone numbers. These charts cover the Atlantic, Gulf, and Pacific coasts, and waters adjacent to Hawaii, Puerto Rico, the Virgin Islands, Alaska, and Guam. Sold by FAA Distribution Division AVN-530, Riverdale, MD 20737-1199; 800-638-8972; http://acc.nos.noaa.gov (VISA or MasterCard accepted); also available from local sales agents listed in NOS Chart Catalogs.

MISCELLANEOUS PUBLICATIONS

The Nautical Almanac. Compact publication from the United States Naval Observatory contains all ephemeris matter essential to the solution of problems of navigation position; star chart is included. Sold by the Superintendent of Documents, P.O. Box 371954, Pittsburgh, PA 15250-1954; http://bookstore.gpo.gov.

INFORMATION

Phone 202-512-1800 from 0730 until 1630 ET Monday through Friday; fax 202-512-2250, 24 hours daily (VISA, MasterCard or Discover/NOVUS accepted); also available from authorized sales agents.

CHARTS OF VARIOUS WATERWAYS

U.S. Coastal Waters and Great Lakes. Atlantic, Pacific, and Gulf coasts; the Atlantic and Gulf Intracoastal Waterways; the Hudson River north to Troy, New York; the Great Lakes and connecting rivers; Lake Champlain; New York State canals; and the Minnesota-Ontario Border Lakes. Sold by FAA Distribution Division AVN-530, Riverdale, MD 20737-1199; 800-638-8972; http://acc.nos.noaa.gov (VISA or Master Card accepted); also available from local sales agents listed in chart catalogs.

New York State Canals. NOS Chart 14786; bound booklet of charts of the Champlain, Erie, Oswego, and Cayuga-Seneca canals. Sold by FAA Distribution Division AVN-530, Riverdale, MD 20737-1199; 800-638-8972; http://acc.nos.noaa.gov; or local sales agents.

Mississippi River and Tributaries. Middle and Upper Mississippi, Cairo, Illinois, to Minneapolis, Minnesota; Middle Mississippi River from Cairo, Illinois, to Grafton, Illinois; Mississippi River from Cairo, Illinois, to Gulf of Mexico; Small Boat Chart, Alton, Illinois, to LaGrange, Illinois, on the Illinois River. Illinois Waterways from Grafton, Illinois, to Lake Michigan at Chicago and Calumet Harbor. Available from Army Engineer District, 1222 Spruce Street, St. Louis, MO 63103-2833.

Mississippi River and Connecting Waterways, North of the Ohio River. U.S. Army Engineers, Northwestern Division, 12565 W, Center Road, Omaha, NE 68144-3869.

Ohio River and Tributaries; Pittsburgh, Pennsylvania, to the Mississippi River. U.S. Army Engineers, Great Lakes & Ohio River Division, P.O. Box 1159, Cincinnati, OH 45201-1159.

Tennessee and Cumberland Rivers. U.S. Army Engineer District, P.O. Box 1070, Nashville, TN 37202-1070; also Tennessee Valley Authority, Maps and Engineering Records Section, 102A Union Building, Knoxville, TN 37902-1116.

Missouri River. Publication in two volumes, the upper one covering from Sioux City to Kansas City; the lower one, from Kansas City to the mouth (at St. Louis). District Engineer, U.S. Army Engineer District, 215 N. 17th Street, Omaha, NE 68102-4970.

Canadian Waters. Charts include coastal waters; Canadian sections of the Great Lakes including Georgian Bay; the St. Lawrence River; Richelieu River; Ottawa River; the Rideau Waterway; and other Canadian lakes and waterways. Chart prices and details are given in several catalogs. Available from Chart Sales & Distribution Office, Canadian Hydrographic Services, P.O. Box 8080, 1675 Russell Rd., Ottawa, Ont. K1G 3H6, Canada; 613-998-4931; www.chs-hsc.dof-mpo.gc.ca/chs_hq/purchase_chs.html.

Waters of Other Nations. NIMA charts are now sold by the Superintendent of Documents, P.O. Box 371954, Pittsburgh, PA 15250-1954; http://bookstore.gpo.gov. Phone 202-512-1800 from 0730 until 1630 ET Monday through Friday; fax 202-512-2250, 24 hours daily (VISA, MasterCard or Discover/NOVUS accepted); also available from authorized sales agents. A general catalog (free) and nine regional catalogs are available.

INFORMATION

CRUISING GUIDES

Waterway Guide. Waterway Guide, 6151 Powers Ferry Road, N.W., Atlanta, GA 30339-2941; 770-618-0320; http://waterwayguide.com. Annual guidebook for boaters traveling the East and Gulf Coasts by boat. Detailed information on marinas, shore services, and repair services. Includes navigational advice on harbors, anchorages, and the entire Intracoastal Waterway, plus spot charts for all marinas. Three regional editions.

Intracoastal Waterway Booklets. Comprehensive descriptions of the Intracoastal Waterway, with data on navigation, charts, distances. Prepared by U.S. Army Corps of Engineers in two sections: (1) Atlantic, Boston to Key West; (2) Gulf, Key West to Brownsville, Texas. Available from Superintendent of Documents, P.O. Box 371954, Pittsburgh, PA 15250-1954; http://bookstore.gpo.gov. Phone 202-512-1800 from 0730 until 1630 ET Monday through Friday; fax 202-512-2250, 24 hours daily (VISA, MasterCard or Discover/NOVUS accepted).

Intracoastal Waterway Bulletins. Frequent bulletins giving latest information on the conditions of the Intracoastal Waterway are published by the U.S. Army Corps of Engineers; available from District Offices at: 803 Front St., Norfolk, VA 23510-1096; P.O. Box 1890, Wilmington, NC 28402-1890; P.O. Box 919, Charleston, SC 29402-0919; P.O. Box 889, Savannah, GA 31402-0889; P.O. Box 4970, Jacksonville, FL 32232-OO19; P.O. Box 2288, Mobile, AL 36628-0001; and P.O. Box 1229, Galveston, TX 77553-1229.

Yachtsman Guide to the Bahamas. All Bahamas Islands and Turks & Caicos Islands. Updated annually. Tropic Isle Publishers, Inc., Editor's Office, P.O. Box 15397, Plantation, FL 33318-5397. Phone 305-893-4277; fax 954-321-0806. Orders to P.O. Box 610938, North Miami, FL 33261-0938.

Yachtsman Guide to the Virgin Islands and Puerto Rico. U.S. and British Virgin Islands, and Puerto Rico. Tropic Isle Publishers, Inc. (see addresses and phone numbers above).

Cruising Guide to Abaco, Bahamas. White Sound Press, 379 Wild Orange Drive, New Smyrna Beach, FL 32168-8379; www.wspress.com.

Maryland Cruising Guide. Williams & Heintz Map Corp., 8119 Central Ave., Capital Heights, MD 20743-3538; 800-338-6228. Reproductions of NOS charts of the Maryland portion of Chesapeake Bay and tributaries, and of the Maryland seacoast. Tidal current information, marina and launching ramp locations, and other useful information.

Canadian Cruising Guides. Chart Sales and Distribution Office, Canadian Hydrographic Services, P.O. Box 8080, 1675 Russell St., Ottawa, Ont. K1G 3H6, Canada; 613-998-4913; www. chs-shc. dof-mpo.gc.ca/chs_hq/purchase_chs.html.

Schools and Courses

PILOTING AND SEAMANSHIP
American Red Cross National Headquarters, Health, Safety, and Community Services, 8111 Gatehouse Road, Falls Church, VA 22042-1213; www.redcross.org. Safe-boating classes offered at local Red Cross chapters include Basic Rowing, Basic Canoeing, Basic Sailing, and Basic Outboard Boating. Swimming and water-safety courses are also offered, ranging from Beginner to Advanced, as well as a variety of first-aid courses and training in CPR.

INFORMATION

American Institute of Navigation, Seafarer Group, Inc., 927 Mountain Meadows Rd., Boulder, CO 80302-9252; 303-444-2307. Courses in seamanship and navigation seminars.

Annapolis Powerboat School, P.O. Box 3334, Annapolis, MD 21403-0334; 800-638-9192; www.annapolispowerboat.com. Basic boat handling and navigation—hands-on, no classroom. Two- and five-day courses. Private instruction available.

Boat Owners Association of the United States, 880 Pickett St., Alexandria, VA 22304. On-line boating safety course at www.boatus.com.

Florida Sailing & Cruising School, 3444 Marinatown Lane, N.W., North Ft. Myers, FL 33903-7050; 800-262-7939; www.swfyachts.com. Various on-water classes from one-day to twelve-day courses.

National Small Craft Schools. For information write: American National Red Cross, Washington, DC 20006.

United States Coast Guard Auxiliary, Washington, DC 20593-0001. The Coast Guard Auxiliary offers public courses covering many boating subjects. For information about courses in your area, or the Auxiliary in general, contact your local Coast Guard unit.

YACHT DESIGN

Westlawn Institute of Marine Technology, 733 Summer St., Stamford, CT 06904; 203-359-0500; www.westlawn.org. A distance-education school offering a professional diploma in yacht design, plus a lesser course for non-professionals.

SAILING INSTRUCTION

Annapolis Sailing School, Box 3335, Annapolis, MD 21403-0335; 800-638-9192; www.annapolissailing.com. Branches in Florida and the Virgin Islands. Courses range from two-day beginner courses to eight-day offshore passages. Children's programs and private instruction also available.

Seafarer Sailing, Seafarer Group, Inc., 927 Mountain Meadows Rd., Boulder, CO 80302-9259; 303-444-2307. Courses on cruising under sail; local sailing classes; "sail & learn" bluewater cruises.

CHAPTER FOURTEEN

Useful Tables

One way of presenting much useful information quickly and easily is through the use of tables. On the following pages are tables covering nautical mile–statute mile conversions; time, speed, and distance problems; propeller selection for inboard engine propulsion; rope, cable, and chain strengths and uses; strengths of metals and woods; metric conversions; and weights and measures.

TABLE 14-1
Conversion Tables—Nautical and Statue Miles

Nautical	Statute	Nautical	Statute	Nautical	Statute		Statute	Nautical	Statute	Nautical	Statute	Nautical
1.00	1.151	8.75	10.075	16.50	18.999		1.00	0.868	9.00	7.815	17.00	14.763
1.25	1.439	9.00	10.363	16.75	19.287		1.25	1.085	9.25	8.032	17.25	14.980
1.50	1.729	9.25	10.651	17.00	19.575		1.50	1.302	9/50	8.249	17.50	15.197
1.75	2.015	9.50	10.939	17.25	19.863		1.75	1.519	9.75	8.467	17.75	15.414
2.00	2.303	9.75	11.227	17.50	20.151		2.00	1.736	10.00	8.684	18.00	15.632
2.25	2.590	10.00	11.515	17.75	20.439		2.25	1.953	10.25	8.901	18.25	15.849
2.50	2.878	10.25	11.803	18.00	20.727		2.50	2.171	10.50	9.118	18.50	16.066
2.75	3.166	10.50	12.090	18.25	21.015		2.75	2.387	10.75	9.335	18.75	16.283
3.00	3.454	10.75	12.378	18.50	21.303		3.00	2.604	11.00	9.552	19.00	16.500
3.25	3.742	11.00	12.666	18.75	21.590		3.25	2.821	11.25	9.769	19.26	16.717
3.50	4.030	11.25	12.954	19.00	21.878		3.50	3.038	11.50	9.986	19.50	16.934
3.75	4.318	11.50	13.242	19.25	22.166		3.75	3.256	11.75	10.203	19.75	17.151
4.00	4.606	11.75	13.530	19.50	22.454		4.00	3.473	12.00	10.420-	20.00	17.369
4.25	4.893	12.00	13.818	19.75	22.742		4.25	3.690	12.25	10.638	20.25	17.586
4.50	5.181	12.25	14.106	20.00	23.030		4.50	3.907	12.50	10.855	20.50	17.803
4.75	5.469	12.50	14.393	20.25	23.318		4.75	4.124	12.75	11.072	20.75	18.020
5.00	5.757	12.75	14.681	20.50	23.606		5.00	4.341	13.00	11.289	21.00	18.237
5.25	6.045	13.00	14.969	20.75	23.893		5.25	4.599	13.25	11.507	21.25	18.454
5.50	6.333	13.25	15.257	21.00	24.181		5.50	4.776	13.50	11.724	21.50	18.671
5.75	6.621	13.50	15.545	21.25	24.468		5.75	4.994	13.75	11.941	21.75	18.888
6.00	6.909	13.75	15.833	21.50	24.757		6.00	5.211	14.00	12.158	22.00	19.105
6.25	7.196	14.00	16.121	21.75	25.045		6.25	5.428	14.25	12.376	22.25	19.322
6.50	7.484	14.25	16.409	22.00	25.333		6.50	5.645	14.50	12.593	22.50	19.539
6.75	7.772	14.50	16.696	22.25	25.621		6.75	5.862	14.75	12.810	22.75	19.756
7.00	8.060	14.75	16.984	22.50	25.909		7.00	6.079	15.00	13.027	23.00	19.973
7.25	8.348	15.00	17.272	22.75	26.196		7.25	6.296	15.25	13.244	23.25	20.191
7.50	8.636	15.25	17.560	23.00	26.484		7.50	6.513	15.50	13.461	23.50	20.408
7.75	8.924	15.50	17/848	23.50	27.00		7.75	6.730	15.75	13.678	23.75	20.625
8.00	9.212	15.75	18.136	24.00	27.636		8.00	6.947	16.00	13.895	24.00	20.842
8.25	9.500	16.00	18.424	24.50	28.212		8.25	7.164	16.25	14.112	24.25	21.060
8.50	9.787	16.25	18.712	25.00	28.787		8.50	7.381	16.50	14.329	24.50	21.277
—							8.75	7.598	16.75	14.546	25.00	21.711

1 nautical mile=1.151 statute miles
1 statute mile=0.869 nautical mile

TABLE 14-2
Time-Speed Distance

	TIME TAKEN TO TRAVEL 1 NAUTICAL MILE (OR STATUTE MILE)								
MIN	1	2	3	4	5	6	7	8	9
SEC	**SPEED OF BOAT IN KNOTS (OR STATUTE MILES PER HOUR)**								
0	60.00	30.00	20.00	15.00	12.00	10.00	8.57	7.50	6.67
2	58.06	29.51	19.78	14.88	11.92	9.95	8.53	7.47	6.64
4	56.25	29.03	19.56	14.75	11.84	9.89	8.49	7.44	6.62
6	54.55	28.57	19.36	14.63	11.76	9.84	8.45	7.41	6.59
8	52.94	28.13	19.15	14.52	11.69	9.78	8.41	7.38	6.56
10	51.43	27.69	18.95	14.40	11.61	9.73	8.37	7.35	6.54
12	50.00	27.27	18.75	14.29	11.54	9.68	8.33	7.32	6.52
14	48.65	26.87	18.56	14.17	11.47	9.63	8.29	7.29	6.50
16	46.37	26.47	18.37	14.06	11.39	9.57	8.26	7.26	6.48
18	46.15	26.09	18.18	13.95	11.32	9.52	8.22	7.23	6.45
20	45.00	25.71	18.00	13.85	11.25	9.47	8.18	7.20	6.43
22	43.90	25.35	17.82	13.74	11.18	9.42	8.15	7.17	6.41
24	42.86	25.00	17.65	13.64	11.11	9.38	8.11	7.14	6.38
26	41.86	24.66	17.48	13.53	11.04	9.33	8.07	7.12	6.36
28	40.90	24.32	17.31	13.43	10.98	9.28	8.04	7.09	6.34
30	40.00	24.00	17.14	13.33	10.91	9.23	8.00	7.06	6.32
32	39.13	23.68	16.98	13.24	10.84	9.18	7.97	7.03	6.29
34	38.30	23.38	16.82	13.14	10.78	9.14	7.93	7.00	6.27
36	37.50	23.08	16.67	13.04	10.71	9.09	7.90	6.98	6.25
38	36.74	22.79	16.51	12.95	10.65	9.05	7.86	6.95	6.23
40	36.00	22.50	16.36	12.85	10.59	9.00	7.83	6.92	6.21
42	35.29	22.22	16.22	12.77	10.53	8.96	7.79	6.90	6.19
44	34.62	21.95	16.07	12.68	10.47	8.91	7.76	6.87	6.16
46	33.96	21.69	15.93	12.59	10.40	8.87	7.73	6.84	6.14
48	33.33	21.43	15.79	12.50	10.35	8.82	7.69	6.82	6.12
50	32.73	21.18	15.65	12.41	10.29	8.78	7.66	6.79	6.10
52	32.14	20.93	17.52	12.33	10.23	8.74	7.63	6.77	6.08
54	31.58	20.69	17.38	12.25	10.17	8.70	7.60	6.74	6.06
56	31.03	20.45	17.25	12.16	10.11	8.65	7.56	6.72	6.04
58	30.51	20.23	17.13	12.08	10.06	8.61	7.53	6.69	6.02
60	30.00	20.00	17.00	12.00	10.00	8.57	7.50	6.67	6.00

TABLE 14-3
Inboard Engine Propeller Selection—Diameter

This table, by Columbian Bronze, can be used to determine approximate diameter of normal three-blade propeller that will best match engine horsepower and propeller shaft speed.

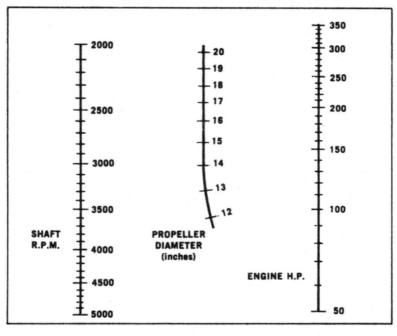

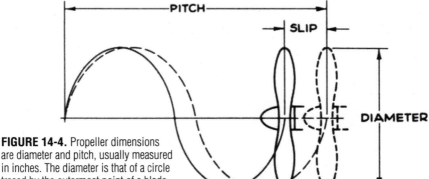

FIGURE 14-4. Propeller dimensions are diameter and pitch, usually measured in inches. The diameter is that of a circle traced by the outermost point of a blade. Pitch is the distance a propeller would move in one revolution (dotted line) if turned as a screw in solid material. Actual movement is less than theoretical pitch distance; the difference between actual movement (solid line) and theoretical pitch is the propeller slip. Slip is expressed as a percentage of pitch distance. Depending on vessel type, slip varies between 10 and 35 percent.

TABLE 14-5
Inboard Engine Propeller Selection—Pitch

RPM	SLIP	8 IN.	10 IN.	12. IN	14 IN.	16 IN.	18 IN.
700	10%	4.16	5.18	6.22	7.27	8.31	9.32
	20%	3.68	4.61	5.53	6.45	7.38	8.28
	30%	3.23	4.03	4.83	5.64	6.46	7.27
800	10%	4.76	5.92	7.12	8.32	9.48	10.64
	20%	4.20	5.28	6.32	7.36	8.44	9.48
	30%	3.68	4.60	5.52	6.44	7.40	8.32
900	10%	5.35	6.66	8.00	9.35	10.68	11.98
	20%	4.73	5.93	7.11	8.29	9.49	10.65
	30%	4.15	5.18	6.21	7.49	8.31	9.35
1,000	10%	5.94	7.41	8.88	10.38	11.85	13.32
	20%	5.27	6.58	7.90	9.22	10.55	11.83
	30%	4.62	5.76	6.91	8.06	9.23	10.38
1,200	10%	7.13	8.89	10.65	12.46	14.22	15.98
	20%	6.32	7.90	9.48	11.06	12.66	14.20
	30%	5.54	6.91	8.29	9.67	11.08	12.46
1,400	10%	8.32	10.37	12.43	14.54	16.59	18.64
	20%	7.37	9.22	11.06	12.09	14.77	16.57
	30%	6.46	8.06	9.67	11.52	12.93	14.54
1,600	10%	9.51	11.85	14.21	16.52	18.96	21.30
	20%	8.42	10.54	12.64	14.74	16.98	18.94
	30%	7.38	9.21	11.05	13.13	14.78	16.62
1,800	10%	10.70	13.33	15.99	18.70	21.33	23.96
	20%	9.47	11.86	14.22	16.58	18.99	21.31
	30%	8.30	10.36	12.43	14.74	16.63	18.70
2,000	10%	11.89	14.81	17.77	20.78	23.70	26.62
	20%	10.52	13.18	15.80	18.42	21.10	23.68
	30%	9.22	11.51	13.82	16.12	18.46	20.76
2,200	10%	13.08	16.29	19.55	22.86	26.07	29.28
	20%	11.57	14.50	17.38	20.26	23.21	26.05
	30%	10.14	12.66	15.20	17.73	20.31	22.84
2,400	10%	14.27	17.77	21.33	24.94	28.44	31.94
	20%	12.62	15.87	18.96	22.10	25.32	28.42
	30%	11.06	13.81	16.58	19.34	22.16	24.92
2,600	10%	15.46	19.25	23.11	27.02	30.81	34.60
	20%	13.67	17.19	20.54	23.94	27.43	30.79
	30%	11.98	14.96	17.96	20.95	24.01	27.00
2,800	10%	16.65	20.73	24.89	29.10	33.18	37.26
	20%	14.72	18.51	22.12	25.78	29.54	33.16
	30%	12.90	16.11	19.34	22.56	25.86	29.08
3,000	10%	17.84	22.21	26.67	31.18	35.55	39.92
	20%	15.77	19.83	23.70	27.62	31.65	35.53
	30%	13.82	17.26	20.72	24.17	27.71	31.16

TABLE 14-5. This table can be used to determine the approximate pitch a propeller should have to permit a boat to operate at its optimum cruising speed, or the approximate speed that will result from use of a propeller of a given pitch. Propeller shaft revolutions per minute (rpm) and the boat's slip factor must be known. Light, fast racing boats have a slip of about 10 percent; runabouts, 12 to 20 percent; fast cruisers, 18 to 30 percent; and heavy cruisers, 20 to 35 percent. Shaft speed is engine rpm divided by any reduction gear ratio present.

TABLE 14-6
Inboard Engine Propeller Shaft Selection

SHAFT DIAMETER (INCHES)		ENGINE DISPLACEMENT (CU. IN.)/ REDUCTION GEAR RATIO				
MONEL, NAVAL OR TOBIN BRONZE	STAINLESS STEEL, OR ALUMINUM BRONZE	1:1 (DIRECT DRIVE)	1:5:1	2:1	2:5:1	3:1
⅞	¾	100-175				
1	⅞	175-250	100-175			
1⅛	1	250-325	175-250	100-175		
1¼	1⅛	325-400	250-325	175-250	100-175	
1⅜	1¼	400-500	325-400	250-325	175-250	100175
1½	1⅜		400-500	325-400	250-325	175-250
1⅝	1½			400-500	325400	250-325
1¾	1⅝				400-500	325-400
2	1¾					400-500

These figures are for gasoline engines. For diesel engines, add ⅛ inches diameter to all shaft size recommendations.

TABLE 14-7
Weight and Strength—Nylon and Chain

APPROX. EIGHT OF 100' IN AIR			ROPE—BREAKING STRENGTH		CHAIN—PROOF TEST	
DIAMETER	NYLON ROPE	BBB GALV. CHAIN	FIBER-CORE WIRE ROPE	6 X 19 NYLON YACHT ROPE	BBB GALV. CELL CHAIN	HIGH ALLOY CHAIN
¼	1.6	76	100	1,300	2,700	6,500
5⁄16	2.6	115	160	2,000	3,700	
⅜	3.8	170	230	2,900	4,600	13,000
7⁄16	5.2	225	310	3,900	6,200	
½	6.9	295	400	5,000	8,200	22,000
9⁄16	8.8	350	510	6,200	10,200	
⅝	10.8	430	630	7,500	12,500	33,000
¾	15.8	600	900	10,700	17,700	46,000
⅞	21.8	810	1230	14,200	24,000	
1	28.5	1050	1600	18,500	31,000	

TABLE 14-8

Fiber Cordage—Typical Weights and Minimum Breaking Strengths (pounds)

NOMINAL SIZE (INCHES) DIA. CIRC.	NYLON			DACRON			POLYPROPYLENE			NYLON DOUBLE BRAID			DACRON DOUBLE BRAID		
	NET WT. 100'	FT. PER LB.	BREAKING STRENGTH	NET WT. 100'	FT. PER LB.	BREAKING STRENGTH	NET WT. 100'	FT. PER LB.	BREAKING STRENGTH	NET WT. 100'	FT. PER LB.	BREAKING STRENGTH	NET WT. 100'	FT. PER LB.	BREAKING STRENGTH
¼ ¾	1.5	66.6	1,700	2.1	47.5	1,700	1.24	80	1,250	1.66	60.3	2,100	1.7	60.2	1,700
⅜ 1⅛	3.6	28	3,650	4.7	21.3	3,500	2.9	34.5	2,600	3.33	30	4,200	3.5	38.5	3,500
½ 1½	6.6	15	6,650	8.2	12.2	6,100	4.9	20.4	4,150	6.67	14.9	7,500	6.8	15	6,800
¾ 2¼	14.5	6.9	14,600	17.9	5.6	13,200	11.1	9	7,900	15.0	6.7	17,000	15	6.7	15,000
1 3	26	3.84	25,000	30.4	3.3	22,000	18.6	5.4	13,000	25.0	4	28,500	28	3.6	28,000

TABLE 14-9
Weight and Strength of Wire Rope (Black)

SIZE CIRCUMFERENCE	FLEXIBLE STEEL WIRE ROPE 6 STRANDS, EACH 12 WIRES			EXTRA-FLEXIBLE STEEL WIRE ROPE 6 STRANDS, EACH 24 WIRES		SPECIAL EXTRA-FLEXIBLE STEEL WIRE ROPE			
	WEIGHT PER FATHOM APPROX.	GUARANTEED BREAKING STRAIN	DIAMETER OF BARREL OR SHEAVE AROUND WHICH IT MAY BE AT A SLOW SPEED WORKED	WEIGHT PER FATHOM APPROX.	GUARANTEED BREAKING STRAIN	6 STRANDS, EACH 37 WIRES		BULLIVANT'S SPECIAL MAKE	
						WEIGHT PER FATHOM APPROX.	GUARANTEED BREAKING STRAIN	GUARANTEED BREAKING STRAIN	SIZE CIRCUMFERENCE
INCHES	POUNDS	TONS	INCHES	POUNDS	TONS	POUNDS	TONS	TONS	INCHES
1	.63	1.75	6	.88	2.95	1.0	—	—	1
1¼	1.06	2.5	7½	1.31	4.45	1.56	—	—	1¼
1½	1.44	4.0	9	1.88	6.7	2.0	7.25	—	1½
1¾	2.0	5.5	10½	2.5	8.75	2.88	10.0	—	1¾
2	2.44	7.0	12	3.5	11.85	4.0	13.0	—	2
2¼	3.37	9.0	13½	4.5	14.6	4.88	15.75	—	2¼
2½	4.19	12.0	15	5.44	18.55	5.88	19.75	—	2½
2¾	5.25	15.0	16½	6.25	21.95	7.0	24.0	—	2¾
3	6.25	18.0	18	7.63	25.7	8.25	29.0	—	3
3¼	7.06	22.0	19½	9.37	30.8	10.38	33.5	—	3¼
3¾	9.87	29.0	22½	12.19	41.1	13.38	44.5	—	3¾
4	11.25	33.0	24	13.62	46.3	15.25	51.0	—	4
4¼	12.35	36.0	25½	15.69	52.9	17.12	58.0	—	4¼
4½	13.44	39.0	27	17.75	58.6	19.0	63.5	—	4½
4¾	—	—	—	19.98	66.4	21.69	71.25	—	4¾
5	—	—	—	22.5	74.2	24.38	79.25	—	5
5¼	—	—	—	23.25	82.88	27.69	87.75	—	5¼
5½	—	—	—	24.5	91.55	31.0	96.75	—	5½
5¾	—	—	—	—	—	33.75	103.75	—	5¾
6	—	—	—	—	—	36.5	113.75	—	6

TABLE 14-10
Rope Comparison Chart

	NYLON	DACRON	POLYOLEFINS
Relative Strength	4	3	2
Relative Weight	2	4	1
Elongation	4	2	3
Relative Resistance to Impact or Shock Loads	4	2	3
Mildew and Rot Resistance	Excellent	Excellent	Excellent
Acid Resistance	Fair	Fair	Excellent
Alkali Resistance	Excellent	Excellent	Excellent
Sunlight Resistance	Fair	Good	Fair
Organic Solvent Resistance	Good	Good	Fair
Melting Point	410°F.	410°F.	About 300°F.
Floatability	None	None	Indefinite
* Relative Abrasion Resistance	3	4	1

(*Depends on many factors — whether wet or dry, etc.)
Key to Ratings: 1 Lowest — 4 Highest

TABLE 14-11
Recommended Rope for Various Uses

	TIE-UP OR MOORING LINES	ANCHOR LINES OR MOORING PENNANTS	SHEETS AND HALYARDS	FLAG HALYARDS	SEIZING AND WHIPPING	BOLT ROPE SYNTHETIC SAILS	TOWING	WATER SKIING
Nylon	•	•		•			•	
Dacron	•		•	•		•		
Polyolefin	•						•	•
Braided Dacron			•	•				
Braided Nylon	•	•		•	•		•	
Wire (Stainless)	Pennants	•						
Braided Cotton			•	•				

TABLE 14-12
Weight and Strength of Metals

METAL	SPECIFIC GRAVITY	POUND IN A CUBIC FOOT	TEARING FORCE POUNDS ON SQUARE INCH	CRUSHING FORCE POUNDS ON SQUARE INCH	MODULUS OF ELASTICITY POUNDS ON SQUARE INCH
Aluminum, cast	2.560	160.0	—	—	—
Aluminum, sheet	2.670	166.9	—	—	—
Brass, cast	8.396	524.8	18,000	10,300	9,170,000
Brass, sheet	8.525	532.8	31,360	—	—
Brass, wire	8.544	533.0	49,000	—	14,230,000
Bronze	8.222	513.4	—	—	—
Copper, bolts	8.850	531.3	36,000	—	—
Copper, cast	8.607	537.9	19,000	—	—
Copper, sheet	8.785	549.1	30,000	—	—
Copper, wire	8.878	548.6	60,000	—	—
Iron, cast, average	7.125	445.3	16,500	112,000	17,000,000
Iron, wrought, average	7.680	480.0	60,000	36,000	28,000,000
Lead, cast	11.352	709.5	1,792	6,900	—
Lead, sheet	11.400	712.8	3,328	—	720,000
Nickel, cast	7.807	487.9	—	—	—
Steel, hard	7.818	488.6	103,000	—	42,000,000
Steel, soft	7.834	489.6	121,700	—	29,000,000
Zinc, cast	7.028	439.3	8,500	—	13,500,000
Zinc, sheet	7.291	455.7	7,111	—	12,650,000

TABLE 14-13

Stainless Steel, Monel, and Copper-Nickel in Marine Use

MATERIAL	APPLICATION	YIELD STRENGTH	TENSILE STRENGTH %	ELONGATION IN 2 INCHES
302 S.S.	rails, trim, cable, hardware	40 KSI	90 KSI	50
304 S.S.	galley equipment	42 KSI	84 KSI	55
305 S.S.	bolts, nuts, screws, fasteners	35 KSI	85 KSI	50
316 S.S.	general use, preferred choice in salt spray	42 KSI	84 KSI	50
316L S.S.	preferred choice for welding	34 KSI	81 KSI	50
17-4 PH S.S.	propeller shafts	175 KSI	205 KSI	15
Monel Alloy 400	pump parts, water boxes, valves, tubing, fasteners	35 KSI	80 KSI	45
Monel Alloy K-500	valves, pump shafts, high-strength applications	130 KSI	160 KSI	22
70/30 Copper-Nickel	pipe, tubing, water boxes, etc.	25 KSI	60 KSI	45
90/10 Copper-Nickel	pipe, tubing, water boxes, etc.	16 KSI	44 KSI	42

TABLE 14-14
GALVANIC SERIES OF METALS IN SEA WATER

ANODIC OR
LEAST NOBLE — ACTIVE

Magnesium and magnesium alloys
CB75 aluminum anode alloy
Zinc
B605 aluminum anode alloy
Galvanized steel or galvanized wrought iron
Aluminum 7072 (cladding alloy)
Aluminum 5456, 5086, 5052
Aluminum 3003, 1100, 6061, 356
Cadmium
2117 aluminum rivet alloy
Mild steel
Wrought Iron
Cast iron
Ni-Resist
13% chromium stainless steel, type 410 (active)
50-50 lead tin solder
18-8 stainless steel, type 304 (active)
18-8 3% NO stainless steel, type 316 (active)
Lead
Tin
Muntz metal
Manganese bronze
Naval brass (60% copper — 39% zinc)
Nickel (active)
78% Ni.-13.5% Cr.-6% Fe. (Inconel) (Active)
Yellow brass (65% copper — 35% zinc)
Admiralty brass
Aluminum bronze
Red brass (85% copper — 15% zinc)
Copper

CATHODIC OR
MOST NOBLE — PASSIVE

Silicon bronze
5% Zn. — 20% Ni. — 75% Cu.
90% Cu. — 10% Ni.
70% Cu. — 30% Ni.
88% Cu. — 2% Zn. —10% Sn (composition G-bronze)
88% Cu. — 3% Zn. — 6.5% Sn. —1.5% Pb (composition M-
    bronze)
Nickel (passive)
78% Ni. — 13.5% Cr. — 6% Fe. (Inconel) (Passive)
70% Ni. — 30% Cr.
18-8 stainless steel type 304 (passive)
18-8 3% Mo. stainless steel, type 316 (passive)
Hastelloy C
Titanium
Platinum

TABLE 14-15
Weight of Water

FRESH WATER

A cubic foot = 0.0312 ton = 62.39 lb. = 998.18 avd. oz. = 7.481 gal.
A cubic inch = 0.0362 lb. = 0.5776 avd.oz. = 0.0043 gal
A gallon = 0.00417 ton = 8.340 lb. = 133.44 avd. oz. = 0.1336 cu. ft
A ton = 32.054 cu. ft. = 2000 lb. = 239.79 gal.
Weight of fresh water = weight of salt water x .9740

SALT WATER

A cubic foot = 0.0320 ton = 64.05 lb. = 1024.80 avd. oz. = 7.481 gal.
A cubic inch = 0.0371 lb. = 0.5930 avd. oz. = 0.0043 gal.
A gallon = 0.00428 ton = 8.561 lb. = 136.97 avd. oz. = 0.1336 cu.ft.
A ton = 31.225 cu. ft. = 2000 lb. = 233.59 gal.
Weight of salt water = weight of fresh water x 1.026

TABLE 14.16
Weight of Liquid Fuels

FUEL	AVERAGE POUNDS PER GALLON
Diesel fuel	7.1
Gasoline	6.0

TABLE 14-17
Velocity of Sound
In miles for intervals from one to twenty seconds, at average summer temperature

IINTERVAL, SECONDS	DISTANCE, MILES	INTERVALS, SECONDS	DISTANCE, MILES
1	.21	11	2.33
2	.42	12	2.54
3	.63	13	2.75
4	.85	14	2.96
5	1.06	15	3.18
6	1.27	16	3.40
7	1.48	17	3.61
8	1.70	18	3.82
9	1.91	19	4.03
10	2.12	20	4.24

TABLE 14-18

Visibility at Sea

Approximate distance of sea horizon from height above sea level

HEIGHT IN FEET	DISTANCE, NAUTICAL MILES	HEIGHT IN FEET	DISTANCE, NAUTICAL MILES
4	2.3	100	11.5
10	3.6	120	12.6
15	4.4	140	13.6
20	5.1	150	14.1
30	6.3	200	16.25
40	7.25	250	18.2
50	8.1	300	19.9
60	8.9	350	21.5
70	9.6	400	23.0
80	10.3	450	24.4
90	10.9	500	25.7

TABLE 14-19

Metric Conversions

1 mile	1.609 km	1 km	0.621 miles
1 nautical mile	1.852 km	1 m	1.094 yards/3.281 feet
1 yard	0.914 m	1 cm	0.394 inches
1 foot	0.305 m	1 cm^2	0.155 sq. in.
1 inch	25.4 mm	1 m^2	10.76 sq. ft.
1 square inch	6.452 cm^2	1 cm^3	0.061 cu. in.
1 square foot	0.836 cm^2	1 m^3	35.315 cu. ft.
1 cubic inch	16.39 cm^3	1 m^3	1.307 cu. yd.
1 cubic foot	0.283 m^3	1 liter	0.264 gallons
1 gallon (U.S.)	3.785 liters	1 liter	2.119 pints
1 pint (U.S.)	0.472 liters	1 kg	35.27 ounces
1 ounce	28.35 grams	1 kg	2.205 pounds
1 pound	0.454 kg	1 kgm	7.233 lb. ft.
1 pound foot	0.138 kgm	1 km/hour	0.621 mph
1 mile per hour	1.609 km/hour	10 liters/100 km.	0.042 gpm
1 gallon per mile	235.2 liters/100 km		

TABLE 14-20

The Decimal Equivalents of the Divisions of the Foot

In.	0	1/16	1/8	3/16	1/4	5/16	3/8	7/16	1/2	9/16	5/8	11/16	3/4	13/16	7/8	15/16
0		.0052	.0104	.0156	.0208	.0260	.0313	.0365	.0417	.0469	.0521	.0573	.0625	.0677	.0729	.0781
1	0.833	.0885	.0937	.0990	.1042	.1094	.1146	.1198	.1250	.1302	.1354	.1406	.1458	.1510	.1563	.1615
2	.1667	.1719	.1771	.1825	.1875	.1927	.1979	.2031	.2083	.2135	.2188	.2240	.2292	.2344	.2396	.2448
3	.2500	.2552	.2604	.2656	.2708	.2760	.2813	.2865	.2917	.2969	.3021	.3073	.3125	.3177	.3229	.3281
4	.3333	.3385	.3437	.3490	.3542	.3594	.3646	.3698	.3750	.3802	.3854	.3906	.3958	.4010	.4063	.4115
5	.4167	.4219	.4271	.4323	.4375	.4427	.4479	.4531	.4583	.4635	.4688	.4740	.4792	.4844	.4896	.4948
6	.5000	.5052	.5104	.5156	.5208	.5260	.5313	.5365	.5417	.5469	.5521	.5573	.5625	.5677	.5729	.5781
7	.5833	.5885	.5937	.5990	.6052	.6094	.6146	.6198	.6250	.6302	.6354	.6406	.6458	.6510	.6563	.6615
8	.6667	.6719	.6771	.6823	.6875	.6927	.6979	.7031	.7083	.7135	.7187	.7240	.7292	.7344	.7396	.7448
9	.7500	.7552	.7604	.7656	.7708	.7760	.7813	.7865	.7917	.7969	.8021	.8073	.8125	.8177	.8229	.8281
10	.8333	.8385	.8437	.8490	.8542	.8594	.8646	.8698	.8750	.8802	.8854	.8906	.8958	.9010	.9063	.9115
11	.9167	.9219	.9271	.9323	.9375	.9427	.9479	.9531	.9583	.9635	.9688	.9740	.9792	.9844	.9896	.9948

TABLE 14-21
Technical Values and Equations

1 horsepower = 33,000 foot pounds per minute.

1 atmosphere (technical expression for pressure) = 14.223 lb./sq. in. = 1 kg/cm² = water column of 10 meters.

The circumference of a circle = diameter x 3.1416.

The diameter of a circle = circumference x 0.3183.

The area of a circle = radius x radius x 3.1416 (πr^2).

The area of a cylinder = circumference x height + end areas as determined above.

The area of an ellipse = $\dfrac{\text{largest length x largest width x 3.1416}}{2}$

The area of a parallelogram = base x vertical height.

The area of a parallel trapezoid = half the total length of the parallel sides x vertical height.

The volume of a sphere = diameter x diameter x diameter x 0.5236 (or $\frac{4}{3}\pi r^3$)

The area of a sphere = diameter x diameter x 3.1416 (or $4\pi r^2$).

The area of a triangle = base x vertical height divided by two.

The volume of a cube = base x side x side. (Also applies to a right-angled parallelepiped.)

The volume of a pyramid = side x height divided by three.

The volume of a cone = radius x radius x height x 3.1416 divided by three.

TABLE 14-22
Astronomical Data

1 light-second = 186,000 miles.

1 light-minute = 11 million miles.

1 light-year - 5.88 x 10^{12} miles

1 parsec = 3.26 light-years.

The distance from the earth to the nearest solar system = 4.3 light-years.

The distance of the sun from the earth = 8.3 light-minutes = approximately 93 million miles = 108 sun diameters.

The distance of the moon from the earth = 1.25 light-seconds = approximately 240,000 miles.

The diameter of the earth = 7,928 miles statute miles (equator) / 7,902 statue miles (polar axis).

The diameter of the sun = 864,000 miles.

The diameter of the moon = 2,158 miles.

The area of the earth = 197 million square miles.

Land area of earth = 29 percent of total area.

Sea area of earth = 71 percent of total area.

The mass of the earth = 6.6 x 10^{21} tons.

The mass of the sun = approximately 333,000 times that of the earth.

The mass of the moon = 1/81 of that of the earth.